Islamic Banking and Finance

To
Dr Mohammad Omar Zubair,
who is a source of inspiration for all those working
in the field of Islamic economics and finance

Islamic Banking and Finance

New Perspectives on Profit-Sharing and Risk

Edited by
Munawar Iqbal
Islamic Development Bank, Saudi Arabia

David T. Llewellyn
Loughborough University, UK

Edward Elgar
Cheltenham, UK • Northampton, MA, USA

In association with:

International Association of Islamic Economics

Islamic Development Bank

The Islamic Foundation

Published by
Edward Elgar Publishing Limited
Glensanda House
Montpellier Parade
Cheltenham
Glos GL50 1UA
UK

Edward Elgar Publishing, Inc.
136 West Street
Suite 202
Northampton
Massachusetts 01060
USA

This book has been printed on demand to keep the title in print.

A catalogue record for this book is available from the British Library

Library of Congress Cataloguing in Publication Data
Islamic Banking and Finance: New Perspectives on Profit-Sharing and Risk / edited by Munawar Iqbal, David T. Llewellyn
p. cm.
"Some of the papers were presented at the Fourth International Conference on Islamic Economics and Banking, held at Loughborough University, UK, 13–15 August 2000" —Pref.
Includes bibliographical references and index.
1. Banks and Banking—Islamic countries—Congresses. 2. Finance—Islamic countries—Congresses. I. Iqbal, Munawar. II. Llewellyn, David T. III. International Conference on Islamic Economics and Banking (4th: 2000: Loughborough University)

HG3368.A6I852 2001
332.1'0917'671—dc21 2001053235

ISBN 1 84064 787 6

Contents

Contributors

Mohammad Abalkhail, Assistant Professor of Business Finance, Imam Mohammad Ibn Saud Islamic University, Dammam, Saudi Arabia

Sultan Abou-Ali, Professor of Economics, Zagazig University, Zagazig, Egypt

Habib Ahmed, Economist, Islamic Research and Training Institute, Islamic Development Bank, Jeddah, Saudi Arabia

Sami Ibrahim Al-Suwailem, Director, Research Centre, Al-Rajhi Banking and Investment Corporation, Riyadh, Saudi Arabia

M.I. Bagsiraj, Director, Indian Institute of Islamic Financial Institutions, Bangalore, India

Abdel-hameed Bashir, Professor, Department of Economics, Grambling State University, Grambling, LA 71245, USA

M. Umer Chapra, Research Adviser, Islamic Research and Training Institute, Islamic Development Bank, Jeddah, Saudi Arabia

Mohamed Ali Elgari, Executive Manager, National Management Consultancy Centre, Jeddah, Saudi Arabia

Fazlur Rahman Faridi, President, Indian Association for Islamic Economics, Aligarh, India

Sule Ahmed Gusau, Department of Economics, Usmanu Danfodiyo University, Sokoto, Nigeria

Said Al Hallaq, Vice Dean, School of Economics and Administrative Sciences, Yarmouk University, Jordan

Munawar Iqbal, Chief of Research, Islamic Banking and Finance Division, Islamic Research and Training Institute, Islamic Development Bank, Jeddah, Saudi Arabia

Zamir Iqbal, Senior Information Officer at the Treasury Operations Department of the World Bank, Washington DC, USA

Abdul Azim Islahi, Associate Professor, Department of Economics, Aligarh Muslim University, Aligarh, India

Monzer Kahf, Former Senior Economist at the Islamic Research and Training Institute, Islamic Development Bank, Jeddah, Saudi Arabia. Now retired

Adiwarman A. Karim, Vice President, Muamalat Institute, Bank Muamalat, Indonesia

Abdel-Fattah A.A. Khalil, University of Birmingham, Birmingham, UK

Abdurrahman Lahlou, President, Moroccan Association of Islamic Economics, Morocco

David T. Llewellyn, Professor of Money and Banking, and Chairman of the Loughborough University Banking Centre, Loughborough University, UK

Muhammad Abdul Mannan, former Chairman, Social Investment Bank Limited, Dhaka, Bangladesh

Victor Murinde, University of Birmingham, Birmingham, UK

John R. Presley, Professsor of Economics, Loughborough University, UK

Colin Rickwood, University of Birmingham, Birmingham, UK

Kazem Sadr, Associate Professor, School of Economics and Political Sciences, Shahid Beheshti University, Tehran, Iran

John G. Sessions, Reader, Department of Economics and Finance, Brunel University, UK

Muhammad Nejatullah Siddiqi, Former Professor of Economics, King Abdulaziz University, Jeddah, Saudi Arabia. Now retired

Rodney Wilson, Professor of Economics, University of Durham, Durham, UK

Ali Yasseri, Vice President, Iran Banking Institute, Tehran, Iran

List of tables

Preface

This volume includes some of the papers presented at the Fourth International Conference on Islamic Economics and Banking held at Loughborough University, UK, during August 13–15, 2000. The theme of the Conference was 'Islamic Finance: Challenges and opportunities in the 21st Century'. Several papers presented at the conference dealt with profit-sharing as an alternative way of providing finance that can be used by financial intermediaries. This is an area that has considerable potential. Papers included in the volume highlight some of the key features of the sharing-based contracts as compared to the debt-based contracts and how they can help improve efficiency and stability of a financial system. At a time when the reform of the global financial system is being actively discussed at both the theoretical and policy levels, it is hoped that this volume will bring some new ideas into the ongoing discussion.

The Academic Committee for the Conference reviewed all the papers submitted to it and accepted only 23 out of 74. The ten papers included in this volume were further refereed after the conference and in some cases revised. All contributors were very cooperative, for which we are grateful to them.

Since many Arabic terms have been used in the papers, we have prepared and included a glossary of such terms for the benefit of readers.

Several people helped in preparing this volume. We are grateful to Dr Mabid Ali Al-Jarhi and Dr M. Umer Chapra (Director and Research Adviser respectively of the Islamic Research and Training Institute, Islamic Development Bank) and Dr M. Anas Zarqa, Chairman of the Academic Committee of the Conference, who gave useful advice at every stage. Thanks are also due to Mr Jaleel Asghar and Mr Shaikh Amanul Hoque for secretarial assistance and for painstakingly going through several drafts to ensure accuracy and consistency of style in various papers. Last, but not least, we are grateful to Elizabeth Teague for her competent and efficient copy editing of the volume.

Munawar Iqbal
David T. Llewellyn
April 30, 2001

Glossary of Arabic terms

Al-Qur'ān (Also written as Qur'ān)	The Holy Book of Muslims, consisting of the revelations made by God to Prophet Muhammad (peace be upon him). The Qur'ān lays down the fundamentals of the Islamic faith, including beliefs and all aspects of the Islamic way of life.
Awqāf	Plural of *waqf.* For meaning, see below.
Āyah	A verse of al-Qur'ān.
*Bay*ʿ	Stands for sale. It is often used as a prefix in referring to different sales-based modes of Islamic finance, like *murābaḥah, ijārah, istiṣnā*ʿ, and *salam.*
*Bay*ʿ *al-dayn*	Sale of debt. According to a large majority of *fuqahā'*, debt cannot be sold except at its face value.
*Bay*ʿ *al-salaf*	An alternative term for *bay*ʿ *al-salam.*
*Bay*ʿ *al-salam*	A sale in which payment is made in advance by the buyer and the delivery of the goods is deferred by the seller.
Falāḥ	Literally means to become happy, to have success. Technically, means achieving success in the life hereafter.
Fatāwā	Plural of *fatwa*. Religious verdicts by *fuqahā'*.
Fiqh	Refers to the whole corpus of Islamic jurisprudence. In contrast with conventional law, *fiqh* covers all aspects of life, religious, political, social, commercial or economic. The whole corpus of *fiqh* is based primarily on interpretations of the Qur'ān and the *Sunnah* and secondarily on *ijmā*ʿ (consensus) and *ijtihād* (individual judgment). While the Qur'ān and the *Sunnah* are immutable, *fiqhī* verdicts may change due to changing circumstances.
Fuqahā'	Plural of *faqīh* meaning jurist who gives opinion on various juristic issues in the light of the Qur'ān and the *Sunnah.*
Gharar	Literally means deception, danger, risk and uncertainty. Technically, means exposing oneself to

excessive risk and danger in a business transaction as a result of uncertainty about the price, the quality and the quantity of the counter-value, the date of delivery, the ability of either the buyer or the seller to fulfill his commitment, or ambiguity in the terms of the deal, thereby exposing either of the two parties to unnecessary risks.

Ghish — Literally means deception, fraud. Technically, means trying to deceive someone by concealing vital information in a deal.

Ḥadīth — Sayings, deeds and reactions of Prophet Muhammad (peace be upon him) narrated by his companions.

Ḥalāl — Things or activities permitted by the *Sharīʿah.*

Ḥarām — Things or activities prohibited by the *Sharīʿah.*

Ḥikmah — Wisdom.

Ḥisbah, al- — Literally means reward, calculation. Technically, refers to an institution that existed through most of the Islamic history for implementing what is proper and preventing what is improper. The main role of *al-ḥisbah* was the regulation and supervision of markets to ensure proper market conduct by all concerned.

Ḥawālah — Literally means bill of exchange, cheque, draft. Technically, refers to an arrangement whereby a debtor passes on the responsibility of payment of the debt to a third party who owes former a debt.

Ijārah — Leasing. The subject matter in a leasing contract is an asset, such as machinery, airplanes, cars, or ships, which generates usufruct over time. This usufruct is sold to the lessee at a predetermined price. The lessor retains the ownership of the asset with all the rights and the responsibilities that go with ownership.

Ijtihād — In technical terms, refers to the endeavour of a jurist to derive a rule or reach a judgement based on evidence found in the Islamic sources of law, predominantly the Qur'ān and the *Sunnah.*

Istiṣnāʿ — Refers to a contract whereby a manufacturer (contractor) agrees to produce (build) and deliver a well-described good (or premise) at a given price on a given date in the future. As against *salam*, in *istiṣnāʿ* the price need not be paid in advance. It may be paid in instalments in step with the preferences

	of the parties or partly at the front end and the balance later on as agreed.
Ju'ālah	Performing a given task against a prescribed fee in a given period.
Kafālah	A contract whereby a person accepts to guarantee or take responsibility for a liability or duty of another person.
Khilāfat al-Rāshidah	The period of the first four caliphs after the Prophet (peace be upon him), ranging from the year 11 AH (632 AC) to the year 41 AH (661 AC).
Khiyār al-sharṭ	Option to rescind a sales contract. One of the parties to a sales contract may stipulate certain conditions, which, if not met, would grant a right to the stipulating party an option to rescind the contract.
Muḍārabah	A contract between two parties, capital owner(s) or financiers (called *rabb al-māl*) and an investment manager (called *muḍārib*). Profit is distributed between the two parties in accordance with the ratio upon which they agree at the time of the contract. Financial loss is borne only by the financier(s). The entrepreneur's loss lies in not getting any reward for his services.
Muḍārib	Investment manager in a *muḍārabah* contract.
Murābaḥah	Sale at a specified profit margin. The term, however, is now used to refer to a sale agreement whereby the seller purchases the goods desired by the buyer and sells them at an agreed marked-up price, the payment being settled within an agreed time frame, either in instalments or in a lump sum. The seller bears the risk for the goods until they have been delivered to the buyer. *Murābaḥah* is also referred to as *bay' mu'ajjal*.
Musāqah	A contract in which the owner of a garden agrees to share its produce with someone in an agreed proportion in return for the latter's services in irrigating and looking after the garden.
Mushārakah	A *mushārakah* contract is similar to a *muḍārabah* contract, with the difference that in the former both the partners participate in the management and the provision of capital, and share in profit and loss. Profits are distributed between the partners in accordance with the ratios initially set, whereas loss

	is distributed in proportion to each one's share in capital.
Muzāraʿah	A contract whereby one party agrees to till the land owned by the other party in consideration for an agreed share in the produce of the land.
Qarḍ or Qarḍ al-ḥasan	A loan extended without interest or any other compensation from the borrower. The lender expects a reward only from God.
Qiyās	Derivation and application of a rule/law on the analogy of another rule/law if the basis (*ʿillah*) of the two is the same. It is one of the secondary sources of Islamic law.
Qurūḍ ḥasanah	Plural of *qarḍ al-ḥasan.*
Rabb al-māl	Capital owner (financier) in a *muḍārabah* contract.
Ribā	Literally means increase or addition, and refers to the 'premium' that must be paid by the borrower to the lender along with the principal amount as a condition for the loan or an extension in its maturity. It is regarded by a predominant majority of Muslims to be equivalent to interest as commonly known today.
Salaf	Short form of *bayʿ al-salaf.*
Salam	Short form of *bayʿ al-salam.*
Sharīʿah	Refers to the corpus of Islamic law based on divine guidance as given by the Qur'ān and the *Sunnah* and embodies all aspects of the Islamic faith, including beliefs and practices.
Sunnah	The *Sunnah* is the most important source of the Islamic faith after the Qur'ān and refers to the Prophet's (peace be upon him) example as indicated by his practice of the faith. The only way to know the *Sunnah* is through the collection of *aḥādīth*, which consist of reports about the sayings, deeds and reactions of the Prophet (peace be upon him).
Sūrah	A chapter of Al-Qur'ān.
Takāful	An alternative for the contemporary insurance contract. A group of persons agree to share certain risk (e.g. damage by fire) by collecting a specified sum from each. In case of loss to anyone of the group, the loss is met from the collected funds.
Tawakkul	Trust in God for results after one has undertaken all necessary effort. It is one of the important values for

	Muslims. After making all necessary efforts, a Muslim believes that the results are in the hand of God.
Wadīʿah	A contract whereby a person leaves valuables with someone for safekeeping. The keeper can charge a fee, even though in Islamic culture it is encouraged to provide this service free of charge or to recover only the costs of safekeeping without any profit.
Wakālah	Contract of agency. In this contract, one person appoints someone else to perform a certain task on his behalf, usually against a fixed fee.
Waqf	Appropriation or tying up a property in perpetuity for specific purposes. No property rights can be exercised over the corpus. Only the usufruct is applied towards the objectives (usually charitable) of the *waqf*.
Zakāh	The amount payable by a Muslim on his net worth as a part of his religious obligations, mainly for the benefit of the poor and the needy.

1. Introduction

Munawar Iqbal and David T. Llewellyn

The Islamic financial system has a centuries-old history. As noted by Chapra and Khan (2000), 'From the very early stage in Islamic history, Muslims were able to establish a financial system without interest for mobilising resources to finance productive activities and consumer needs. The system worked quite effectively during the heyday of Islamic civilization and for centuries thereafter.' However, as the centre of economic gravity shifted over the centuries to the Western world, Western financial institutions (including banks) became dominant and the Islamic tradition remained dormant.

In recent years, however, there has been a significant revival of interest in developing a modern version of the historic Islamic financial system in the wake of Muslims' desire to stay clear of interest, which is prohibited according to the Islamic *Sharīʿah*. Some countries (notably Iran, Pakistan and Sudan) are attempting complete elimination of the role of interest from their financial systems. Other countries have allowed the establishment of Islamic banks alongside what will be termed 'conventional' banks. There are now more than 200 Islamic financial institutions around the globe working under different economic and social milieux. Even in secular countries where legal systems do not allow establishment of Islamic banks, Muslim communities have found alternative provisions within the law to establish substitute institutions to fulfil the financial needs of Muslims in accordance with their faith. Bagsiraj (Chapter 9, this volume) offers a valuable survey of the experience of Islamic financial institutions in the secular system of India. He notes that although the financial laws of India do not allow establishment of Islamic banks, some Islamic financial institutions have been established as non-bank financial companies, which offer financial services without the use of interest. He provides instructive highlights of the working of several such institutions in India. Wilson (Chapter 10) reviews some similar institutions working in both Muslim and Western countries using non-bank provisions of the laws there. Recently, several Western multinational banks, including Citibank, Hong Kong and Shanghai Banking Corporation and Chase Manhattan, have also started offering Islamic financial products.

The Islamic financial industry is already one of the fastest-growing industries and has great potential. It has been estimated that the market size of Islamic transactions was about $160 billion in 1997 and was rising at an annual rate of 10–15 per cent (*Islamic Banker*, 1997). The re-emergence of Islamic banking and different types of Islamic financial institutions and products is to be welcomed because in many ways global financial arrangements can benefit from diversity and having banking institutions with a different *modus operandi*, and different risk-sharing characteristics associated with the types of contracts that they offer.

The papers at the Conference[1] (a selection of which are included in this volume) address some of the key analytical and practical issues in Islamic finance in general and banking in particular. Although, as mentioned above, Islamic banking has its roots in centuries-old history, formal analysis of Islamic finance is a comparatively recent phenomenon. Papers presented at the conference testify that it has developed significantly in a short period of time. There is richness in the analysis in the conference papers, which contributes substantially to enhancing our understanding of Islamic finance and its role in economy and society.

While the progress made by Islamic banks may be impressive, they should not be viewed in isolation. This could make them become marginalized. In this regard the contribution by Wilson (Chapter 10) is particularly welcome. In this chapter he considers, *inter alia*, how conventional banks can offer Islamic financing facilities, and whether or not Islamic and conventional banks are converging or becoming increasingly distinctive. He also considers whether Islamic banks can learn lessons from the experience of conventional banks and vice versa. In particular, he argues that conventional banks can learn useful lessons from the experience of Islamic banks with respect to developing more enduring and trusting relationships with their customers. His final conclusion, with which we fully concur, is that Islamic and conventional banks should not view each other as threats.

In order to set an analytical context to the wide variety of chapters in this volume, it is instructive to return to some first principles. In this Introduction, we review some of the key analytical issues that confront all financial systems. In particular, we consider the basic and universal functions of a financial system irrespective of its particular form, the nature of financial contracts, and the common problems encountered in all financial systems.

The functions of financial systems are universal, whether these relate to developed or less developed economies, or to Islamic or conventional economies. Similarly, the practical problems encountered in performing these functions are also common to all financial systems. Where different paradigms diverge, relates to precisely how the universal functions are performed (the different modes of finance, for instance) but more importantly to the mechanisms for solving the universal problems in practice. The latter relates largely to the type of contracts issued. It is in these two dimensions that the key differences between Islamic and conventional finance lie.

1. UNIVERSAL FUNCTIONS OF A FINANCIAL SYSTEM

Four key roles are performed in a financial system. First, it provides financial intermediation services, channelling funds from ultimate savers to ultimate borrowers and in the process removing budget constraints. This in turn facilitates the movement of resources between agents, over time and across space. Second, the system provides a wide range of other financial services not immediately related to financial intermediation: payments services, insurance, fund management, and so on. Third, it creates a wide range of assets and liabilities, each of which has different characteristics with respect to, for instance, liquidity, maturity, the type of return generated, and risk-sharing. The fourth central role of any financial system is the creation of incentives for an efficient allocation of resources within an economy, and the allocation of scarce financial and real resources between competing ends. These key roles of the financial system are not specific to conventional or Islamic-based systems. It is in how these roles are performed that differences arise. This can be illustrated by giving some examples.

The function of financial intermediation requires providing mechanisms for saving and borrowing so that agents in the economy can alleviate budget constraints. This involves creating a variety of financial assets and liabilities with different characteristics that appeal to different savers and borrowers. The conventional commercial banks provide the financial intermediation services on the basis of rate of interest on both the assets and the liabilities side. Since interest is prohibited in Islam, Islamic banks have developed several other modes through which savings are mobilized and passed on to entrepreneurs, none of which involves interest. Yasseri (Chapter 8) describes several of these modes being used in Iran. These include *muḍārabah*, *mushārakah*, *murābaḥah*, *muzāraʿah*, *bayʿ al-salam*, and so on. Islamic banks in other countries are also, by and large, using the same modes, though the degree of use of a particular mode may differ from one bank to another. Similarly, for performing the function of providing other financial services, such as payment services, insurance, fund management and the like, Islamic banks have developed contracts such as *juʿālah*, *takāful* and *mushārakah*. Some of these are also discussed by Yasseri.

The third and fourth common functions require creation of a wide variety of instruments and incentives for an efficient allocation of scarce financial and real resources between competing ends. An efficient allocation of resources requires an accurate assessment and efficient pricing of risk. Somehow, the price of finance needs to include an allowance for the risks involved. Similarly, the rates of return to the suppliers of finance should also reflect the risks taken. In conventional systems a major route for this is through the rate of interest, with risks of alternative projects or loans being reflected in different risk premia incorporated in interest rates on different loans. Clearly, this route is not relevant in Islamic finance, which means that alternative mechanisms are needed.

It must be noted here that the prohibition of interest in Islam does not mean that capital is not to be rewarded nor that risk is not to be priced. The Islamic system has both fixed and variable return modes to price the capital and add risk premia according to the degree of risk involved. Islamic banks provide financing using two methods. The first is based on profit-sharing and the second involves modes which depend on fixed return (mark-up) and often end in creating indebtedness of the party seeking finance. The modes of finance used by Islamic banks are, however, unique for two reasons. First, debt associated with financing by way of mark-up modes results from real commodity sale/purchase operations, rather than the exchange of money for interest-bearing debt. Unlike conventional debt, such debt is not marketable except at its nominal value. Second, the introduction into banking of modes that depend on profit-sharing is an innovation that brings important advantages. (See Mirakhor, 1997.)

2. NATURE OF FINANCIAL CONTRACTS

Financial instruments, contracts, institutions and markets are needed for these functions to be performed. Risk and uncertainty are at the centre of financial contracts and the way they are constructed. If there were no uncertainty about the future, the specific contractual form in which financial markets and institutions channel funds from savers to lenders would have no significance. The chapter by Suwailem (Chapter 2) discusses the problems of decision-making under uncertainty. He quotes from several authors to show that in conventional textbook presentations of decision-making under uncertainty, no distinction is made between investment and gambling. Chance and skill are treated equally in this framework. It is not clear how gambling differs from entrepreneurship, and why taking risk in some instances is praised and in others blamed. He argues that this framework is not suitable from an Islamic perspective. Instead, he suggests that the proper starting point for the subject is causality, whereby decisions are based on proper causes to achieve the desired outcome. The most likely outcome of a certain action determines its causal value, so if an action is more likely to lead to failure than to success, it is considered as a cause of failure, regardless of the desirability of the outcome. Because of the moral value of causes, the decision-maker shall not be deceived by the size of return when it is unlikely to materialize. Incorporating a moral value of cause, he argues that from an Islamic perspective, decision-making under uncertainty requires implementing proper causes to achieve desired outcomes. Investment differs from gambling: investment is a decision to implement appropriate causes, while gambling is to take pure chance. The former is eulogized in Islam, while the latter is condemned.

In practice, uncertainty does matter and three alternative types of contracts are available to deal with it: debt, equity and insurance contracts. In comparing conventional and Islamic financial systems, the first two of these contracts have been the focus of several chapters in this volume. Debt contracts create a defined obligation to repay irrespective of the performance of the borrower. The rate of return paid by the borrower and received by the lender is independent of performance except in the extreme case of default. Equity contracts are where the return to the holder of the contract is determined by the performance of the issuer. The rate of return cannot be specified in advance, but is determined by the outcome of the project. As in the conventional system, both kinds of contract exist in the Islamic financial system. Relative preferences may, however, differ.

In conventional banking, debt has been found to be an efficient risk-sharing mode in the face of asymmetric information and when the costs of verifying the rate of return of a project become excessive in relation to potential benefits. At the same time, debt contracts minimize monitoring costs because the lending bank is not interested in the degree of success of the project so long as it does not fail to an extent that causes the borrower to default. Debt contracts also have lower transactions costs.

Due to these attractive features, conventional banks have a natural preference for debt contracts. However, the contract also has several undesirable features. One of these is that the bank does not share in the potential upside gain (the return is fixed even in the event that the project is extremely, and possibly unexpectedly, successful) but does share in the extreme downside potential loss in the event of bankruptcy of the borrower. For the financial system as a whole, it has been argued that excessive reliance on debt-financing is both inefficient and unstable. Analysing several financial crises, Chapra (Chapter 11) argues that the primary cause of these crises is inadequate market discipline resulting from debt-based borrowing and lending. He points out that:

> Instead of making the depositors and the bankers share in the risks of business, it assures the depositors of the repayment of their deposits or loans with interest. This makes the depositors take little interest in the soundness of the financial institution. It also makes the banks rely on the crutches of the collateral to extend financing for practically any purpose, including speculation. The collateral cannot, however, be a substitute for a more careful evaluation of the project financed. This is because the value of the collateral can itself be impaired by the same factors that diminish the ability of the borrower to repay the loan. The ability of the market to impose the

> required discipline is thus impaired, which leads to an unhealthy expansion in the overall volume of credit, to excessive leverage, and to living beyond means. (p. 221)

He poses the question as to why a rise in debt, and particularly short-term debt, should accentuate instability. In this respect, he points out that:

> One of the major reasons is the close link between easy availability of credit, macroeconomic imbalances, and financial instability. The easy availability of credit makes it possible for the public sector to have a high debt profile and for the private sector to live beyond its means and to have a high leverage. If the debt is not used productively, the ability to service the debt does not rise in proportion to the debt and leads to financial fragility and debt crises. The greater the reliance on short-term debt and the higher the leverage, the more severe the crises may be. This is because short-term debt is easily reversible as far as the lender is concerned, but repayment is difficult for the borrower if the amount is locked up in loss-making speculative assets or medium- and long-term investments with a long gestation period. (p. 222)

However, debt remains a useful contract both in conventional and Islamic systems. Chapra himself points out that 'there may be nothing basically wrong in a reasonable amount of short-term debt that is used for financing the purchase and sale of real goods and services.' The point here is that debt ought to be linked with real transactions and that it is not used for pure speculative purposes.

As compared to debt contracts, profit-sharing contracts are where the return to the holder of the contract is determined by the performance of the issuer. In contrast to a debt contract, the financier and entrepreneur share symmetrically (though not, of course, necessarily equally) in profits and losses. There are four key differences between the debt contracts and equity or equity-type contracts: the degree and form of risk-sharing; the absence of any ownership stake in debt contracts but its presence to some degree in equity contracts; the incentives that exist for the lender to monitor the borrower's post-contract behaviour; and the fact that default on debt contracts can trigger bankruptcy whereas poor performance on equity contracts does not trigger insolvency. Chapra argues (Chapter 11) that more equity financing would enhance the stability characteristics of financial systems because, through the resultant risk-sharing contracts, financiers would have a greater incentive both to assess risks at the outset and to monitor borrowers after finance had been given.

Theoretical studies in the early 1960s, which formed the basis for the establishment of Islamic banks, built their vision on profit-sharing finance. Several strong arguments in favour of profit-sharing finance over fixed return modes of finance were provided. However, in practice the modes of financing being used by most Islamic banks are dominated by fixed-return modes such as *murābaḥah* and leasing (see Iqbal et al., 1998). This divergence between theory and practice needs an explanation. Several chapters in this volume address this issue.

There are practical reasons for the profit/loss-sharing (PLS) contracts not to be as popular as expected. Problems of moral hazard, adverse selection, high information requirements and higher transactions costs are some of these. Abalkhail and Presley (Chapter 6) note that constraints on PLS contracts in Islamic banking derive essentially from problems of asymmetric information and the nature of banks as essentially short-term finance institutions. Similarly, Ahmed (Chapter 3) highlights the moral hazard problems in PLS contracts. In order for Islamic finance to deliver its full promise, the share of profit-sharing finance in the financial system must be increased. However, in order for this to happen the features of a profit-sharing contract which are compatible with the incentive requirements of both suppliers and seekers of funds must be identified and incorporated in the contracts. Some authors in this volume argue that while equity or equity-type contracts are to be preferred in Islamic finance, there are major obstacles in the way of their widespread use. They have pointed out several problems along with possible solutions. Some of these are discussed below.

3. COMMON PROBLEMS

Just as the role and basic functions of financial systems are universal, so too are the problems that are encountered in performing these functions. However, there are differences in the way they are handled. Many chapters in this volume focus on the ways of addressing these problems in Islamic finance. It is instructive to outline the nature of at least the most important of the common problems. A brief consideration is given to six problem areas that are discussed in different chapters included in this volume: (1) the problem of asymmetric information and the costs involved in reducing it; (2) the problem of verifying, *ex ante*, the promises and intentions that are frequently involved in financial transactions (adverse selection problem); (3) problems of moral hazard; (4) incentive problems and the issue of aligning incentives between counterparties; (5) agency costs when direct or indirect principal–agent relationships arise in financial transactions; and (6) the need for monitoring of counterparties' behaviour.

3.1 Asymmetric Information

Information is at the centre of all financial transactions and contracts. Three problems are pertinent: not everyone has the same information; everyone has less than perfect information; and some transactors have 'inside' information which is not made available to counterparties to transactions. Decisions are therefore made *ex ante* on the basis of less than complete information and sometimes with counterparties who have superior information with the potential for exploitation. In any financial system, information is not symmetrically distributed across all agents, which implies that different agents have different information sets. Put another way, full and complete information is not uniformly available to all interested parties. In addition, not all parties have the same ability to utilize the information that is available to them. In particular, parties have more information about themselves (including their intentions and abilities) than do others. The problem arises because information is not a free good and the acquisition of information is not a costless activity. If either were the case, there would never be a problem of asymmetric information. Information problems have been addressed in many of the chapters included in this volume. This is not particularly surprising, as asymmetric information and the problems this gives rise to are central to financial arrangements and the way financial institutions behave to limit and manage risk.

One general solution to information problems, of course, is for transactors to invest in information, although, as already noted, this is not a costless activity and free-rider problems may emerge as, in some cases, no one transactor can appropriate the full value of the costly information acquired. However, in some areas public policy can assist by requiring disclosure of relevant information. Ahmed (Chapter 3) emphasizes the role that governments can play in alleviating asymmetric information problems in Islamic finance by requiring information disclosure. He also observes that information disclosure, along with other measures that governments can adopt, is required not only to bolster profit-sharing modes of finance but also in the interests of efficiency in the financial system in general. There are also international standards of information disclosure set by the Basel Accords. These need to be given serious attention.

Markets can also sometimes create incentives for disclosure as, for instance, when the cost of capital is lowered when complete information is made available to market participants. It is also an option to screen counterparties and attempt to verify the information given. And yet none of this is costless, which implies that the rational transactor will continue to acquire information until the marginal cost of acquisition is equal to the marginal benefit derived from it. This is easy to state in principle but difficult to measure in practice. A key question, therefore, in many financial transactions (most especially in loan arrangements) is what information is necessary before a considered judgement about risks can be made.

Abalkhail and Presley (Chapter 6) remind us that, without effective information transfer, markets perform poorly and inefficiently. A somewhat different, but very useful, perspective is offered in their chapter, where they discuss asymmetric information problems in PLS contracts in the informal risk capital market of Saudi Arabia. They present empirical evidence with respect to how attempts are made to solve these problems in this particular market. The chapter presents the first-ever empirical investigation in Saudi Arabia of informal investors' decision-making behaviour. The authors present a theoretical framework, based on asymmetric information, principal–agent analysis, and incomplete contracts that characterize this market. They use this framework to test empirically how informal investors attempt to reduce the inefficiencies and risks associated with asymmetric information problems that exist in PLS contracts.

3.2 Contractual Promises and Adverse Selection Problem

Financial transactions often involve a set of promises or undertakings from one party to another. The problem is that intentions cannot be observed and there may be incentives to lie to or mislead a counterparty. For example, in the case of PLS contracts, Ahmed (Chapter 3) points out that 'as the profit is shared between the firm and the bank at an agreed-upon ratio, there may be an incentive on the part of an amoral entrepreneur to report lower profit to keep a larger share of it for himself'. He then goes on to give a theoretical exposition of a profit-sharing contract that may reduce the inducement to cheat through a reward/punishment mechanism. The fact that intentions cannot be observed in essence implies that financial contracts are necessarily incomplete contracts. As argued by Abalkhail and Presley (Chapter 6), this implies that 'investors may be unable to predict future events in order to write complete contracts that specify each party's obligations in all contingencies'. The central problem is how one party can ensure that the counterparty delivers on promises or intentions. This may involve sanctions or creating incentive structures that align the interests of the counterparties. This is discussed in section 3.4 below.

3.3 Moral Hazard Problems

Moral hazard is a particular incentive problem that often arises from asymmetric information. Superior information may enable one party to work against the interest of another. In general, moral hazard arises when a contract or financial arrangement creates incentives for parties to behave against the interest of others. The skill in devising financial contracts is to limit the potential for moral hazard behaviour.

There are inherent moral hazards in profit-sharing contracts, which is one reason for their lack of popularity even in Islamic banks. One problem, for example, is the incentive the borrower may have in concealing the true level of profits or absorbing some of the profits through unauthorized perquisites. However, these problems are not unique to profit-sharing contracts. They are similar to those that arise in any equity contract in conventional systems.

The solution to moral hazard problems can lie in a combination of incentive-compatible contracts, the imposition of penalties on bad behaviour, effective monitoring of behaviour, and the enforcement of contracts if ever a moral hazard arises which creates an incentive for one party not to deliver on a contract. One solution in conventional banking, which may have only limited use in Islamic banking, is the pledging of collateral against loans whereby the borrower loses the collateral in the event of default.[2] This is a mechanism for aligning the incentives of the borrower with the interest of the lender.

In the Islamic system a particular consideration is the extent to which reliance can be placed on good behaviour dictated by the norms of Islam itself. This is an interesting area and useful discussion is given in the chapter by Wilson (Chapter 10). He argues that there is a higher level of trust between Islamic banks and their clients than is the case with conventional banks and hence the moral hazard risks are less. This is because there is a greater degree of shared values, including ethical values related to honesty. He makes the important point that higher levels of trust reduce risk and uncertainty, which in turn results in lower monitoring costs for Islamic banks. A similar line is offered in the chapter by Khalil, Rickwood and Murinde (Chapter 4), who argue that 'religion, and in particular Islam, demands specific codes of behaviour to be followed, adherence to which would reduce the agency problems'.

3.4 Incentive Structures

A key problem in many financial transactions is how to create incentives for good behaviour, and in particular incentives not to behave against the interests of a counterparty in a transaction. A central issue in any financial system is the structure of incentives that arise and how contracts can be constructed in such a way as to align incentives. Some of the chapters discuss a particular route to solving incentive problems: the creation of incentive-compatible contracts. These are extensively discussed in the literature in conventional finance. The key is to construct contracts that align the incentives of counterparties. Obvious mechanisms include profit- or reward-sharing arrangements, imposing costs and penalties on bad behaviour, and ensuring that contracts are enforced and that all parties know that contracts will be enforced. The chapter by Karim (Chapter 5) considers optimal contracts to deal with the problems of asymmetric information and the resultant danger of moral hazard and how risk-sharing can be structured optimally. He emphasizes the requirement to construct incentive-compatible contracts for Islamic banking and, using a valuable case study of Bank Muamalat, Indonesia, proceeds to describe how this can be done. He stresses four conditions for incentive-compatibility in contracts: the entrepreneur or recipients of funds having a higher stake in net worth and/or collateral; low operating costs; having a low degree of unobservable cash flow; and having a low proportion of non-controllable costs. He discusses the nature of optimal contracts and, using the case study of Bank Muamalat in its *muḍārabah* contracts, shows how the proportion of profit-sharing financing increased significantly after 1998 when the bank introduced its pilot project based on incentive-compatible contracts for profit-sharing modes of finance. This chapter is particularly interesting because it extends the analysis beyond the theoretical plane and illustrates a practical application of theoretical constructs.

The literature on this topic as related to conventional finance also includes reference to reputation as at least a partial solution to incentive problems. This becomes relevant in repeat games where a bad reputation gained in one contract is carried through to subsequent contracts, which means that the terms of subsequent contracts are less advantageous and sometimes contracts are refused altogether. Abalkhail and Presley (Chapter 6) discuss how the investors in the informal sector evaluate the reputation of the entrepreneur through consultation with other investors. They find that for Saudi informal investors the track record of the entrepreneur is the best method of preventing the selection of low-quality entrepreneurs. This may have important lessons for Islamic banks. They can institute a mechanism through which amoral entrepreneurs are singled out and blacklisted by all banks.

3.5 Principal–Agent Problems

Financial transactions frequently create principal–agent problems of one sort or another. This is also related to the problem of incentive structures in that the central issue is how a principal is able to rely on the agent acting in the interests of the principal employing him rather than his own selfish interest and against those of the principal. The problem arises because the agent often has superior information and expertise (which may be the reason the principal employs him). The agent can choose his behaviour after the contract has been established, and because of this the agent is often able to conceal the outcome of a contract. Agency problems also arise because the agent cannot be efficiently or costlessly monitored. Unless these problems can be solved, the agency costs involved can act as a serious deterrent to financial contracting with resultant welfare losses. The challenge is to create contracts or arrangements that align the interests of the principal and the agent. As many of the authors establish, one way of solving this is through a standard profit/loss-sharing arrangement whereby the agent shares the profits with the principal and so has an incentive also to behave in the interest of the principal.

Abalkhail and Presley (Chapter 6) remind us that the literature has identified two main approaches to reducing agency problems. In the principal–agent approach, the focus is on the optimal contract between principal and agent. In contrast, in the incomplete contract approach emphasis is given to how contracts can be made less incomplete. The particular agency costs associated with *muḍārabah* contracts are discussed by Khalil, Rickwood and Murinde (Chapter 4), who present substantial empirical evidence on the problems encountered in such contracts. The authors have applied survey methods to collect primary data on the practice of Islamic banking and in the process have produced what is probably one of the most comprehensive empirical tests of PLS contracts to date. The authors extensively consider the agency characteristics and problems in PLS contracts such as overconsumption of perquisites by the entrepreneur, the under-reporting of profits, risk avoidance and shirking of effort by the agent. They go on to propose a robust contractual governance structure to cope with the agency problems encountered in PLS contracts.

3.6 Monitoring

The need for post-contract monitoring is generally greater in finance than in other areas of economic activity. Because of the asymmetric information problems, the behaviour of counterparties needs to be monitored after a contract has been agreed to ensure that information asymmetries are not exploited by one party against the interest of the other, and also because frequently a fiduciary relationship is created by a financial contract. In both cases, agents need to be monitored to ensure that their behaviour is consistent with the interests of principals. A special characteristic of many financial contracts is that the value cannot be observed or verified at the point of purchase, and that the post-contract behaviour of a counterparty determines the ultimate value of the contract. This also creates a need for monitoring. In addition, monitoring is needed because many financial contracts are long-term in nature and information acquired before a contract is agreed may become irrelevant during the course of the contract as circumstances and conditions change. Above all, the value of a contract or financial product cannot be ascertained with certainty at the point the contract is made or the product is purchased. This often distinguishes financial contracts from other economic contracts such as purchases of goods. While the need for monitoring is accepted, it too is an expensive activity (see Khalil, Rickwood and Murinde, Chapter 4) and transactors need to balance the marginal costs and benefits of incremental monitoring.

An interesting way of safeguarding against the asymmetry of information at the post-investment stage is staging of finance. Abalkhail and Presley (Chapter 6) show how informal investors resort to this method to minimize adverse selection. Another way is supervision and monitoring of the entrepreneur. In their chapter (Chapter 7), Sadr and Iqbal show the importance of returns to information-gathering and monitoring of recipients of funds and entrepreneurs in order to reduce asymmetric information and resultant moral hazard problems. They provide a useful case study of the Agricultural Bank of Iran and show that there are huge benefits for an Islamic financial institution investing in supervision and monitoring.

4. CONCLUSION

Several potential benefits can arise from the emergence of Islamic banks, beside their desirability from an Islamic point of view. These include:

1. The range of contracts available to customers is widened. This is an example of the efficiency-enhancing characteristics of spectrum filling (Llewellyn, 1992).
2. It would create a financial system populated by financial institutions with a different *modus operandi*, which has the effect of widening choice for consumers.
3. The widening of the range of financial contracts available, and differences in the *modus operandi* of conventional and Islamic banks, have the effect of enhancing competition between alternative banking models which is expected, in turn, to increase efficiency of the financial system.
4. It would enable Islamic religious beliefs to be reflected in financial arrangements and transactions, thereby fulfilling the financial needs of Muslims in accordance with their faith.
5. Allocation of financial resources on the basis of profit/loss-sharing gives maximum weight to the profitability of investment, whereas an interest-based allocation gives it to creditworthiness. We may expect the allocation made on the basis of profitability to be more efficient than that made on the basis of interest.
6. Because of the nature of the contracts on the liabilities side of the balance sheet, Islamic banks are often less vulnerable to external shocks and are less susceptible to insolvency. This is because a wider range of liability holders share in the risks of the bank as compared with the conventional banks.
7. Because holders of investment deposits share in the risks of an Islamic bank (for example through PLS contracts) and are not offered guarantees, incentives are created for a wider range of stakeholders in the bank to monitor its behaviour and risk-taking.
8. By creating more systemic diversity, the stability of the financial system may be enhanced because the behavioural characteristics of different types of banks are likely to vary.
9. In the case of both the PLS and *murābaḥah* contracts, since bank assets are created in response to investment opportunities in the real sector of the economy, the real factors related to the production of goods and services (in

contrast with the financial factors) become the prime movers of the rates of return to the financial sector.

During the last two decades, the Islamic financial industry as well as the Islamic theory of finance has made significant progress. However, as an evolving reality the industry is still faced with many problems. Some of these have been noted by the contributors to this volume. Islamic finance as a discipline is also in its early phases of development. A number of theoretical issues need to be researched. One of the most important issues that captured the attention of several contributors to the conference relates to the role of profit/loss-sharing under Islamic finance. Despite several theoretical studies showing the benefits of profit-sharing, in practice it has not been adopted by Islamic banks to any significant degree. Contributors to this volume have mentioned some reasons for this divergence between theory and practice. The attention given to this issue is very welcome. An important area in the development of the Islamic theory of finance is to identify the features of a profit-sharing contract that are compatible with the incentive requirements of both suppliers and seekers of funds. Therefore, a great deal more research is needed in this area.

NOTES

1. The Fourth International Conference on Islamic Economics and Banking, Loughborough University, UK, 13–15 August 2000.
2. In the Islamic system, such recourse is possible only in the case of default or loss caused by negligence or wilful misconduct.

REFERENCES

Chapra, M.U. and Tariqullah Khan (2000), *Regulation and Supervision of Islamic Banks*, Occasional Paper No. 3, Jeddah, Saudi Arabia: Islamic Research and Training Institute, Islamic Development Bank.

Iqbal, Munawar, Ausaf Ahmad and Tariqullah Khan (1998), *Challenges Facing Islamic Banking*, Occasional Paper No. 2, Jeddah, Saudi Arabia: Islamic Research and Training Institute, Islamic Development Bank.

Islamic Banker (1997) (9), August.

Llewellyn, David T. (1992), 'Financial Innovation: A Basic Analysis', in H. Cavanna (ed.), *Financial Innovation*, London: Routledge.

Mirakhor, Abbas (1997), 'Progress and Challenges of Islamic Banking', *Review of Islamic Economics*, **4** (2).

2. Decision-making under uncertainty: an Islamic perspective

Sami Ibrahim Al-Suwailem

> Although theories of choice tend to treat gambling as a prototypic situation of decision-making under risk, decision-makers distinguish between 'risk-taking' and gambling, saying that while they should take risks, they should never gamble. They react to variability more by trying actively to avoid it or control it than by treating it as a trade-off with expected value in making a choice. March (1994, p. 54)

1. INTRODUCTION

Textbook presentation of decision-making under uncertainty does not distinguish between investment and gambling. 'We structure the uncertainty facing an agent by interpreting risky situations as gambles' (Jehle, 1991, p. 193). Writers start with how an entrepreneur chooses among different investment projects and end up with the lottery ticket as a 'concrete example' of the problem (for example Sinn, 1983, pp. 4–5). After defining a lottery to be a prize received with a given probability, Varian (1992, p. 172) writes: 'Most situations involving behaviour under risk can be put into this lottery framework.' Allais (1976) reports that he started analysing random choice by 'thinking about a method for successful race-course betting, based on the use of newspaper forecasts' (p. 445).

Thus decision-making under uncertainty is viewed as choosing among lotteries. Chance and skill appear to be treated equally in this framework. It is not clear how gambling differs from entrepreneurship, and why taking a risk in some instances is praised and in others blamed.

Studies on decision-making under uncertainty from an Islamic perspective are quite rare. Further, despite the central position of *gharar* and risk in Islamic principles of exchange, there is no framework for studying such transactions within an integral theme of decision-making under risk.

This chapter is an attempt to address these problems in a suggestive manner. It is argued that the proper starting point for the subject is causality, whereby decisions are based on proper causes to achieve the desired outcome. The most likely outcome of a certain action determines its causal value, so if an action is more likely to lead to failure than to success, it is considered as a cause of failure, regardless of the desirability of the other outcome. Because of the moral value of causes the decision-maker shall not be deceived by the size of return when it is unlikely to materialize. The relationship between causality and *gharar* points to the existence of a general framework for individual and interactive decisions.

2. RISK AND ACTION

2.1 The Act of Choice and Process-regarding

Neoclassical economics distinguishes three concepts in decision theory under risk:[1] states of nature, actions of the decision-maker, and consequences of these actions. 'Individual choices relate solely to consequences' (Malinvaud, 1972, p. 286).

Several studies have criticized neoclassical economics for ignoring the process of choice in decision-making. The act of choice, or the way a decision-maker chooses, is not evaluated in the conventional theory of decision-making.

Knight (1921) is among the early economists to explain how the process of choice becomes important under uncertainty:

> With uncertainty absent, man's energies are devoted altogether to doing things; it is doubtful whether intelligence itself would exist in such a situation; in a world so built that perfect knowledge was theoretically possible, it seems likely that all organic readjustments would become mechanical, all organisms automata. With uncertainty present, doing things, the actual execution of activity, becomes in a real sense a secondary part of life; the primary problem or function is deciding what to do and how to do it ... *the task of deciding what to do and how to do it takes the ascendancy over that of execution* (emphasis added). (p. 268)

More recently, Sen (1997) argued that the act of choice differentiates human maximization from natural maximization:

> The formulation of maximizing behaviour in economics paralleled the modelling in physics and related disciplines. But maximizing behaviour differs from non-volitional maximization because of the fundamental relevance of the choice act, which has to be placed in a central position in analysing maximizing behaviour. (p. 745)

Sen calls for 'including the choice act in comprehensive analysis of decisions, and the connection between choosing and responsibility' (p. 746).

Ben-Ner and Putterman (1998) take a similar position:

> Individuals care about the manner in which they themselves and others behave, including the ways in which they attain outcomes of interest. ... Uncommon is the individual who is indifferent about whether he has achieved his income through honest work or blind luck, whether he has cheated others or treated them fairly. (p. 20)

These remarks are supported by empirical studies concerning business decision-making under risk. We review below some of these studies.

2.2 Adjusting Risk

Experimental studies in choice under uncertainty focus almost exclusively on pure selection among lotteries. Subjects are presented with risky options and asked simply to choose among them. This framework is neither realistic nor desirable. Decision makers in real-life situations more often than not seek to adjust risky situations to have the odds in their favour. MacCrimmon and Wehrung (1986) arrive at this conclusion after receiving extensive questionnaires filled in by more than 500 senior business managers. Among these questionnaires was what they call the 'risk in-basket' model. In this model, each participant is presented with a certain problem and asked to take decisions to solve it. The consequences, however, are uncertain. The main finding is that managers consistently attempt to control or adjust the risks they face, and do not simply take them as given. Only 4 per cent of the sample did not modify any of the situations they were presented with (p. 88). The authors point out that the 'prevalence of attempts to modify risk suggests the desirability of expanding existing theories of risk beyond a narrow focus on choice' (p. 101).

In a similar study, Shapira (1995) surveys more than 700 business managers on issues related to risk and decision-making under uncertainty. An important finding is that managers made a sharp distinction between risk-taking and gambling. The former involves judgement and skill, while the latter is merely accepting risk. Risk adjustment is not restricted to the pre-decision stage; it extends to the post-decision period. 'Managers see themselves as taking risks, but only after modifying and working on the dangers *so that they can be confident of success*' (p. 74, emphasis added). In contrast to gambling, risk-taking 'is an endeavour where a manager can use his judgement, exert control, and utilize skills'. This is absent from gambling (p. 48). Shapira concludes that the 'gambling metaphor appears as an inadequate description of managerial risk taking' (p. 120).

On the basis of these studies, we can conclude that the lottery or gambling framework is not a proper starting point for the analysis of decision-making under risk. We need a framework that is closer to real-life business decisions. In an Islamic framework, it also has to be consistent with Islamic rules and principles.

2.3 Controllable and Uncontrollable Risk

It is first necessary to differentiate between two types of risks:[2]

1. Uncontrollable risk or chance. The decision-maker has no control whatsoever over this type of risk.
2. Controllable or responsive risk. This type of risk can be controlled and affected by the decision-maker.

Whenever risk taking is praised for promoting growth and economic development, it is responsive risk, not chance. The reason is that such risk creates incentives for entrepreneurial efforts and value-adding work. From an Islamic point of view, risk as such, like hardship, is not desirable for its own sake. The Prophet (peace be upon him) clearly states: 'Avoid what causes suspicions and choose what does not' (Albānī al-, 1986, No. 3378). Muslim scholars state that 'if one affords certainty he may not resort to conjecture' (Quarāfī al-, undated, vol. 3, p. 274; Ashathrī, 1997, vol. 2, p. 507; Miqarī al-, undated, vol. 2, p. 370; Azzarkashī, 1982, vol. 2, p. 354). Risk becomes desirable only when it stimulates productive efforts and value-adding activities.

3. THE CAUSALITY APPROACH

3.1 Uncertainty and Causality

Uncertainty is intrinsic to all economic activities. However, uncertain rewards are governed by certain causes that control or affect the probabilities of their occurrence. So if an agent seeks an uncertain return, he should implement the actions that control the occurrence of the return.

Factors that control the probability of a random outcome are considered as causes (*asbāb*) of that outcome. In Islamic cultures, uncertainty is strongly linked to causes. Once a decision-maker is faced with an uncertain decision problem, he will take care of the causal factors and leave the final result to the will of Allah, the Almighty. This behaviour is well established in Islamic principles. In this regard, the saying of the Prophet (peace be upon him) about protecting one's camel in the desert, 'Tie it and entrust [it to God]' (Albānī al-, 1986, No. 1068), is frequently cited. This rule is compatible with the types of risks mentioned above. The cause, tying the camel, addresses controllable risk, while entrusting (*tawakkul*) addresses uncontrollable risk.

Here we argue that the causality principle represents an important landmark in the Islamic approach to decision-making under uncertainty.

3.2 How to Identify Causes

Identifying a casual relationship can be based on one or more of the following:

1. An explicit statement from the Qur'ān or *Sunnah* of the Prophet (peace be upon him). Such assertion might be in the form '*x* causes *y*,' as in the Qur'ānic phrase concerning honey: 'In it is a cure for mankind' (16:69). Or, it might be in the form '*x* does *not* cause *y*,' like the *ḥadīth*: 'The sun and the moon are two signs of Allah. They do not eclipse for the birth of a person nor for his death' [Albānī al-, 1986, No. 1644).
2. Experimental evidence, whereby statistical and quantitative methods are used to evaluate causality relations (for example Pearl, 2000).
3. Intuitive judgement, whereby an agent would assess the plausibility of different scenarios to conclude which is more likely to be the cause of a certain effect (for example Einhorn and Hogarth, 1987).

3.3 Moral Value of Causes

From an Islamic perspective, a cause becomes of value because it leads to the desired (beneficial) outcome. Muslim scholars state that 'means are treated in the same manner as ends' (Quarāfi al-, undated, vol. 3, p. 111), and the Prophet (peace be upon him) states: 'deeds are evaluated based on the objectives (intentions) behind them' (Albānī al-, 1986, p. 10). He further states that: 'if a jurist seeks the truth and achieves it, he is rewarded twice; if not he is rewarded once' (Albānī al-, 1986, No. 493). This shows that proper seeking of the truth (*ijtihād*) is rewarded, even when the desired (uncertain) outcome is missed. Thus causes are valued in themselves as long as the outcome they determine is valuable.

The cause is valued in its own right because its usefulness is not limited to a single trial or a particular instance, where the desired outcome may or may not be realized. Rather, it is based on *a priori* information that such an act, overall and in general, leads to the desired return. This explains what might at first glance appear as a contradiction; namely, the value of the cause is certain while its effect is uncertain. The reason is that describing an act *x* as a cause for result *y* does not mean that for every occurrence of *x* the result *y* will follow. It is a probabilistic relationship whereby *x*, more likely than not, leads to *y*.[3]

When a certain action may lead to different consequences, the one with the highest likelihood determines the value of that action. Driving to school or to work exposes one to risk of accident, but more probably one would arrive safely. Such actions, therefore, are valued because they lead successfully to the desired outcome more probably than to loss or failure. (Ibn Abdus-Salam pointed to this result a long time ago. See his book (2000), vol. 2, p. 109; also vol. 1, pp.

6–7, 138; vol. 2, pp. 35, 242–3.) Although this appears intuitive, conventional models of choice violate this result, as will be explained later.

It is, therefore, more appropriate to construct the objective function of decision-making in accordance with the causal contribution of the action considered. This approach is consistent with the importance of act of choice and process-regarding discussed by Sen (1997) and Ben-Ner and Putterman (1998). However, here the act is introduced because of the causal relationship between it and final outcomes. This logical linkage appears a natural extension to rationality, rather than a substitute for it.

3.4 Circle of Influence versus Circle of Concern

Everyone has a wide set of concerns, for example health, family, prices and so on. Only a subset of these issues can be influenced by the decision-maker, which can be classified into 'circle of influence'. According to Covey (1990), by focusing on the circle of influence, one becomes proactive, able to take initiatives, act positively, and able to determine one's condition. Those who focus instead on concerns beyond their influence become reactive to outside factors. Over time, the circle of influence for a reactive individual shrinks, while that for a proactive one expands. A reactive person eventually becomes conditioned by outside factors. His life becomes a function of circumstances.

A gambler is a clear example of a reactive person. His fortune is determined purely by luck. His circle of influence is effectively void, and he is totally dependent on outside circumstances. An entrepreneur, on the other hand, is a good example of a proactive individual. He focuses on his circle of influence and does not allow outside factors to totally determine his fortune. His objective is to maximize his circle of influence and minimize concerns beyond that.

Thus proactivity is consistent with the causality approach to decision-making under risk. Both lead to desirable behaviour, not only in economic matters, but in personal and social matters as well.

3.5 Causes and Ethics

More than 600 years ago, Al-Shāṭibī pointed to the relationship between causes and ethics. By focusing on the certain cause rather than on the uncertain outcome, Al-Shāṭibī argues, an individual will be able to implement the cause in a proper manner. If he were to focus on the uncertain outcome instead, he might implement the cause improperly, or seek inappropriate means, leading to dishonesty and unethical behaviour (Shāṭibī al-, 1997, vol. 1, pp. 348–9).

More recently, Dawes (1988) writes: 'If there were no uncertainty about consequences of behaviour, ethics and morality would not exist. ... To a large degree, an individual concerned with ethics wishes to do "the right thing" because the consequences of choice are not immediately obvious' (Dawes, 1988, pp. 267–8).

'The right thing' simply describes the thing that one may not regret doing, had the desired outcome not materialized. Obviously, it includes natural and logical causes of the desired outcome. It follows that adopting proper causes is an integral part of ethical behaviour. This approach integrates ethics into economics without attacking utility-maximizing or pursuing self-interest (see Sen, 1988).

Improper means need not be more effective in terms of causality than proper causes. To the contrary, there is a reason to believe that causality of the former is less effective than that of the latter. For example, an improper means might lead to the result 40 per cent of the time, while the proper cause leads to it 75 per cent of the time. This can be inferred from the saying of the Prophet (peace be upon him) concerning wine: 'It is not a cure; it is a disease', and: 'Allah did not put your cure in what He prohibited for you' (Ibn Al-Qayyim, 1992, vol. 4, pp. 154–8; Mawṣilī al-, 1992, vol. 10, p. 402). Consequently, 'the right thing' is the more effective cause, and vice versa. Ethics and rationality are more likely to be in harmony than in conflict.

4. CAUSAL DECISION-MAKING

4.1 Islamic Maxim of Certainty

A valuable guideline to decision-making under uncertainty is based on the Islamic legal maxim: 'certainty cannot be overruled by doubt'.[4] 'Certainty' in this maxim means firm belief based on sufficient evidence that the subject exists (or is true). 'Doubt', on the other hand, implies that the subject is at least as likely to exist (be true) as not to exist (be false).

The maxim implies that if:

1. at time t_0, state a prevails with certainty; and
2. at time t_1 state a' is doubtful;

then, state a is assumed to prevail at time t_1.

For example, we know that Mars exists in the solar system. It is theoretically possible that at any moment it is destroyed by a massive cosmic body. Since this is quite unlikely, we can safely assume that Mars still exists in the solar system.

This maxim is unanimously accepted by Muslim scholars, and it is based on statements of the Prophet (peace be upon him) as well as on pure logic. It simply states that a rational agent should not change his belief unless there is sufficient reason to do so.[5]

To see how this maxim is related to causality, recall that we defined a cause as a factor that makes the outcome more likely to obtain than not. So if an action x can lead to two different (mutually exclusive) outcomes, y and y', with y more likely to obtain than y', then such an action is considered overall as a cause of y, because this is the most likely of its outcomes. (We may alternatively describe x as a *net cause* of y.)

Consider buying a lottery ticket today in the hope of winning a prize tomorrow. This action involves a certain loss today. Winning the lottery tomorrow, however, is a remote possibility. Thus the state of loss is quite likely to prevail tomorrow. It follows that buying the lottery ticket is a net cause of loss.

We can evaluate any investment project on the same grounds. A project which requires an upfront investment, whereby subsequent gain is very likely, is a net cause of gain. If gain is unlikely, then it is a net cause of loss. An agent who engages in a losing project must be relying on luck rather than effective causes to gain. Obviously, what promotes such reliance is the magnitude of gain. If this magnitude is quite large, he might accept such an investment even if it is a cause of loss. We turn to this point in the following sub-section.

4.2 Wishful Behaviour

The concept of causality is independent of the magnitude or desirability of the outcome. We cannot change our beliefs regarding a future event simply because we like or dislike that event. If it is very likely to be raining tomorrow, then we should act accordingly, no matter how much we dislike rainy weather. It is irrational to plan to walk outside in this case simply because we prefer to walk in the sun. Similarly, winning a lottery prize is a very unlikely event, no matter how large the prize is. The size of the prize has no impact on its likelihood. That we prefer to win the prize should not deceive us into believing that we are likely to win. Unfortunately, the expected utility rule (and many competing rules in this regard) leads to such 'wishful behaviour'. If the utility of walking in sunny weather is, say, 10, and the disutility of walking in the rain is, say, –1, then the expected utility rule suggests we go walking even if the probability of rain is as large as 90 per cent.[6] Simply because we much prefer walking in the sun to walking in the rain, we behave as if it will be sunny, when in fact it is almost certain that it will not be. This is exactly what 'deception' is. Objectivity, however, requires that we behave according to the most likely outcome, independent of how much we dislike that outcome.

This is not to say that magnitudes of loss and gain have no effect on decision-making under uncertainty. Naturally, the more costly a project is, the more likely the gain should be, and/or the larger the magnitude of the gain should be. But this is considered only within the set of valid causes, that is, only for projects for which gain is more likely than loss.[7]

4.3 Retrospective Evaluation

How would a decision-maker know whether he is relying on chance or on causes to achieve the desired outcome? One way to find out is to ask the following question: supposing the desired outcome is not realized, would the decision-maker still be satisfied that he took the proper course of action for achieving the desired objective? Or would he feel that it was a waste of effort and resources? If the answer is the former, then he values the cause sufficiently to offset its costs, and thus it is a valuable cause. If it is the latter, then the decision-maker is relying on luck inasmuch as the value of the cause falls short of incurred costs.

To elaborate, suppose you are planning to invest in a project whose return is uncertain. Then you should ask yourself the following question: What if the project fails? If the answer is: 'the odds are in my favour; if it fails, it would only be bad luck' or 'it is worth the effort' then you are addressing the problem appropriately. By feeling satisfied even if the project fails, you are valuing the cause itself, and thus feel that the effort is not spent wastefully. Obviously, this does not mean that one is not hurt by failure. It only means that the value of the cause was sufficient to counter the pain. When appropriate causes are enacted, failure can be safely attributed to 'bad luck', whereby the agent is not blamed for it. For a Muslim, belief in destiny (*qadar*) would provide a justified excuse in this case, but only if proper causes were enacted. It is for this reason that the Prophet (peace be upon him) said:

> Seek what is good for you, look for Allah's help, and do not lax. Then if something (undesired) happens to you, do not say: 'had I done so and so I would have gotten so and so,' but say: 'it is Allah's will, and He does what He wills.' This is because 'had I' brings up Satan's work. (Albānī al-, 1986, No. 6650)

If, on the other hand, the answer to the question 'what if the project fails?' is: 'Oh no! I don't want to think of that possibility!' or 'this will never happen to me,' then one should think carefully before engaging in such a project. Such a response indicates that the agent is overestimating the likelihood of success, thereby not handling the relevant causes properly. He is relying on luck being on his side. So if he fails, the pain of failure is not counteracted by the value of enacted actions. Whatever costs the agent incurs can be compensated for only in the case of success; in the case of failure, they represent a source of sorrow and regret.

4.4 Cost of Passive Behaviour

A decision-maker who takes a non-causal action is effectively relying on chance to succeed. Such a position creates a fertile environment for disappointment and regret, because the decision-maker had known in advance that failure was more likely to occur. By relying on chance one is betting that luck will be on one's side, and this is the essence of gambling. Gambling might lead to serious psychological stress and frustration. According to one study, problem gamblers were shown to have a suicide rate five to ten times higher than the rest of the population (Goodman, 1995, p. 51). Experimental evidence shows that a passive response to stress factors leads to a higher probability of disease and mortality than a positive response. In an animal experiment, two cages of rats were set to receive an electrical shock randomly. In one cage rats had a switch that they could use to shut off the shock. Although both cages received exactly the same number and extent of shocks, rats in the first cage demonstrated significantly lower incidence of clinical diseases and significantly lower mortality rate (Becker, 1990, pp. 103–4). This teaches us a valuable lesson: having control over risky outcomes markedly reduces stress and improves personal well-being.

Reliance on chance and luck, therefore, leads to stress and frustration. It is irrational behaviour, since mere hope is not a natural means for achieving the desired outcome.

4.5 Chance and *Gharar*

Muslim scholars call the hope to achieve a desired objective without enacting appropriate causes *tamannī*. When it is combined with enacting proper causes, it is called *rajā'* (Assaʿdī, 1995, p. 298). *Tamannī*, therefore, leads an individual to ignore natural means, and rely on blind luck. After uncertainty is resolved, such hope passes away, and the individual faces the reality without having made any real attempt to influence it. Such hope deceives the decision-maker into behaving irrationally.

There is evidence that people tend to think that they have control over chance, even though it is uncontrollable. Several experiments have been performed, and results support the existence of 'the illusion of control' (see Langer, 1975; Langer and Roth, 1975; Plous, 1993). For example, gamblers tend to throw dice with greater force when they are attempting to roll high numbers than they do for low numbers. This illusion would distract the individual's attention from real causes to pure chance. According to Camerer (1995): 'The illusion of control is one kind of "magical thinking", a misunderstanding of casual relationship, akin to rain dance and superstitions' (p. 615). This illusion is described as *gharar*. The Qur'ān states that *amānī* (plural of *tamannī*) leads to deception or *gharar*: '*amānī* have deceived you' (57:14).

Thus *gharar* is deception that distracts the decision-maker from real causes to reliance on pure chance to achieve desired objectives. This deception develops as a result of *tamannī* and the illusion of control, leading to unjustified optimism.

5. CAUSALITY IN INTERACTIVE DECISIONS

5.1 Chance and the Zero-sum Measure

In gambling, each player relies on pure chance to win. However, chance will favour only one player; it is therefore a zero-sum game. Thus there is a connection between chance and zero-sum games. With some reflection, one can arrive at the following result: *A zero-sum exchange with uncertain payoffs is a game of chance.*

Elsewhere (Suwailem al-, 1999), it is argued that a *gharar* exchange is equivalent to a zero-sum game with uncertain payoffs. Here we argue that such a contract can be described as a game of luck or chance.

If the risk involved in a game is uncontrollable, and none of the players can influence the likelihood of his payoff, then it is obvious that such a game is a game of chance. If players follow the expected utility rule, the paid price would represent the expected value of the random return, given all available information. By design, any deviation of the realized return *ex post* from the expected value is due to chance. If the realized *ex post* return is greater than the expected value, the seller would be giving up the difference, so he loses and the buyer wins. If the realized return is less than the expected value, the buyer loses the difference, while the seller saves himself the loss. If the distribution of returns is continuous, then the probability that realized returns would be exactly equal to the paid price is trivial. Thus the realized return would be either greater than or less than the paid price, and such deviation is due to chance. Therefore, a *gharar* game is a game of chance.

This result holds even if the game involves skill, as in the sale of a lost camel. The buyer may search for the camel, and this would improve the likelihood that the buyer would win, and the seller would lose. In response, the seller would ask for a higher price in order that expected payoffs remain constant. Again, since deviations from the expected payoff are due to chance, the winner is determined by chance.

Note that if both players adopt a causal decision rule, then they may not play a zero-sum game. If each player insists that he is more likely to win than to lose, then there is no way in a zero-sum game that both can reach this condition. By design, if one party is more likely to win, the other must be more likely to lose.

That zero-sum games with uncertain payoffs are in fact games of chance can be deduced from the nature of the game. Suppose the game is certain. Then there is no point in playing the game, as it is known in advance who wins and who loses. The losing party will have no interest in playing the game. The game may be played only if chance is introduced (see Rapoport, 1960, pp. 137–8). In contrast, cooperative games may be played even under certainty, as both players are able to win.

The moral behind this result is that prohibition of *gharar* is established on the general principle that a decision-maker shall not rely on pure chance to achieve desired outcomes. The causality approach is suitable not only for personal decisions, but also for interactions with others. It is a principle that governs general human behaviour under risk.

5.2 Market Value of Causes

If causality is measured objectively, then what one individual values as a cause can be valued in a similar manner by another. Hence such a cause can be exchanged, and a market can develop for it, where equilibrium determines its price.

Even though the causality of a certain factor is only probabilistic, it is still valuable, just like a medicine. A medicine is not valued because it works for a particular patient. It is valued because it is a determinant of the cure, which means that, over a large number of patients, cure happens more frequently than not. Hence the market overall values it.

The same logic applies to economic causes or factors of return. Although in a given project a factor of production may not produce the desired returns, but overall it does, and thus is valued in the market. In this framework we can understand why a labour market exists. Labour is a factor of production, and therefore is a cause of return. Given its value as a cause, it can be exchanged, and thus has a market. A similar reasoning applies to capital. Does this mean that interest is justified as a price for a factor of production?

5.3 *Ribā*

A capital market is perfectly rational, since capital is a factor of production and a cause of return. But such a market need not be based on interest. It can be based either on price or rent, but not necessarily interest.

Many writers on *ribā* and interest argue that money is not a factor of production, and therefore cannot be valued as such. Although this is true for money, it is not true for wheat, for example, where *ribā* still applies. It is pure *ribā* to lend, say, 100 kg of wheat and receive 110 kg. Here we argue that, despite the fact that the principal has a causality value, the charged interest doesn't.

The borrower is required to pay back: (1) an amount of wheat equal to what he borrowed (principal, 100 kg), and (2) an extra amount as interest (10 kg). To simplify the argument, assume that the loan must be repaid within a single period of time (for example at the end of the season) so that the time factor is not included in the analysis. Only the causality factor is.

The borrowed wheat has a productivity value that by no means exceeds that of the principal. Productivity of 100 kg, by design, cannot exceed the productivity value of an identical 100 kg. Remember that time value is ignored in this analysis; only productivity or causality is considered. The interest that the borrower is charged does not contribute to the productivity of the principal. Thus interest is pure cost with no corresponding value in production. The borrower, by accepting this contract, is relying on the hope that realized output will be sufficient to recover such a cost. He is, therefore, relying on chance, by which it becomes a *gharar* transaction.

Now consider a monetary loan. The entrepreneur uses the loan to obtain factors of production, generate return, and then repay the principal plus interest. Other things constant, the productivity value of the principal is identical to that of the loan. By design, the borrower cannot use the interest to obtain factors of production, and thus, obviously, interest cannot be valued as a factor of production. Thus interest is pure cost without a corresponding productive asset. In the case of failure, it becomes a source of regret.

Interest, therefore, represents a cost that is borne for the mere hope that the project succeeds, and such behaviour is consistent with *gharar* and the tendency to gamble. Hence we can see how *ribā* and *gharar* can be motivated by the same improper motive: reliance on chance, not real causes.

6. CONCLUSION

The key difference between investment and gambling is confidence of success. An entrepreneur starts a project because he is rationally confident that the project will succeed. A gambler knows in advance that he is more likely to lose than to win. However, the size of the prize deceives him into engaging in such a losing project.

This difference is consistent with the concept of causality, at least from an Islamic point of view. An action that leads to failure more frequently than to success cannot be considered as a cause of success. It is a cause of failure. This reasoning is also consistent with the Islamic maxim 'certainty cannot be overruled by doubt'.

The expected utility rule does not differentiate between a cause and a non-cause. It mixes the likelihood of the outcome with its magnitude, and the decision is based on the final result. No attention is given to how this outcome is reached, whether systematically or by blind luck.

The causality approach not only improves individual decision-making; it also leads to avoidance of Islamically unacceptable contracts, mainly *gharar* contracts. By establishing the principle of causality, Islamic teachings attack *gharar* and similar social ills at their roots. Islamic economics, therefore, is an integral part of a comprehensive system that leads to optimal decisions, not only in economic matters but in social life in general.

There are certainly other important aspects of decision-making under uncertainty from an Islamic perspective. Muslim economists are strongly encouraged to investigate the subject to develop a coherent framework for its analysis.

NOTES

1. The terms 'risk' and 'uncertainty' are used interchangeably.
2. This distinction is ubiquitous in the literature; see, for example, Bernstein (1996), p. 14.
3. Compare with Hitchcock (1997).
4. In Arabic, '*Al yaqīn la yazalu bish-shak*'. See Aba-Hussein (1996).
5. Compare this maxim to the 'principle of insufficient reason' discussed in the philosophy of science. See Honderich (1995) p. 410; Schlesinger (1994), pp. 93–6; and Keynes (1921), ch. 4.
6. This follows from solving for probability of rain, p, that satisfies non-negative expected utility in the inequality: $-p + 10(1-p) \geq 0$. The result is $p \leq 0.91$.
7. A decision rule that satisfies the causality criterion and allows for risk–return trade-off is discussed by Suwailem al- (2001).

REFERENCES

Aba-Hussein, Y. (1996), *Qa'idat Al-Yaqīn La Yazalu Bish-shak*, Riyadh, Saudi Arabia: Maktabatul-Rushd.

Albānī al-, N. (1986), *Ṣaḥiḥ Al-Jamiʿ Aṣṣaghīr*, Beirut, Lebanon: Al-Maktab Al-Islamī.

Allais, M. (1976), 'The so-called Allais Paradox and Rational Decisions under Uncertainty', in M. Allais and O. Hagen (eds), *Expected Utility Theory and the Allais Paradox*, The Netherlands: D. Reidel Publishing, pp. 437–682.

Assaʿdi, A. (1995), *Ṭariqul Wusūl*, edited by S. Madhi and Y. Bakri, Amman, Jordan: Ramadi Linnashr.

Ashathrī, N. (1997), *Al-Qaṭ Waz-zann iʿndal Uṣouliyyīn*, Riyadh, Saudi Arabia: Dar Al-ḥabib.

Azzarkashī, M. (1982), *Al-Manthūr fil Qawāiʿd*, edited by A. Abu Ghouddah and T. Fai'q, Kuwait: Ministry of Islamic Affairs.

Becker, R.O. (1990), *Cross Currents*, New York: Penguin Putnam Inc.

Ben-Ner, A. and L. Putterman (1998), 'Values and Institutions in Economic Analysis', in A. Ben-Ner and L. Putterman (eds), *Economics, Values, and Organization*, Cambridge, UK: Cambridge University Press, pp. 3–69.

Bernstein, Peter L. (1996), *Against the Gods: The Remarkable Story of Risk*, New York: John Wiley & Sons.

Camerer, C. (1995), 'Individual Decision Making', in J. Kagel and A. Roth (eds), *Handbook of Experimental Economics*, Princeton, NJ: Princeton University Press, pp. 587–703.
Covey, S. (1990), *The Seven Habits of Highly Effective People*, New York: Simon & Schuster.
Dawes, R.M. (1988), *Rational Choice in an Uncertain World*, New York: Harcourt Brace College Publishers.
Einhorn, H. and R. Hogarth (1987), 'Decision Making: Going Forward in Reverse', *Harvard Business Review*, January/February. Reprinted in *On Managing Uncertainty* (1999), Boston, MA: Harvard Business School Press, pp. 131–46.
Goodman, R. (1995), *The Luck Business*, New York: The Free Press.
Hitchcock, C. (1997), 'Probabilistic Causation', *Stanford Encyclopaedia of Philosophy*. Online: http://plato.stanford.edu.
Honderich, T. (ed.) (1995), *The Oxford Companion to Philosophy*, Oxford: Oxford University Press.
Ibn Abdus-Salam, A. (2000), *Al-Qawāiʿd Al-Kubrā*, edited by N. Hammad and O. Dhumairiyyah, Beirut, Lebanon: Darul Qalam.
Ibn Al-Qayyim, M. (1992), *Zādul-Maʿād*, edited by A. Al-Arna'out and S. Al-Arna'out, Beirut, Lebanon: Dar Arrisālah.
Jehle, G.A. (1991), *Advanced Microeconomic Theory*, Englewood Cliffs, NJ: Prentice Hall.
Keynes, J.M. (1921), *A Treatise of Probability*, London: Macmillan.
Knight, F.H. (1921), *Risk, Uncertainty and Profit*, New York: Houghton Mifflin.
Langer, E.J. (1975), 'The Illusion of Control', *Journal of Personality and Social Psychology*, **32**, 311–28.
Langer, E.J. and J. Roth (1975), 'Heads I Win, Tails is Chance: The Illusion of Control is a Function of the Sequence of Outcomes in a Purely Chance Task', *Journal of Personality and Social Psychology*, **32**, 951–5.
MacCrimmon, K. and D. Wehrung (1986), *Taking Risks: The Management of Uncertainty*, New York: The Free Press.
Malinvaud, E. (1972), *Lectures in Microeconomic Theory*, Amsterdam: North-Holland.
March, J. (1994), *A Primer on Decision Making*, New York: The Free Press.
Mawṣilī al-, A. (1992), *Al-Musnad*, edited by Hussein Asad, Beirut, Lebanon: Dar Althaqāfah Al Arabiyyah.
Miqarī al-, M. (undated), *Al-Qawāiʿd* edited by M. ibn Humaid, Makkah, Saudi Arabia: Ummul-Qura University.
Pearl, J. (2000), *Causality: Models, Reasoning, and Inference*, Cambridge, UK: Cambridge University Press.
Plous, S. (1993), *The Psychology of Judgment and Decision Making*, New York: McGraw-Hill.
Quarāfī al-, *Al-Forūq* (undated), Beirut, Lebanon: ʿAllāmul-Kutub.
Rapoport, A. (1960), *Fights, Games, and Debates*, Ann Arbor, MI: University of Michigan Press.
Schlesinger, G. (1994), 'A Central Theistic Argument', in J. Jordan (ed.), *Gambling on God: Essays on Pascal's Wager*, Lanham, MD: Rowman & Littlefield Publishers, pp. 83–100.
Sen, A. (1988), *On Ethics and Economics*, Oxford: Blackwell Publishers.
Sen, A. (1997), 'Maximization and the Act of Choice', *Econometrica*, **65** (4), 745–79.
Shapira, Z. (1995), *Risk Taking: A Managerial Perspective*, New York: Russell Sage Foundation.

Shāṭibī al-, I. (1997), *Al-Muwāfaqāt*, edited by M. Salman, Al-Khubar, Saudi Arabia: Dar Ibn Affān.

Sinn, H. (1983), *Economic Decision Under Uncertainty*, Amsterdam: North-Holland.

Suwailem al-, Sami I. (1999), 'Towards an Objective Measure of *Gharar* in Exchange', *Islamic Economic Studies*, **7** (1&2), 61–102.

Suwailem al-, Sami I. (2001), 'A Causal Decision Rule Under Risk', mimeo, unpublished.

Varian, H. (1992), *Microeconomic Analysis*, 3rd edn, New York: W.W. Norton.

COMMENTS

Monzer Kahf

This chapter is thought-provoking. It deals with an interesting and very important subject that is rarely touched upon in Islamic economics writings. My comments will focus on areas that raise questions and discussion rather than the areas of merits. Overall, the chapter has a great deal of merit. I will begin my comments from the end of the chapter.

1. *Ribā* and *Gharar*

In the last section of the chapter, the writer argues that *ribā* has a great deal of *gharar* on the grounds that interest represents a cost borne in the mere hope that the project succeeds. This argument seems to be in contradiction with the common wisdom and the predominant argument in both *fiqh* (Islamic jurisprudence) and Islamic economics with regard to *ribā*. *Ribā* is prohibited because it is a contract that contains certainty while real life is not certain. As some of the commentators on the Qur'ān put it: it is a payment that is sure and certain while real life is neither sure nor certain about the outcome of the use of capital.

A *ribā* contract contains no *gharar* whatsoever, nor a tendency to gamble. Except for the risk of inability to repay, it is a risk-free contract. That is exactly why it is prohibited.

If we go along with the argument of the chapter that interest is a price of the principal, and that it therefore contains *gharar*, we must also prohibit wages as a price for labour, because we do not know the result of the project. The chapter's argument on interest looks exactly similar to the argument that the writer provides in a preceding paragraph about the price of labour. If wage is a price of labour, then following that same line of argument, interest must also be a price of capital, be it monetary or physical.

In my humble understanding, the prohibition of interest in the *Sharīʿah* is based on a different argument that does not even come close to the concept of *gharar* or a tendency to gamble. Rather, it goes in the opposite direction. *Ribā* is a price put on a loan, whether monetary or physical, and in a lending relationship, the lender ceases to be the owner of lent assets. She becomes an owner of an abstract right called debt. An abstract right is not capable of growth; it is fixed. It can only grow by popular convention and in an operation whose only place is in the minds of men and women, not in the real world. This stands in direct opposition to contributing capital to a project in which the owner maintains his ownership because in this case the principal, be it physical or monetary, contributes directly or through its conversion into physical assets, to the production process, and therefore deserves a portion of the outcome of that process. What is the return other than a growth of a property? This is why *muḍārabah* is just and permissible, while lending on interest is not.

In a lending contract, the borrower becomes the owner of the principal amount. All changes in what one owns must fairly belong to the owner, and not the lender. The lender only owns an abstract interpersonal right on the borrower.

A *ribā*-based contract clearly specifies the obligations and rights of both parties. It does not contain any *gharar*. Yet it is a prohibited contract because it is not balanced. It involves 'eating the funds of others in vanity and with no reason'. This is so because the counterpart of the interest in a loan contract is only a presumed benefit, not a real one. The *gharar* that the writer refers to, under the subtitle of *ribā*, is in the mind of the borrower, not in the contract between him and the lender, and what matters is the contract and not the mental exercise of calculation, estimation, and approximation of the future.

2. Chance and *Gharar*

The learned writer discusses the relationship between chance and *gharar*. At this point, we need to put forward a few definitions in a clear manner:

- Ibn Faris (1979) says in his *Maqāyis al-lughah* that *tamannī* is an expected or estimated hope or things that are hoped; that is *tamannī* is *rajā'* and is estimation. In his commentary of Verse 14, *Surah* 57, Al-Qurṭubī (1947) says that *amānī* (plural of *tamannī*) are the false hopes or deceits of Satan or of the worldly life.
- As for *gharar*, Al-Dareer (1995) says that *gharar* in Arabic is *khaṭar*, which is risk. He quotes from *Al-Qaḍi Iʿāḍ* that *gharar* are things that have a likeable appearance but undesired in reality. Ibn Faris supports this meaning. He says, '*al-gharar* is the risk that we do not know whether it happens or not'.
- As for the definition of *gharar* in *fiqh*, Al-Dareer says that '*gharar* is when there is an unknown outcome in an exchange'. *Gharar* is very often used interchangeably with ignorance, as *gharar* is either ignorance related to the very existence of an outcome or ignorance about the characteristics of an outcome that is well known to have existed. *Gharar* relates to contracts, not to the calculation in the mind. There is an important point here. The *Sharīʿah* does not go beyond the contract to read the minds of the parties. In other words, *gharar* is not deception, as emphasized by the writer. It is a risk that results from the unknown. *Gharar* in contracts may contain the meaning of deception where there is a great deal of ignorance about an exchange relationship, whether with regard to the existence of the object of the contract or to its main characteristics.

Taking chance in decision-making is not *gharar*. It is an estimation or anticipation of a person, and it is only a mental operation that takes place within one party. It is not part of a contract. A chance may be random or pure, or it may be calculated by putting together in a scientific sequence probable causes for a future course of events. Taking a chance, whether calculated or not, is not prohibited in the *Sharīʿah*. *Gharar* in *fiqh* only happens in contracts. Illusions and deceptions are mental operations that have nothing to do with *gharar*, unless they are put down on paper in a form creating ignorance surrounding the object of the contract. Deception in a contract is called *ghish*, and is prohibited for its own sake.

Now let's come to the zero-sum arrangement, and let us see how, in analogy with the chapter's line of analysis, it applies to *salam*. In *salam*, you pay a price, and you get a well-defined quantity with future delivery. The future price at the time of delivery of that quantity is not known. No matter what estimation the two players have in their minds, it is very seldom that the *ex post* equals exactly the *ex ante*. Therefore, if the price in the future turns out to be higher than what is expected, the seller loses and the buyer gains, and vice versa. Let us compare this with the zero-sum game described in the chapter. The paid price represents the expected value of the unknown 'random return', and if the realized return is greater than the expected value, the seller would be giving up the difference, so he loses and the buyer wins. If the realized return is less than the expected value, the buyer loses the difference while the seller saves himself the loss. It is exactly the same zero-sum measure. Yet there is no disagreement that *salam* is permissible. Is it a *gharar*-based contract? The answer is no. *Salam* is permissible because it is a contract that has no *gharar*, nor any other reason for prohibition. This is in spite of the fact that each party is susceptible to gains or losses. What one gains equals exactly the loss of the other, hence, zero-sum. It is human nature that we always attribute to chance the entire residual in an outcome that results from unknown 'random' factors. In *gharar*, there is a great deal of ignorance about the object of the contract, not about the expected return of entering into it. Selling a lost camel is prohibited not because of a zero-sum feature, but because you don't know whether the camel exists or not.

What is the difference between *salam* and gambling? Gambling is not prohibited because it contains a zero sum. Real life has many zero-sum exercises. It is prohibited because the outcome is left to artificial or fabricated chance. That is different from the real-life chance arising from unknown or unanticipated factors, uncontrollable residual factors that we call, in their totality, chance. In gambling, the chance contains a vain process, like throwing a coin or rolling a dice. It is the element of vanity that makes gambling prohibited.

A zero-sum game becomes a gambling game when it is based on artificial chance, not on real-life unknown factors that we call chance. This is different from *gharar*. *Gharar* is when the object of a contract is not known, whether the ignorance relates to its very existence or to its main characteristics. Every entrepreneur and every businessman takes chances because they deal with the unknown. They produce for the future, and the future is not known.

Additionally, the morality of the prohibition of *gharar* is that contracts must be definite, with known rights and obligations. This is different from the morality of the prohibition of gambling, which is the refusal of the distribution of wealth and income on the basis of fabricated chances that are created vainly, rather than chances that are part of real life, and that account for all the residual uncontrollable factors that affect an outcome. Therefore, it is not forbidden to roll a dice with my little daughter, with the outcome that the one who gets a higher number is called a winner, without affecting anybody's income.

3. Risk and *Gharar*

Let us go back now to the main point of risk. People by their nature are susceptible to taking different levels of risk. That is why some people are called risk-takers and others risk-averters. In general, rationality and Islam together prefer risk-aversion, and whenever risk is taken, a price or compensation is always expected. Yet the saying 'avoid what causes suspicion and choose what does not' is not relevant for the area of risk-aversion. We have many sayings and many prayers of the Prophet (peace be upon him) that call for safety and security. These indicate more the preference of avoiding risk, and risk is not equivalent to suspicion. Furthermore, it is true that all rational humans, Muslims or not, generally prefer certainty and security as compared to risk and uncertainty. But all rational humans also know that real life has a certain amount of risk that is not avoidable, no matter what you do. So we take two kinds of risks: risk that stimulates productive effort, and risk that is an unavoidable part of real life. All cultures, and all types of rationality, call for 'tying the camel', and not Islamic economics alone. The uniqueness of Islam here is that it adds a concept of relying on God, the Creator, a concept of *tawakkul*, as we believe that Allah is an active Ruler over all things and events and a continuous decision-maker, not a retired one who does not interfere anymore. So we always need His help and we need to rely on His might. I do not agree with the writer in stating that the causality approach to decision-making is a unique characteristic of Islamic thinking. Rather, what is unique to Islam is relying on God, in addition to causality.

4. The Value of Causes

Valuation of causes is insufficient to compensate for risk-taking. Let's take an example of a person who believes in superstition. He goes to a witch or a palm-reader and takes the decision according to the information he obtains. If this person values what he thought as causes, the decision taken is, or becomes, rational if the value of the causes plus the outcome exceeds the price he pays in exchange, or the cost. The causes he had added are false ones; they are not true. What matters is that there ought to be a scientific approach, that is an approach based on knowledge obtained in a correct manner, as stated by the writer, either from revelation or from human experience, that is, a calculation that compares the costs and benefits of a decision. For instance, avoiding losing a battle on the basis of calculating one's resources as compared with the resources available to the enemy was a decision described by the Prophet (peace be upon him) as made by Khalid bin Al-Waleed. He deserved that title because he retreated from a losing battle. This calculation, or rather such a calculation, may be based either on human experience or on knowledge derived from revelation. See, for instance, the verse that compares the number of soldiers that can fairly face each other if the elements of faith and perseverance exist. In other words, had Khalid bin Al-Waleed decided to value the cause of relying on God more than the expected cost of losing a battle, he would have continued the battle of Mu'ta instead of withdrawing, and he would have not been given the title 'A Sword of God'. Hence, controlling one's fear is not sufficient. We must always add to it 'while continuously exercising rational means to improve the outcome', because the outcome does matter; whatever value one may give to causes as causes that are proven wrong may have been thought of (*ex ante*) as real causes at one time.

We also cannot deny that the outcome is extremely important for the valuation of a cause. If, in a single instance, the cause does not lead to the outcome, the value of the cause in that instance is very much limited or even null, as it is in the *ḥadīth* that 'he whose prayer does not prevent him from bad and unacceptable deeds is only increasing his distance from God', and in the *ḥadīth* about fasting: 'there may be some fasting person whose outcome of fasting is only hunger and thirst'. Hence, in considering the value of causes, we cannot rely solely on statistical and generalized information as suggested in the chapter. The value of cause increases if it actually leads to an outcome that is desired and sought. The *ḥadīth* that talks about a judge who makes an effort and yet reaches a wrong verdict getting one reward does not imply that this wrong verdict needs to be accepted. Rather, it implies that some wrong is done and a reverse chain of events needs to be set in motion, otherwise justice remains lost. It has always been said that the road to hell is paved with good intentions.

When it comes to material causes and outcomes, the cause does not have any moral value of its own. All its value is derived from its outcome. If I enter into a project, and the project fails, then that is a loss and a failure, and it can only be calculated on the basis of *ex post* cost and benefit. Only in moral issues, where the cause itself has a moral value of its own because it is ordained by God, can we attribute an independent value to the cause regardless of the outcome. In a material undertaking, I am not required by any moral or religious impulse to undertake project (A) in comparison with project (B). All that matters in my decision is the outcome of the project, and all causes are valued on the basis of that outcome alone.

REFERENCES

Ibn Faris, Abu al-Hasan Ahmad (1979), *Muʿjam Maqāyis al-lughah*, Beirut, Lebanon: Dar al-Fikr.

Ibn Ahmed, Abu Abdullah M. (1947), *Tafsīr al-Qurṭubī*, Cairo, Egypt: Dar al-Shaʿb.

Dareer al-, Al-Saddiq M. Al-Amin (1995), *Al-Gharar Wa Atharuhū fil ʿUqood fil-Fiqh al-Islamī*, Jeddah, Saudi Arabia: Dallah Al-Barakah.

COMMENTS

Mohamed Ali Elgari

Let me, at the outset, congratulate the writer on this exceptional piece of research. Such rigour and depth are rare in Islamic economic research. The subject of this chapter is clearly an important one, not only because it is interdisciplinary, combining elements from economics, positive law and the *Sharī*ʿ*ah*, but also because it is an attempt to develop the basic concepts of the theory of contract in the *Sharī*ʿ*ah* into tools for analysis of economic behaviour. The writer has done a commendable job.

The author starts with an introduction to the subject of decision-making under uncertainty in which he distinguishes between entrepreneurship and gambling, where the first is praised and the second is blamed. Then he emphasizes the importance of 'process', an area he says is not given sufficient attention in the current literature, which focuses on 'consequence'. Then he moves to what he calls controllable and uncontrollable risks (a very evasive distinction) to delve into what he terms 'causality' or *asbāb*, where most of the Islamic perspective is introduced. I enjoyed reading the chapter, and have no doubt that it is a significant contribution to the literature. However, and regardless of how meticulous this chapter is, it is far from impeccable. The following comments are in order:

1. There are those of us who think that no matter what the subject matter of scientific inquiry, the findings will not be valid if they are not supported by narrations from the *Sharī*ʿ*ah* scholars of the past. Not only will such methodology limit the scope of their probing, but it will render their research irrelevant to contemporary application and transform their investigation into a mere inquiry in the history of thought. I am not suggesting that we should advocate a detachment from our rich heritage of jurisprudence. Rather, I am worried that we sometimes enslave our minds to the contribution of our forefathers. We have no hope of even reaching their level of excellence, let alone surpassing our contemporaries, if we don't follow their methodology of liberating our minds from the bondage of history.
2. The writer's distinction between what he calls 'controllable risk' and 'chance' is by no means conclusive. The difference to him is the responsibility of being able to implement factors that influence the uncertain outcome. It is no secret that even compulsive gamblers will do their best to 'implement factors that influence the uncertain outcome'.

   Any attempt to distinguish (from the point of view of economic analysis) 'gambling' from other decisions under uncertainty will be in vain. This is because the difference is only legalistic, not economic. The writer describes the gambler (unlike the entrepreneur) as someone 'whose fortunes are determined purely by luck'. 'His circle of influence', he adds, 'is effectively void and he is totally dependent on outside circumstances.' This could very well be a description of an investor in the stock market (that is, an entrepreneur). On the other hand, the writer's description of an entrepreneur can easily pass for a permanent resident of a Las Vegas casino.

3. Once he is engaged in this 'causation' thing, it becomes rather easy for the writer to 'dig up' citations on the subject of *asbāb*. However, the applicability of these quotes is questionable, if not totally irrelevant. They do not support the distinction between gambling and other decisions under uncertainty, the objective of which is different.
4. In the literature on decision-making under uncertainty it is customary to speak about risk, not *gharar*. It would have been very useful had the writer, before introducing his ideas about decision-making under *gharar*, shown us the difference, if there is any, between the two concepts. I say this because, again, I feel the difference between the two concepts is important to the conclusions reached by the writer. For example, the following statement that the writer makes is not conclusive.

> The moral behind this result is that prohibition of *gharar* is established on the general principle that a decision-maker shall not rely on pure chance to achieve desired outcomes. The causality approach is suitable not only for personal decisions, but also for interactions with others. It is a principle that governs general human behaviour under risk. (p. 26)

A game of chance is one with a relatively high degree of *gharar*, but it may or may not have a high degree of risk. If we follow the writer's advice, we may engage in a *gharar* contract to reduce risk (a deferred payment sale with variable price is *gharar* but less risky than the alternative).

Again, it is important to differentiate between what is economic and what is legalistic. *Gharar* is a legalistic concept, one that arises in contractual relationships independent of the parties to a contract, while risk is individualistic. It concerns the decision-maker. Hence a contract may be risky for one party and not so risky for the other, while *gharar* concerns the contractual relationship.

From the point of view of economic analysis of decision-making under uncertainty, there is no difference between a gambler and an entrepreneur. We all know that the whole theory of probability (so useful for entrepreneurial purposes) was developed as a means to improve one's luck in games of chance.[1] This leads us to say that everything the writer mentioned about causal relationships (*asbāb*) is just as relevant to gambling as it is to entrepreneurship.

NOTE

1. Some writers think this is the reason why Muslims, with all their advances in mathematics, have made no contribution to the theory of probability. See, for example, Peter L. Bernstein (1998), *Against the Gods: The Remarkable Story of Risk*, New York: John Wiley & Sons.

3. Incentive-compatible profit-sharing contracts: a theoretical treatment

Habib Ahmed*

1. INTRODUCTION

With the inception of Islamic banking practices in the mid-1970s academic discourses on the subject highlighted the profit-sharing features of Islamic financing. It was believed that Islamic banking would take the form of the two-tier *muḍārabah* model. Experience, however, shows that there are some inherent problems in applying profit-sharing modes of financing (*muḍārabah* and *mushārakah*). The problems in the application of the profit-sharing model in practice led to the use of other financial instruments. Mark-up financing (*murābaḥah*) became the dominant mode of financing in Islamic banks (Iqbal et al., 1998; Khan, 1995). Studies exploring this phenomenon identify the moral hazard problem in profit-sharing modes of financing as the main cause of its unpopularity. Though an Islamic economy cannot be a 'pure profit-sharing' economy, there is an aspiration among the proponents of Islamic banking to have a balanced mix between mark-up and profit-sharing modes of financing (Jarhi al-, 1999). The success of the use of profit-sharing modes of financing, however, will depend on the resolution of the problems of asymmetric information associated with their use.

A financial system constitutes a series of contracts that resolve the conflicting interests of different parties by addressing incentive problems. Though much has been written on the nature and implications of profit-sharing modes of financing, discussions on contracts that can be used in these transactions are scant.[1] This chapter is a contribution to this issue. In particular, we discuss agency relationships in profit-sharing modes of financing and outline the characteristics of an incentive-compatible contract that addresses the asymmetric

* The author is grateful to M. Umer Chapra, Munawar Iqbal, Tariqullah Khan, Sirajul Haque, the discussant of the chapter, Said Al Hallaq and the participants of the conference for comments. The views and opinions expressed in this chapter are personal and do not represent those of the Islamic Research and Training Institute or the Islamic Development Bank.

information problem arising in this relationship. The theoretical discussions can be a useful guide to formulating *murābaḥah* and *mushārakah* contracts by Islamic banks.

The theoretical framework of the model used in this chapter is similar to that of Khan (1985 and 1987). We, however, add elements from contemporary contract theory to address an important issue raised, but not resolved, by him. Specifically, Khan (1987) points to the problem of moral hazard arising from underreporting of profit by the entrepreneur in a profit-sharing scheme but does not provide any specific solutions to the problem. He suggests that the problem of underreporting may be reduced by the implicit penalty in the form of increasing the probability of monitoring.[2] Being aware that this may not resolve the problem, he suggests seeking solutions from other financial transactions where the moral hazard problem exists and designing incentive-compatible contracts which either eliminate or minimize the incentives for misrepresentation (Khan, W.M., 1987, p. 103). In this chapter we attempt to do the same. We develop an incentive-compatible profit-sharing contract that reduces the moral hazard problem. In doing so, we analyse the conditions under which an entrepreneur may under-report his profit and the steps a bank can take to minimize the problem. We propose using assets of the entrepreneur as collateral that can be used to punish false reporting by the firm to minimize the problem. In addition, we address some other issues related to the profit-sharing mode of financing. The chapter sheds light on the adverse selection problem and choosing the deserving firms for investment. It also endogenously derives the profit-sharing ratio that can be used in the contract and identifies the risk-premium component in this ratio.

The chapter is organized as follows. In the next section, the nature of the asymmetric information problem and its implications for different modes of financing are discussed. The preferences of banks and firms for different modes of financing are outlined. In section 3, we discuss features of a contract that minimize asymmetric information problems in a profit-sharing contract. Other than suggesting the mechanism for identifying the projects that can be financed on a profit-sharing basis to minimize the adverse selection problem, we also discuss an incentive structure of the contract that reduces the moral hazard problem. After explaining the mechanism of determining the profit-sharing ratio endogenously, we outline a repayment function, an auditing rule, and the penalty/reward functions of a profit-sharing contract. Given the incentive structure in the contract, section 4 examines the strategies that a firm takes and analyses the extent of moral hazard problems that result from these decisions. The last section recommends a few policy options for the successful application of profit-sharing modes of financing.

2. ECONOMICS OF PROFIT-SHARING FINANCING

Berger and Udell (1998) discuss the conventional financial growth cycles of different firms. They point out that sources of finance depend on the firm's size, its age and the information available to it. When the firm is new, it starts out as a small enterprise. The new entrepreneurs often do not have any track record or acceptable physical collateral to obtain funds from institutional sources. The only source of finance for these firms is insider finance, where an individual or a group (family members, friends) use their savings to finance the setting up of the project and bear the operating costs. As firms age, they develop a track record. Firms with high growth potentials can finance their expansion either by venture capital or by development credit offered by governmental organizations. Medium and large-sized firms that have a long track record and can provide acceptable physical collateral can get intermediate and long-term credit from institutional sources for setting up new plants. They can also obtain short-term operational credit from the same sources. In addition, larger established firms can borrow funds from the public by selling bonds.

The above discussion indicates that smaller firms hardly have any access to funds from traditional financial institutions. The underlying theoretical explanation for this phenomenon lies in the traditional problems of asymmetric information in financial intermediation. The problems of adverse selection and moral hazard worsen in the case of smaller enterprises in developing countries due to some added problems (Lynn, 1998).[3] These problems make assessment of projects and monitoring the use of funds (to minimize adverse selection and moral hazard problems) very costly.

Given the differences between infant and mature firms, it is argued that there is a dichotomy in the preferences of the firm and the bank in the mode of financing. Small firms have relatively few assets and, being riskier, would prefer the profit-sharing mode of financing to spread their risk. Larger (incorporated) firms have a solid asset base and experience with managing risk. These firms would prefer a fixed mark-up mode of financing (Khan, T., 1995, p. 51). The bank, however, prefers to finance smaller, riskier firms on a relatively risk-free fixed mark-up basis and will be comfortable to fund larger, established firms on profit-sharing basis.

The argument that larger firms will prefer fixed mark-up financing compared to profit-sharing modes implicitly assumes that the profit-sharing ratio is the same for all types of firms. This, however, may not be the case. The bank will use the profit-sharing ratio to distinguish good (low-risk) and bad (high-risk) investors. Another factor that will determine the profit-sharing ratio is the expected return (or profit) from the investment.[4] The bank can offer firms that have relatively low risk and expect a good return on investment a profit-sharing ratio that is comparable to the mark-up alternative. The added advantage in the profit-sharing mode is that the risk is shared with the bank (Khan, T., 1995). Given that smaller firms are relatively riskier, as they lack a track record and experience, Islamic banks will have a tendency to target medium- and large-sized firms for the profit-sharing modes of financing.

As mentioned above, the moral hazard problem in profit-sharing modes of financing has been identified as one of the important factors hindering its use in Islamic banking practices.[5] The moral hazard problem occurs when the entrepreneur's conduct changes after the receipt of the funds from the bank. In the profit-sharing mode of financing, moral hazard problems are similar to those found in agency relationships. They take the form of the principal–agent problem found in equity contracts.[6] The entrepreneur acts as an agent using the funds provided by the bank (the principal). The principal–agent problem arises when the agent (entrepreneur) works in his own interest at the cost of the interest of the principal (bank). This can occur due to asymmetric information. In particular, the moral hazard problem arises in this set-up if the agent misuses the funds, is slack about the management of the firm, and is not honest (Mishkin, 1995, p. 218). The principal–agent problem, therefore, can be resolved if the principal can gather more information on the operations of the firm. One way of doing this is by monitoring. Monitoring, however, is costly in terms of both time and money. An alternative way to reduce the moral hazard problem is to use contracts with an incentive structure that reduces such behaviour.

In this chapter we consider the moral hazard problem arising from dishonesty in reporting the actual figures of profit by the entrepreneur.[7] It should be noted that, ideally, Muslims should be striving to achieve *falāḥ*, which includes rewards in the Hereafter. In such cases, entrepreneurs would be honest and reveal actual profit figures to the bank so that the moral hazard problem arising from under-reporting of profit would not exist. In practice, however, this may not be the case. It has been observed that while depositors' preferences for using an Islamic bank may be due to religious reasons, the investors in these banks may not necessarily have this motive. As the profit is shared between the firm and the bank at an agreed ratio, there may be an incentive on the part of an amoral entrepreneur to report lower profit and thus to keep a larger share of it for himself. This chapter gives a theoretical exposition of a profit-sharing contract that may reduce the inducement to cheat through a reward/punishment mechanism. The nature of this contract is discussed in the next section.

3. INCENTIVE-COMPATIBLE PROFIT-SHARING CONTRACTS

We first outline the guidelines a bank can use in deciding whether to fund a project when it faces adverse selection problems. Then we discuss the format of an incentive-compatible contract that will induce the entrepreneur to reveal true information *ex post*, so that the moral hazard problem is mitigated. The following assumptions form the basis of the analysis:

1. A firm (entrepreneur), possessing assets valued at V, plans to invest in a project in time period $t = 0$.
2. To operate the firm at an efficient level and make optimum profit, the entrepreneur needs an amount of $L < V$.
3. An investment of amount L is expected to yield a profit of y_e in period $t = 1$.
4. The investor (bank) is risk-neutral.
5. Let r be the bank's expected risk-free rate of return.[8]
6. In period $t = 1$, the firm reports a profit of y_r.
7. After the profit is reported, the bank has a right to audit the accounts of the firm at a cost of A.
8. The audit reveals the actual profit value of y_a. This amount (y_a) will not be equal to the reported profit (y_r) in the case of false reporting by the firm.

The conditions under which the bank will fund the entrepreneur on a profit-sharing basis, and the asymmetric information problems that a bank faces in doing so, are discussed next.

3.1 Adverse Selection Problem and Bank's Choice of Firms

Adverse selection problems arise before the contract is signed because the bank has less information on the project than the client (borrower). Let the entrepreneur's information on the project be an index normalized to unity. If the information that the bank has on the firm is given by an index λ ($0 < \lambda < 1$), then $AS = 1/\lambda$, is an index of the adverse selection problem. Note that when the bank has the same information as the borrower, then $\lambda = 1$, giving $AS = 1$, indicating that no adverse selection problem exists. This, however, is not the case. As the information gap between the lender and the borrower increases, λ becomes smaller and AS larger.

In reality, AS is not observable by the bank, as the information relative to that of the entrepreneur is not available and hence an adverse selection problem exists. The bank, however, can take into account the factors that will affect AS by gathering all relevant information. This includes the age and size of the firm (track record) and the length of association of the entrepreneur with the bank (on *murābaḥah* basis). The lack of knowledge on these factors makes AS large, increasing the adverse selection problem.

The entrepreneur applies for funds to the bank by submitting a proposal that contains the details of the project. Other than relevant financial information from past experience, the proposal also indicates the expected return y_e and the amount L required from the bank. Let this financial information provided be assessed by the bank by an index (I). Based on AS and I, the bank categorizes different prospective borrowers with a risk parameter θ. That is,

$$\theta = f(AS, I)\ \theta_{AS}' > 0, \theta_I' < 0; \tag{3.1}$$

Note that the higher the risk, the closer is θ to unity ($0 < \theta < 1$). We define a safety index $\sigma = 1 - \theta$, so that σ is small for riskier projects. Note that $\sigma = 1$ for risk-free investment.

While analysing individual projects for investment, the bank appraises the expected return on the project by the safety index. The risk-adjusted expected return of a project σy_e. The bank may be willing to fund the project if the risk-adjusted expected rate of return is greater than the returns from the risk-free investment. Note that even if a firm is not risky in terms of its financial position (I), it may not be funded due to lack of information. For example, new smaller firms with no past information will have a relatively serious adverse selection problem, making AS large. This will make θ large and σ small. In cases where $\sigma y_e < rL$, the bank will reject the project outright. For larger firms with a track record, AS will be small and I large, giving a higher safety index. The bank will be willing to finance the projects that yield $\sigma y_e > rL$. Once this is decided, the bank has to decide the profit-sharing ratio and ensure the moral hazard problem does not arise from dishonesty (under-reporting of profits) of the firm. A contract that may help in doing so is discussed below.

3.2 Profit-sharing Contract to Reduce the Moral Hazard Problem

The incentive-compatible contract discussed in this section has a similar framework to that used by Townsend (1979) and Gale and Hellwig (1985) to describe debt contracts. These contracts assume that information available to the lender (bank) is less than that of the borrower (entrepreneur). The actual realized profit from a project is not observable by the bank unless a costly audit is undertaken. The contract specifies a repayment function, an auditing rule and a penalty/reward function.

The sequence of events in profit-sharing transactions is the following. A contract between the bank and the entrepreneur is signed based on the *ex ante* expected profit of the project y_e. After completion of the project the firm reports a profit of y_r. The bank has a right to audit the accounts of the project at a cost of A. The *ex post* return of the bank will depend on the profit reported by the firm and the decision on auditing of accounts by the bank. Jensen and Meckling (1976) include bonding costs and residual loss along with monitoring costs as components of agency costs. While auditing expenditures are a part of the monitoring costs, we will point out the nature of the former two costs in the framework of the profit-sharing mode of financing in the text below. We use this backdrop to discuss the attributes of a profit-sharing contract next.

A repayment function

The repayment function defines the transfer promised to the bank by the firm as a function of profit. In particular, it will define the ratio at which profit will be shared between the firm and the bank. Since a profit-sharing arrangement is a partnership, we assume both parties share *ex ante* the auditing cost A equally. Note that the auditing cost is incurred *ex post* and only if the bank decides to undertake an audit. Furthermore, this cost is used to reward (penalize) honesty (dishonesty) of the entrepreneur. Assuming risk-neutrality, the profit-sharing ratio s (the share that goes to the bank) is derived endogenously from the following expression.

$$s\,(\sigma y_e - 0.5A) = rL \tag{3.2}$$

Equation (3.1) states that the expected risk-adjusted profit share from an investment net of auditing cost should equal the opportunity cost of the investment (equal to the risk-free return on investment on amount invested, L). From equation (3.2), we derive the expression for the profit-sharing ratio as follows:

$$s = rL\,/\,(\sigma y_e - 0.5A) \tag{3.3}$$

Ceteris paribus, the profit-sharing ratio s is positively related to the risk-free rate r, the amount of funds invested by the bank L, and the auditing expenses A. It is inversely related to the safety index σ and expected income y_e.

Some important results emerge from equation (3.2). First, note that auditing costs are internalized in the profit-sharing ratio. Specifically, as the auditing cost, A, increases, the bank's profit share, s, becomes larger. This increment in s reflects an implicit compensation for the special nature of risk associated with the moral hazard problem particular to profit-sharing modes of financing.[9]

Second, the risk-premium component, p, in the profit-sharing ratio can be derived by comparing the ratio of a risky project with that of a risk-free project (that is, when $\sigma = 1$). For a given r, L, y_e and A, the profit-sharing ratio for a risk-free project s_b equals

$$s_b = rL\,/\,(y_e - 0.5A) \tag{3.3'}$$

The difference in the profit-sharing ratio of a risky project s and that of a risk-free project s_b reflects the risk premium (p) charged by the bank in a profit-sharing mode of financing. Thus,

$$p = s - s_b \tag{3.4}$$

Note that when the amount of funds invested equals the expected income net of auditing costs (that is, $L = y_e - 0.5A$), the risk-free profit-sharing ratio, s_b, will equal the risk-free rate of return, r.

Finally, we can examine the implications of different modes of financing for the income of the entrepreneur and the bank. Let the rate of mark-up for the project be fixed at $r_m = r + p_m$, where p_m is defined as risk premium in a fixed-income mode of financing like *murābaḥah*. To compare the relative returns and costs from the perspective of the bank and firm respectively, assume $L = \sigma y_e - 0.5A$. In the case of *murābaḥah*, the entrepreneur pays $r_m L$ to the bank in period $t = 1$. Under the profit-sharing mode, the entrepreneur's payment and the bank's return will depend on the actual *ex post* profit from the project y_a. Assuming the firm reports actual profit, then it pays sy_a to the bank. The relative payments made by the firm to the bank in the two modes of financing will depend on the *ex post* actual income, y_a, and the *ex ante* expected income, y_e. If y_a equals y_e, then the entrepreneur's payments to the bank will be the same in both modes of financing (that is, $r_m L = sy_a$). If, however, y_a is less (more) than y_e, then the entrepreneur pays less (more) in the case of the profit-sharing mode than in the *murābaḥah* case. In the case of a negative shock, the profit-sharing mode of financing protects a firm's profitability more than the fixed-income mode of financing. This risk-reducing phenomenon can be an incentive for firms to opt for the profit-sharing mode of financing.

Auditing rule

After the borrower reports a profit of y_r from the project in period $t = 1$, the bank takes a decision on auditing the firm's accounts. The following rules are followed in deciding to undertake an audit.

(i) If $y_r > y_e =\; >$ audit with a probability of $p_1 \approx 0$,
(ii) If $y_r = y_e =\; >$ audit with a probability of $0 < p_2 < 1$,
(iii) If $y_r < y_e =\; >$ audit with a probability of $p_3 \approx 1$.

If the bank decides to undertake the audit, it reveals an actual profit of y_a. The burden of the cost of audit will depend on the outcome of the actual profit, y_a, *vis-à-vis* the reported outcome by the entrepreneur, y_r. This is determined by the reward/punishment function discussed below.

The reward/punishment function

The reward/punishment function defines the reward and punishment (pecuniary and non-pecuniary) structures in the contract after the audit is undertaken. The features in the reward/punishment function should have incentives that will lessen false reporting of profits by the borrower and reduce the moral hazard problem. In the profit-sharing framework, the reward/punishment will depend on the actual profit found in the audit (y_a) relative to the reported profit (y_r) by the firm. Note that reward/punishment cannot be implemented if the bank decides not to audit the accounts of the firm. Though non-pecuniary reward/punishment can be used in an effective way to reduce the moral hazard problem, we focus only on pecuniary reward/punishment in our discussion.[10] The following three possible cases can occur.

1. Wrong reporting: the actual profit found in the audit is less than the reported profit (that is, $y_a < y_r$). This case is not very likely. The bank will, in this case, get sy_a. Note that the firm may benefit from the audit as it will now pay sy_a instead of $sy_r > sy_a$.
2. True reporting: the actual profit found equals the reported profit (that is, $y_a = y_r$). In this case all the auditing cost will be borne by the bank. The payment made by the firm will be $sy_a - 0.5A$. By refunding the share of the firm's audit cost when the firm is truthful in reporting the profit, the bank rewards honesty. This reward can be classified as bonding costs that Jensen and Meckling (1976) include in agency costs.[11]
3. False reporting: the actual profit found in the audit is greater than the reported profit (that is, $y_a > y_r$). This is a case of the moral hazard problem. The under-reporting of profit will lead to a penalty of the following nature. Other than paying back the invested amount L, the firm will bear all the auditing costs (A) and an additional fine $\beta\,(y_a - y_r)$, $\beta > 1$.[12] The total penalty (F) in the case of false reporting is now shown:

$$F = A + \beta\,(y_a - y_r) \tag{3.5}$$

To dissuade the firm from being dishonest, the threat of collecting the penalty should be costly and credible. The threat of collecting the penalty will be costly if the total penalty (F) and the invested amount due to the bank (L) for false reporting are much larger than the payment when true profit is reported. The threat will be credible if the fine can be accounted for from the assets of the firm V. That is,

$$V \geq L + F > L + sy_a \tag{3.6}$$

Note that the assets (V) act as collateral to enforce the penalty, to encourage true reporting of profit, and to minimize the moral hazard problem.

4. STRATEGIES OF THE FIRM AND IMPLICATIONS

Given the nature of the contract discussed above, we discuss the payoffs of the different strategies a firm can take in reporting profit. We will be able to determine the steps a bank can take to reduce the moral hazard problem (that is, false reporting of profit). The payoffs of the firm will depend on whether the firm reports true/false profit and whether the bank decides to audit the accounts of the firm. The payoffs under different situations are shown in Table 3.1. Note that the figures in the payoff matrix are costs to the firm (the amount paid to the bank) and as such smaller amounts are preferable to larger amounts.

Table 3.1 Payoff matrix of the firm and bank

Firm	**True**	**False**
Bank	$(y_a = y_r)$	$(y_a > y_r)$
Audit	$sy_a - 0.5A$ $(= sy_r - 0.5A)$	$A + \beta\,(y_a - y_r)$ $(> sy_a)$
No audit	sy_a $(= sy_r)$	sy_r $(< sy_a)$

Given the above payoff matrix, the strategy of the firm in reporting the profits will depend on the relative expected costs of true and false reporting. If the probability that an audit will be undertaken is p, then the expected costs of false and true reporting are given as follows:

Expected cost of true reporting = $E(C_t)$:

$$E(C_t) = p\,(sy_a - 0.5A) + (1 - p)\,sy_a = sy_a - 0.5Ap \tag{3.7}$$

Expected cost of false reporting = $E(C_t)$:

$$E(C_f) = p[A + \beta(y_a - y_r)] + (1 - p)\,sy_r \tag{3.8}$$

The moral hazard problem will occur when the expected cost of false reporting is less than the expected cost of true reporting. That is, the firm will choose to report a figure less than the actual profit when

$$E(C_f) < E(C_t), \tag{3.9}$$

or

$$p[A + \beta (y_a - y_r)] + (1 - p)sy_r < sy_a - 0.5Ap \tag{3.9^1}$$

From equation (3.9^1), we can derive the cut-off probability of audit (p^*) that will lead to moral hazard behaviour (that is, under-reporting profit) on the part of the firm as

$$p^* = s (y_a - y_r)/[1.5A + \beta (y_a - y_r) - sy_r] \tag{3.10}$$

Let p^* be called moral hazard probability. If $p < p^*$, the firm will have an incentive to report false profit as the expected cost of false reporting will be less than the expected cost of true reporting. A smaller moral hazard probability is preferable to the bank.[13] From equation (3.10) we note that the bank has control on only β to influence the moral hazard probability, as other variables are determined either exogenously (y_a, y_r and A) or endogenously in the model (s). By increasing the weight of the fine β, the bank can reduce the probability of the firm's under-reporting of profit.

To examine the moral hazard problem arising from under-reporting of profit, three cases can be discussed. First, the firm's *ex post* actual profit y_a is greater than the *ex ante* expected profit y_e (that is, $y_a > y_e$). The second case is when the firm's actual profit turns out to be the *ex ante* expected profit (that is, $y_a = y_e$). Finally, the firm's *ex post* actual profit is less than the *ex ante* expected profit (that is, $y_a < y_e$). The moral hazard problem involves reporting a profit below the actual level. The strategies that a firm will follow will depend on the probability of an audit being undertaken. The probabilities of audit, however, depend on the reported profit y_r relative to the expected profit y_e (as discussed under 'Auditing rule' in section 3 above). The strategies followed by the firm under the different situations indicated above are discussed below.

(a) *The actual profit y_a is greater than the expected profit y_e*: The firm knows that when the reported profit is equal to the expected profit (that is, $y_r = y_e$), the probability that the bank will undertake an audit is $p_2 (0 < p_2 < 1)$. If the probability of audit is less than the moral hazard probability (that is, $p_2 < p^*$), then the firm will not reveal the true profit. If, however, the probability of an audit, p_2, is greater than the moral hazard probability (that is, $p_2 > p^*$), the firm will declare true profit. The firm may, however, adopt another strategy in the latter case. Instead of revealing the actual profit, the firm can report a profit that is marginally above the expected profit so that $y_a > y_r > y_e$. In this case the probability of audit falls to $p_1 \approx 0 < p^*$, resulting in no audit. The firm keeps a larger share of the profit by under-reporting and the bank is satisfied with its return, as it is marginally higher than what it expected.[14]

(b) *The actual profit y_a equals the expected profit y_e*: If the firm underreports in this case, the reported profit y_r will be less than expected profit y_e. The probability of an audit will then be $p_3 \approx 1 > p^*$. The optimum strategy in this case will be to reveal the actual profit. Another factor that may induce the firm to report the actual profit is that an audit (if undertaken) will indicate actual profit as being the same as the reported amount. This will result in a reward for the firm as the firm's share of auditing costs will be returned and this potentially increases its return.

(c) *The actual profit y_a is less than the expected profit y_e*: When this is the case, the probability of an audit is high (that is, $p_3 \approx 1 > p^*$), and the firm will report actual profit. As in (b) above, the expected reward of getting back its share of auditing costs will be an additional incentive on the part of the firm to reveal actual profit.

The above discussion shows that moral hazard problems arising from under-reporting of profit will occur only when the actual profit is greater than the expected profit. Even in this case, the bank gets the expected rate of return. In other cases, it is in the firm's interest to report true profits. The step the bank can take to minimize the moral hazard problem is to reduce moral hazard probability p^* relative to probability of audit p. While the bank can influence the probability of audit p directly, it can reduce p^* indirectly by increasing the weight of the fine, β.

5. CONCLUSION

The chapter discusses the asymmetric information problem arising in profit-sharing modes of financing and the ways to deal with it by using incentive-compatible contracts. After discussing how the problem of adverse selection arises in financial dealings, it suggests guidelines for identifying the projects to minimize the adverse selection problem. These include choosing firms that are relatively established and have had previous (*murābaḥah*) dealings with the bank. The chapter derived the profit-sharing ratio that can be used in profit-sharing contracts. A profit-sharing contract that specifies the repayment function, auditing rule, and the reward/penalty functions of a profit-sharing contract was then discussed. Random auditing, along with using the assets of the firm as conditional collateral in the case of false reporting, yields an incentive structure that reduces the moral hazard problem. Specifically, we show that, given the threat of an audit and the reward/penalty thereof, the firm will not have an incentive to under-report profit, except in the case where the actual profit is greater than the expected profit. In this case, the bank still receives the expected rate of return from the investment.

The problem of asymmetric information arises from lack of information about operations of the firms. The financial sector of an economy can run more efficiently if information on the operations of firms is readily available. To enable this, laws and regulations that ensure transparency and certain institutions that can help in information-gathering and dissemination are needed. Governments in Islamic countries can play a vital role in reducing the asymmetric information problem by setting up institutions and enacting laws that increase the availability of information. In particular, policies may include setting up institutions that rate different firms according to different risk criteria (credit-rating institutions), establishing accounting standards that all firms should adhere to (so that verification of the profit by banks is easier), and enacting and enforcing laws that are very strict in their penalties for fraud, perjury and misuse of funds. These steps are not only required to help bolster the use of profit-sharing modes of financing by Islamic banks, but are also prerequisites for an efficient functioning of the financial system.

NOTES

1. Chapra (1985), Bendjilali and Khan (1995), Siddiqi (1981, 1983 and 1991), Khan (1985 and 1987) are the only papers, to the best of my knowledge, that discuss the nature of contracts in profit-sharing modes of financing.
2. Khan, W.M. (1987) also refers to the fear of losing reputation in the credit market in a multi-period framework that can work as a disincentive to false reporting of profit.
3. Lynn (1998) outlines the barriers that arise between financial institutions and their clients. These include physical barriers of poor infrastructure such as lack of markets, roads, power, communications, and so on, socio-economic factors of clients such as low numerical skills due to illiteracy, caste/ethnicity/gender aspects preventing interaction, and entrepreneurs' lack of collateral due to poverty.
4. The mechanism for determining the profit-sharing ratio given the risk and expected return from investment is discussed in the next section.
5. For a discussion, see Khan, T. (1995).
6. See Jensen and Meckling (1976) and Mishkin (1995, pp. 217–23) for a discussion on the moral hazard problem in conventional equity and debt contracts.
7. In a survey of 23 banks, Khalil et al. (2000) find that fear of misreporting the outcome by the agent is the prime reason that prevents banks from adopting *muḍārabah* financing contracts.
8. Though there are some theoretical discussions that indicate a method of determining an Islamic risk-free rate of return (see Khan, M.F., 1999), it is not used in practice yet. In its absence, the conventional risk-free rate (for example LIBOR, London Inter-Bank Offered Rate) can be used as a proxy.
9. Note that in debt contracts, the rate of interest accounts for different kinds of risk, including financial risk arising from fixed financing charges. In profit-sharing modes of financing, the financial risk will not appear, but other kinds of risk, such as the one arising from under-reporting of profit, will exist.

10. Non-pecuniary reward/punishment may include publishing names of dishonest entrepreneurs in the media, deprivation of banking facilities, jail terms, and so on. (See Chapra, 1985, pp. 174–81 and 200–202).
11. Jensen and Meckling (1976) define bonding costs as the resources used by the principal to reduce the harm caused by the agent.
12. The discussant of the chapter suggests determining β endogenously (see the comment following the chapter). While this suggestion can be incorporated in the model, it takes away a tool that the bank can use to influence the moral hazard behaviour of the entrepreneur.
13. A lower probability of audit implies that the bank has to undertake relatively fewer audits, reducing the auditing costs.
14. This loss by the bank can be classified as the residual loss included in agency costs due to the divergence between the agent's decision and the utility of the principal (Jensen and Meckling, 1976).

REFERENCES

Bendjilali, Boualem and Tariqullah Khan (1995), *Economics of Diminishing Mushārakah*, Jeddah, Saudi Arabia: Islamic Research and Training Institute, Islamic Development Bank.

Berger, Allen N. and Gregory F. Udell (1998), 'The Economics of Small Business Finance: The Roles of Private Equity and Debt Markets in the Financial Growth Cycle', *Journal of Banking and Finance*, **22**, 613–73.

Chapra, M. Umer (1985), *Towards a Just Monetary System*, Leicester, UK: The Islamic Foundation.

Gale, D. and M. Hellwig (1985), 'Incentive Compatible Debt Contracts: The One Period Problem', *Review of Economic Studies*, **52**, 647–63.

Iqbal, Munawar, Ausaf Ahmad and Tariqullah Khan (1998), *Challenges Facing Islamic Banking*, Occasional Paper No. 2, Jeddah, Saudi Arabia: Islamic Research and Training Institute, Islamic Development Bank.

Jarhi al-, Mabid Ali (1999), 'Islamic Economics from a Vantage Point', Keynote Lecture, International Conference on Islamic Economics towards the 21st Century, Kuala Lumpur, Malaysia.

Jensen, Michael C. and William H. Meckling (1976), 'Theory of the Firm: Managerial Behaviour, Agency Costs and Ownership Structure', *Journal of Financial Economics*, **3**, 305–60.

Khalil, Abdel-Fattah A.A., Colin Rickwood and Victor Murinde (2001), 'Evidence on agency-contractural problems in *muḍārabah* financing operations by Islamic banks', Chapter 4 in this volume.

Khan, M. Fahim (1999), 'Islamic Benchmarks as Alternative to LIBOR/Interest Rates', unpublished.

Khan, Tariqullah (1995), 'Demand for and Supply of Mark-up and PLS Funds in Islamic Banking: Some Alternative Explanations', *Islamic Economic Studies*, **3** (1), 39–78.

Khan, Waqar Masood (1985), *Towards an Interest-Free Islamic Economic System*, Islamic Economics Series 11, Leicester, UK: The Islamic Foundation, and Islamabad, Pakistan: The International Association for Islamic Economics.

Khan, Waqar Masood (1987), 'Towards an Interest-Free Islamic Economic System', in Mohsin S. Khan and Abbas Mirakhor (eds), *Theoretical Studies in Islamic Banking and Finance*, Houston, TX: The Institute for Research and Islamic Studies.

Lynn, Bennett (1998), 'Combining Social and Financial Intermediation to Reach the Poor: The Necessity and the Dangers', in Mwangi S. Kimenyi, Robert C. Wieland and J.D.V. Pischke (eds), *Strategic Issues in Microfinance*, Aldershot, Hants, UK: Ashgate Publishing.

Mishkin, Frederic S. (1995), *The Economics of Money, Banking, and Financial Markets*, 4th edn, New York: Harper Collins College Publications.

Siddiqi, M.N. (1981), *Banking without Interest*, Lahore, Pakistan: Islamic Publications Limited.

Siddiqi, M.N. (1983), *Issues in Islamic Banking*, Islamic Economics Series 4, Leicester, UK: The Islamic Foundation.

Siddiqi, M.N. (1991), 'Some Economic Aspects of *Muḍārabah*', *Review of Islamic Economics*, **1** (2), 21–33.

Townsend, R. (1979), 'Optimal Contracts and Competitive Markets with Costly State Verification', *Journal of Economic Theory*, **21**, 265–93.

COMMENTS

Said Al Hallaq

The chapter raises several important issues whose implications need to be considered by Muslim scholars to advance knowledge and understanding of the issues in question. The author emphasizes the inherent problems in applying profit-sharing modes of financing (*muḍārabah* and *mushārakah*), that is, asymmetric information and moral hazard problems.

I believe that the following remarks can enrich the contribution of the chapter:

1. An overview of the framework of the Islamic financial system needs to be added to the chapter, since we are not sure that non-Muslim scholars are fully aware of this framework.
2. The author claims that experience indicates some inherent problems in applying profit-sharing modes of financing. I think it is important to provide evidence to convince us about the significance of this problem and where it exists.
3. The chapter highlights the moral hazard problem arising from dishonesty in reporting actual figures by entrepreneurs. The idea is that the audit criterion suggested by the author represents external supervision. But what about internal supervision (that is, religious, social, ethical values)? We cannot ignore that completely; otherwise the analysis could apply to any non-Muslim entrepreneur. It must be emphasized, in this regard, that in an Islamic environment the behaviour of the Muslim entrepreneur is different from that of a non-Muslim. The Muslim firm's ultimate objective is not maximizing profit by exploiting moral hazard, but also achieving *falāḥ* in the Hereafter. Then, by not revealing the actual profit (y_a), he is giving up this spiritual benefit in exchange for pecuniary benefits.
4. In the case of false reporting (that is, $y_a > y_r$), where the actual profit found in the audit is greater than the reported profit, the author indicates that the total penalty (F) in the case of false reporting is given by the formula $F = A + \beta (y_a - y_r)$. However, the additional fine $\beta (y_a - y_r)$ needs more clarification (that is, what determines the value of β which the author assumes to be >1?). To explain this, let us consider the following situation: if y_a = SR 1000, y_r = SR 500, then $\beta (1000 - 500) = \beta (500)$. The question is, what will determine β? Is it 10 per cent of $(y_a - y_r)$, 20 per cent or what? I think the β must be determined by the gap between (y_a and y_r), such that $\beta = (y_a - y_r / y_a) \times 100$.

   Then in the previous example, $\beta = [\{(1000 - 500)/1000\} \times 100]$, that is, β = 50 per cent. The idea is that the higher the gap between y_a and y_r, the higher the ratio of the fine. To complete the picture, if A = SR 1000, then the total penalty is

$$\begin{aligned} F &= 1000 + 0.5\,(1000 - 500) \\ &= 1000 + 250 \\ &= \text{SR } 1250 \end{aligned}$$

4. Evidence on agency-contractual problems in *muḍārabah* financing operations by Islamic banks*

Abdel-Fattah A.A. Khalil, Colin Rickwood and Victor Murinde

1. INTRODUCTION

Islamic banks have developed specific forms of financial contracts to replace the interest rate mechanism in financial transactions. Invariably, these forms are based on profit/loss-sharing relationships between the supplier of funds, on the one hand, and the entrepreneur, on the other. One of the main forms of these financial contracts is the profit-sharing (hereafter, *muḍārabah*) contract. A standard *muḍārabah* contract can be described as a contractual relationship between two parties, the financier (*rabb al-māl*) and the entrepreneur (*muḍārib*), who are governed by the *Sharīʿah* (the Islamic law) and combine human and financial capital in order to set up a risky but profitable joint invesment project. The contract has a prime role in utilizing funds as well as distributing returns to investment without resort to interest. However, in the context of agency theory, the *muḍārabah* contract seems to be inherently characterized by agency problems. In particular, the economic interests of the entrepreneur (the agent) may conflict with those of the Islamic bank (the principal) despite the contractual relationship between the two that requires the former to act in the interest of the latter. Moreover, information asymmetry may exist in the sense that the bank may not be able consistently to monitor the activities of the entrepreneur.

* This chapter was completed while A.A. Khalil was on sabbatical at Birmingham Business School, the University of Birmingham, partly under the auspices of the 'Finance and Development Research Programme' funded by DFID, Contract No. RSC106056. We thank Jim Ford, Roger Groves, John Presley, Munawar Iqbal, Humayoun Dar, Abdel-hameed Bashir (the discussant) and participants at the Fourth International Conference on Islamic Economics and Banking held at Loughborough University during 13–15 August 2000 for useful comments on an earlier version of this chapter. However, the interpretations and conclusions expressed in the chapter are entirely the responsibility of the authors.

This chapter reports the results of a study of the agency theory features of the *muḍārabah* contract between the Islamic bank and the entrepreneur. We used questionnaire survey methods to collect primary data on Islamic banking practices. By analysing the data using non-parametric methods, we are able to disentangle the main variables that underpin the agency theory features of the *muḍārabah* contract. The main four types of variables considered are the key variables that: capture the construction and pricing of *muḍārabah* contracts; underpin the restrictiveness of *muḍārabah* contracts; measure the incidence of agency problems in *muḍārabah* contracts; and underpin monitoring and contractual governance issues in *muḍārabah* contracts.

We then invoke deductive hypothesis-testing methods to investigate the incidence of agency-contractual problems in these contracts. We find that project attributes, the quality of the entrepreneur (or agent), and religious (*Sharīʿah*) considerations are the three most important agency-contractual poblems in *muḍārabah* financing practices by Islamic banks. These results have important policy implications for managers of Islamic banks, entrepreneurs dealing in *muḍārabah* contracts, and central banks that are charged with the regulation of Islamic banks. Bank managers may use the results in order to design strategies for reducing agency problems; for example, to identify good projects and credible entrepreneurs, and to acknowledge the *Sharīʿah* factor. Entrepreneurs must pay attention to maintaining their credibility. Bank regulators should enforce the vigilance of the *Sharīʿah* boards in Islamic banks. In general, however, further empirical research is needed to fully qualify each of these implications.

2. SOME SALIENT AGENCY FEATURES OF A *MUḌĀRABAH* FINANCING CONTRACT

The first party to a *muḍārabah* contract is the financier (*rabb al-māl*), who provides funds needed to establish any venture, trade or service with the purpose of generating profits. The other party, the entrepreneur (*muḍārib*), supplies human capital and fulfils the entrepreneurial role. Arguably, the *muḍārabah* contract reflects the core of Islamic banking, where the sharing of risk and return is the fundamental axiom of the system (see Siddiqi, 1991 and Khan, 1995).

However, in the agency-theoretical framework associated with the work by Jensen and Meckling (1976, 1992), Ross (1973), Fama (1980, 1990) and Stulz (1990), the ideal risk-sharing and profit-sharing contract relates to two parties who have identical probability beliefs with respect to the state of nature. One party is the insider (active) who is identified as the agent (entrepreneur). This party has knowledge about a risky profitable investment project that they wish to undertake, but they have zero initial funds to finance it. The outsider (passive) party is interpreted as the principal (bank), who provides the full initial funds needed to establish the project.

In general, a number of distinctive features can be attributed to the *muḍārabah* contract to reflect its nature and the inherent magnitude of agency-contractual problems. We identify three main features; namely, idiosyncratic uncertainty (risk), extreme linearity and discretionary power. It is argued here that idiosyncratic uncertainty, particularly for the bank, is embodied in profit-sharing contracts. This uncertainty has many sources: the bank's return is assumed to depend solely on the reported future cash flows resulting from operating profitability, which in turn depends entirely on the corporate investment decisions that are made by the agent. Moreover, the agent is not fully supervised, and has a measure of independence.[1] Given that the agent's level of effort may be regarded as unobservable, it cannot be contracted. Moreover, the uncertainty is exacerbated by lack of security over assets. As Khan (1995) argues, the bank normally has no control rights over the assets employed in the project in *muḍārabah* contracts, particularly given the existence (according to Islamic rule) of the restriction to collateralize these assets. If the assets are not easy to re-deploy and human capital is a major component, as is the case in Williamson (1996), then the lack of collateral is further emphasized. In addition, the financial reporting system that is utilized for assessing the outcomes of the contract is mainly chosen and managed by the entrepreneur. Accordingly, uncertainty will be severe and the bank bears very significant risks, particularly in the case of occurrence of losses. This may give rise to high incidence of adverse selection and moral hazard problems, which are facilitated by the ability of entrepreneur, in such contracts, to hide information regarding his abilities and background before contracting and to conceal actions taken after the contract is put in place (see Smith, 1996). In addition, the outcome may not be reported truthfully by the agent. This adverse selection problem arises because of the existence of the *ex ante* asymmetric information between the bank and the agent, while two moral hazard problems may result: first from the entrepreneur's selection of effort; and second due to the reluctance of the agent to report private information.

The second distinctive feature attributable to the *muḍārabah* contract is the extreme linearity (linear-sharing) between the reward and the performance of the project undertaken, where the party's reward is a linear function of the realized outcome. The expected state-contingent final outcome is mainly dependent upon the endowed skill level of the entrepreneur and the level of effort expended, combined with his avoidance of perquisites. Not only are these aspects unobservable by the bank, but also their costs are shared in fixed proportions while the utility gains from shirking and perquisites are enjoyed only by the agent. This makes the entrepreneur compensation scheme a purely concave function of the ultimate outcomes (making the agent a residual claimant). In some circumstances, linearity can be regarded, from an agency-contractual point of view, as an efficient way to spread the risk attached to the contract, as shown in the work by, among others, Holmstrom (1989), Libby and Lipe (1992), Zou (1992) and Mehran (1995). It may provide a perfect alignment of interest between the bank and the entrepreneur and hence induce appropriate incentive for the agent in his activity both to effectively minimize costs and to select investment projects. However, to achieve this, linearity requires effective monitoring and verification technology so that consumption of perquisites and shirking can be fully detected and borne by the agent. Monitoring costs may be incurred in all stages of the contract to ensure compliance with the terms of the contract, and to convey verifiable and informative signals about the entrepreneur's behaviour. Verification costs (for example auditing) are required to check the accuracy of measurement of the performance and the truthfulness of the reported outcome prepared by the agent's financial system (see for example, Penno, 1990a and 1990b; Watts and Zimmerman, 1983; Mehran, 1995 and Lang et al., 1995).

The third distinctive feature of the *muḍārabah* contract represents discretionary power since the agent initially controls the project and enjoys the rights to make decisions concerning investment and distribution of intermediate cash flows. This provides the entrepreneur with full discretion over assets, similar to that assigned to sole owner–manager projects, without bearing the risk of financial losses. By contrast with equity, there are no automatic rights to make appointments to the board of directors using associated voting power, which would give the financier some scope for intrusive oversight of operating activity, as in Grossman and Hart (1988), Jensen and Warner (1988) and Smith (1996). In this setting, it can be argued that the entrepreneur can be characterized as a discretionary agent who, having relinquished ownership of the project in relation to outcomes, may act in self-interest. Therefore, personal qualities (honesty, capability and so on) and other characteristics of the entrepreneur are expected to be vital criteria for such contracts in controlling and mitigating agency problems such as sub-optimal investment policy and the motivation to consume more perks (see Diamond, 1991). The agency-cost reflection of this salient feature is that the bank may have to address these fundamental issues about the entrepreneur. As Diamond (1989, 1991) has argued, costs may be incurred in assessing accurately the relevant qualities of the entrepreneur which might be useful in establishing efficient incentive structures of a Pareto-optimal risk-sharing partnership.

3. KEY QUESTIONS AND HYPOTHESES ON THE PRACTICE OF THE *MUḌĀRABAH* CONTRACT

On the basis of the foregoing discussion on the main features of the *muḍārabah* contract, we identify four of its main characteristics. These relate to construction and pricing, restrictiveness, agency incidence, and monitoring. Below, we investigate a number of questions with respect to each of the four types of characteristics.

The characteristics relating to the construction and pricing of *muḍārabah* contracts derive from the idiosyncratic uncertainty feature of the contract. We aim to investigate three main questions:

1. What are the main variables that underpin the uncertainty that may prevent banks from constructing *muḍārabah* contracts on a large scale?
2. What are the main factors that may influence banks' assessment of *muḍārabah* contracts, that is, in reaching a decision to accept or reject these contracts?
3. What are the main factors used in pricing the *muḍārabah* contract and in determining the profit-sharing rates?

The characteristics relating to restrictiveness of *muḍārabah* contracts derive from the discretionary power feature of the contract. Here, we aim to investigate two main questions:

1. To what extent is the *muḍārabah* contract likely to impose restrictions on the entrepreneur's decision regarding the project's policies and the accounting policy choice?
2. To what extent does the entrepreneur have discretion regarding production, investment and financing decisions under the *muḍārabah* contract?

The characteristics relating to the incidence of *muḍārabah* contracts derive from the idiosyncratic uncertainty feature as well as the discretionary power feature of the contract. In this context, we aim to investigate two main questions:

1. What are the main variables that underpin the incidence of agency problems in *muḍārabah* contracts?
2. Which party should bear losses in the event of the project resulting in negative net present values?

The characteristics relating to monitoring of *muḍārabah* contracts derive from the extreme linearity feature of the contract. Jensen and Meckling (1976) argue that agency problems associated with financial contracts can be diminished by expenditure on monitoring. However, as Watts and Zimmerman (1983, 1990) have shown, expenditure on monitoring is an increasing function of the proportion of the firm's assets that is financed by outsider capital. The authors suggest that the expenditure and benefits of monitoring depend on the asset structure of the firm and the composition of financial claims. In this case, we aim to investigate three main questions:

1. What are the aims of the monitoring system in *muḍārabah* contracts?
2. What are the main areas of activity to be monitored?
3. What are the main devices which agents use in monitoring the *muḍārabah* contract?

In addition to the above questions, the discussion (in section 2) on the three main features of the *muḍārabah* contract have important implications for the nature and magnitude of agency-contractual problems, as well as the determination of the associated contractual governance structure. In this section, we use the discussion to propose three hypotheses relating to the *muḍārabah* contract.[2] In deriving the hypotheses, we explore the theoretical implications for the design of the contract. We also identify the key factors in practice and relate them to the agency-contracting cost expectation.

We interpret the agency-contracting cost expectation to predict that *muḍārabah* contracts are particularly susceptible to generating agency-contractual problems and associated costs. Standard agency theory implies a positive relation between the level of agency problems and the magnitude of asymmetric information in contracts. The asymmetric information is inherent in *muḍārabah* contracts, where two types may exist. The adverse selection agency problem (hidden characteristics) is expected to emerge as a result of the existence of *ex ante* asymmetric information with regard to the agent's type (talent, skill, experience, ingenuity, leadership and so on) and about the validity of the project. Moral hazard associated with hidden action and hidden information is predicted to be high as a result of the existence of the *ex post* information asymmetries, the discretionary power of the agent, the unobservability of agent's actions, and the existence of a linear relationship between reward and performance. Therefore, opportunistic behaviour (particularly the shifting of risk) is more likely in the *muḍārabah* setting as a result of the interplay of adverse selection and moral hazard problems. The significance of these agency-contractual costs of *muḍārabah* contracts may restrict the use of profit-sharing contracts. Adverse selection and moral hazard problems are predicted to be very significant and to exert a profound impact on the profit-sharing paradigm. It follows that information about a project's attributes is of significance at the pre-contractual screening stage. Hence, hypothesis 1 (H1) can be stated as follows:

Banks will give high ranking to the specific attributes of the project in accepting or rejecting a muḍārabah *contract* ex ante.

In addition, the entrepreneurs' reputation for competence and integrity is considered potentially to affect the incidence and pricing of a *muḍārabah* contract. The entrepreneurial role in a profit-sharing contract and, hence, the creation of value through the entrepreneurial process is likely to be important where the entrepreneur utilizes his abilities (talent, skill, experience, ingenuity, leadership and so on) to combine and deploy tangible and intangible assets in ways that could not be imitated easily. In *muḍārabah* contracts, the personal qualities (for example honesty) and the characteristics of the entrepreneur are vital criteria in relation to the decision by the provider of funds to accept or reject the project. In this context, the bank will be concerned to minimize the moral hazard problems in relation to the agent's actions and will also affect the reliability of the agent's reporting *ex post*. Hence, hypothesis 2 (H2) can be stated as follows:

Banks will give high ranking to the specific attributes of the entrepreneur in a muḍārabah *contract.*

Islam demands specific codes of behaviour to be followed. Adherence to these codes may reduce agency problems. The codes represent voluntary adoption of self-constraint to avoid certain opportunistic behaviour, including dishonesty and other activities that take advantage of moral hazard imperfections. Placing emphasis on obedience to religious principles attempts to use voluntary self-constraint. It can benefit from informal policing by society at large, acting as observers, as well as observation by religious officials both informally and formally in their role as members of the *Sharī*ʿ*ah* board. Evidence of this emphasis provided by contractual provisions may be expected in the face of the significant agency problems. Hence, hypothesis 3 (H3) can be stated as follows:

In relation to accepting or rejecting project (or investment) decisions, compliance with the Sharīʿah *considerations is a significant requirement in* muḍārabah *contracts.*

4. METHODOLOGY

4.1 The Data

In order to address the research questions of this study in a logical way, it was necessary to focus on generating relevant, detailed primary data on *muḍārabah* contracting practices, rather than relying on secondary data. It was decided that primary data would be generated by means of a survey. It was also decided that the most appropriate research technique to be employed to obtain the required data was a structured postal questionnaire.[3] These decisions were based on four main considerations. First, the whole population (sampling frame or working population) of Islamic banking is very limited, amounting to only about 52 Islamic banks worldwide. These banks exhibit differences in their treatment of Islamic banking and the *muḍārabah* contract. Hence, the survey method was applied to the whole population in order to accurately represent and describe the characteristics of the phenomena and avoid the problems of random sampling errors. Second, Islamic banks are not geographically concentrated but are widely spread across the world. So it would have been prohibitively costly in terms of time and money to adopt the case-study method or to conduct in-depth interviews or a self-administered questionnaire for this population. Third, the postal questionnaire offers a feasible alternative in the sense that it avoids the bias that the interviewer might introduce in using the case-study or interview technique. Fourth, the nature and the environment of the banking industry in general, and Islamic banking in particular, raises issues of confidentiality which restrict access and may prevent the widespread use of interview techniques.

We paid attention to questionnaire design first in order to ensure that the questionnaire would lead to the collection of adequate data concerning the *muḍārabah* contracting activities. Considerable attention was given to the selection of areas, question content and the wording of questions in aiming to get clear, unambiguous and useful questions. It was also recognized that the overall size of the questionnaire had to be limited if it was to be acceptable by its recipients. This required special attention to limit its content to only those questions that were expected to result in useful data. The questionnaire was designed to obtain information on the agency problem, contracting cost and the contractual governance role of accounting and auditing.

After pilot-testing work had been carried out, inside and outside the UK, a questionnaire with 32 questions grouped into three sections was finalized to explore the bankers' views on the agency-contractual problems of *muḍārabah* contracts. The postal questionnaires were dispatched to 52 Islamic banks worldwide, which represented the whole of the population that could be identified at the time of mailing. A satisfactory response rate (44 per cent) was obtained from the survey of this study. No evidence of potential non-response biases seems to appear in the response patterns.

After coding and preparing variables in the questionnaire for analysis, SPSS was employed as an appropriate statistical package to carry out the initial as well as the main statistical analysis.

4.2 Statistical Analysis

After coding the questionnaire data into a form suitable for analysis, our first step in the initial analysis was to obtain descriptive statistics of each of the main variables (univariate analysis), giving particular attention to any unexpected results. The calculation of the mean and the standard deviation for most individual questions, and the joint frequency distribution of selected variables, was carried out to generate some preliminary results. In general, we considered four types of variables: the key variables used to capture the construction and pricing of *muḍārabah* contracts; the key variables that underpin the restrictiveness of *muḍārabah* contracts; the key variables that measure the incidence of agency problems in *muḍārabah* contracts; and the key variables that underpin monitoring and contractual governance issues in *muḍārabah* contracts.

In addition, bivariate analysis was used to measure both the strength and direction of relationships, if any, between pairs of variables that represent the agency-contractual relationship in a *muḍārabah* contract. Specifically, we undertook cross-tabulation analysis for the relationship between the incidence of agency problems, on the one hand, and each of the key variables that prevent the Islamic bank from adopting *muḍārabah* financing contracts, on the other. Since the measurement levels of most of the variables in this study are nominal and ordinal, cross-tabulation was used in conjunction with a chi-square test of significance, and correlation coefficient methods based on Spearman's rho or Kendall's tau, as appropriate techniques for detecting whether pairs of selected variables were associated or not.

We also used correlation analysis to measure the degree of relationship between variables in the study. The idea was to present the whole set of bivariate correlations by using a correlation matrix.[4] To be consistent with the prediction of the agency-contractual paradigm, the type of the agent and the characteristics of the project are expected to have a substantial effect on the construction and the shaping of the governance of the financial contracts.[5] By studying the association between selected pairs of ordinal variables, we were seeking to explore the relationship between the characteristics of the agent and the project, the devices used in monitoring, and the areas to be monitored in *muḍārabah* contracts.

Finally, the deductive hypothesis-testing (hypothetico-deductive) method was adopted here on the grounds that the absence of previous empirical work on the *muḍārabah* contract makes it necessary to adopt an exploratory approach. The three hypotheses in this chapter were tested against the null hypothesis in each case. The chi-square (one-tailed level) test was used as a non-parametric statistical test of the significance of the difference between the ranks and the variance of the population.[6]

5. INITIAL RESULTS: DESCRIPTIVE STATISTICS

5.1 Results from Univariate Analysis

The results from univariate analysis are reported here in terms of the main four types of variables considered, namely: the key variables used to capture the construction and pricing of *muḍārabah* contracts; the key variables that underpin the restrictiveness of *muḍārabah* contracts; the key variables that measure the incidence of agency problems in *muḍārabah* contracts; and the key variables that underpin monitoring and contractual governance issues in *muḍārabah* contracts.

5.1.1 The construction and pricing of *muḍārabah* contracts

Panel A of Table 4.1 reports results relating to the main reasons that prevent banks from entering into *muḍārabah* contracts on a large scale. The results show that misreporting (MISREPT) of the result of the project (87 per cent) and the uncertainty and variability (UNCRTNTY) of the return from these contracts (83 per cent) represent the two most important variables that prevent the banks from constructing *muḍārabah* contracts. These results reflect some moral hazard problems in the nature of the *muḍārabah* contract. The implications relate to the importance of assessing the quality of the agent and the feasibility of the project.

Panel B presents descriptive statistics of the main determinants in relation to the banks' assessment in reaching a decision to accept or reject a *muḍārabah* contract. It is shown that RPUTATON, EXPRNCE and ISLMRULE are the most important variables in accepting or rejecting *muḍārabah* decisions. The mean of these variables is close to 1.00 with a small standard deviation. PRFPRJCT, FNLRCRD, CREDWRTH and UNCTPRJT variables represent considerable importance, while SOCIALLY, TIMPROFT and SECURITY factors have moderate importance.

The results are consistent with the expected characteristics of *muḍārabah* contracts. It is useful to note that the agent in a *muḍārabah* contract has considerable discretionary power, is assigned all control rights of the project and contributes only the effort and entrepreneurial role. It is therefore not surprising that banks place great emphasis on the agent's qualification and reputation, given the need for compliance with Islamic rule (as a determinant factor to accept or reject such contracts). Moreover, the results in Panel B support hypothesis 2, which predicts that banks will give high ranking to the specific attributes of the entrepreneur. In addition, the results support hypothesis 3, which predicts that compliance of the project with the *Sharīʿah* considerations is a significant requirement for banks to accept or reject decisions.

Panel C of Table 4.1 shows that DGRISK is the highest-rated (83 per cent) factor in determining the profit-sharing rates for the distribution of cash flow. TYPPOJCT, TIMPOJCT, SIZPOJCT and INTRSTRT are rated at about 70 per cent. In *muḍārabah* contracts, a fixed return on the use of the funds is not acceptable, rights to the repayment of the funds invested are not granted, and the funds are not secured by any charge on assets. Accordingly, the banks assess the riskiness of an investment, type, size and time horizon of the project, and

Table 4.1 Evidence based on univariate analysis

Panel A: Descriptive statistics of key variables which prevent the banks from adopting *muḍārabah* financing contracts (the range is from 0 to 1)

Variable	Mean	Std dev.
MISREPT: misreporting of the outcome by the agent	0.87	0.34
UNCRTNTY: variability and uncertainty of the return	0.83	0.39
RKLOSS: the bank bears the risk of losses	0.70	0.47
HMONTCST: the high costs required for monitoring	0.70	0.47
UNCECUR: the lack of legal repayment requirement	0.52	0.51
NOCONTRL: the lack of right of control	0.30	0.47
INFORMAT: no access to information	0.30	0.47
LPROFIT: the risk of low profit	0.09	0.29
ACONTING: the demand for rigorous accounting	0.00	0.00

Panel B: Descriptive statistics of the decision variables in accepting or rejecting *muḍārabah* contracts (note: 1 = very important; 2 = reasonably important; 3 = important; 4 = neutral; 5 = unimportant

Variable	Mean	Std dev.	Minimum	Maximum
RPUTATON: reputation	1.00	0.00	1	1
EXPRNCE: experience and qualification	1.09	0.29	1	2
ISLMRULE: compliance with Islamic rules	1.17	0.49	1	3
PRFPRJCT: profitability of project	1.26	0.45	1	2
FNLRCRD: the financial track records	1.30	0.63	1	3
CREDWRTH: current financial position	1.35	0.65	1	3
UNCTPRJT: degree of uncertainty of project	1.52	0.73	1	3
SOCIALLY: social and environmental	1.91	0.85	1	4
TIMPROFT: the time horizon of profits	2.00	0.67	1	3
SECURITY: the security offered by the assets	2.13	1.01	1	4

Panel C: Descriptive statistics of factors used in determining the profit-sharing rates

Variable	Mean	Std dev.
DGRISK: degree of risk	0.83	0.39
TYPPOJCT: type of project	0.78	0.42

Table 4.1 (continued)

Panel C: Descriptive statistics of factors used in determining the profit-sharing rates

Variable	Mean	Std dev.
TIMPOJCT: time horizon of the project	0.78	0.42
SIZPOJCT: size of project	0.70	0.47
INTRSTRT: interest rate level	0.61	0.50
LEVCOLAT: level of collateral	0.43	0.51

Panel D: Descriptive statistics of the restrictions imposed on the agent's decisions

Variable	Mean	Std dev.
RSTDSPS: restriction on disposition of assets	0.96	0.21
RFINANCE: restriction on additional financing	0.83	0.39
RSTMRGE: restriction on mergers	0.78	0.42
RSTWCAP: restriction on working capital	0.65	0.49
RSTSECRT: restriction on purchase securities	0.30	0.47
RDIVDIND: restriction on payment dividends	0.26	0.45
RSTOTHER: other restrictions	0.17	0.39

Panel E: Descriptive statistics of the agent's discretionary power regarding production, investment and financing decisions

Variable	Mean	Std dev.
PRODDECN: production decisions	0.98	0.10
INVSTDES: investment decisions	0.87	0.34
FINCDESN: financing decisions	0.26	0.45

Panel F: Descriptive statistics of the incidence of agency problems in *muḍārabah* contracts

Variable	Mean	Std dev.
OVRINVST: overinvestment problem	0.82	0.39
PRSNLPF: overconsumption of personal benefits	0.73	0.46
PERKS: incentive to consume more perks	0.59	0.50
REDEFFRT: reduction of effort (shirking)	0.36	0.49
UNDRINVS: underinvestment problem	0.18	0.39

Table 4.1 (continued)

Panel G: Descriptive statistics of the party which should bear the losses in *muḍārabah* contracts

Variable	Mean	Std dev.
LOSSBANK: borne mainly by the bank	0.78	0.42
PERFORM: depending on the agent's performance	0.78	0.42
LOSASPRF: shared on the same basis as profit	0.09	0.29
LOSDIFPF: shared on a different basis	0.04	0.21
LOSSAGNT: borne mainly by the agent	0.04	0.21

Panel H: Descriptive statistics concerning the responsibility of the agent towards the losses resulting from the project

Variable	Mean	Std dev.
NEGLIGNC: from the negligence of the agent	0.91	0.29
BREACH: loss resulting from breach of the contract	0.91	0.29
INEFICNT: because of the inefficiencies	0.43	0.51
NOLOSS: none	0.04	0.21

Panel I: Descriptive statistics of the importance of taking an active role in monitoring the project in *muḍārabah* contracts

Variable	Mean	Std dev.	Minimum	Maximum
PREPORT: periodical management reports	1.48	1.16	1	5
ADVICE: making available help and advice	1.78	1.13	1	5
REPBOARD: representation on the board	2.30	1.29	1	5
DINVOLVE: involvement in strategic decisions	2.35	1.27	1	5
MANGSTAF: providing management staff	3.78	1.38	1	5
NOROLE: not to play any role in management	4.43	1.16	1	5

Table 4.1 (continued)

Panel J: Descriptive statistics of the aims of the monitoring system in *muḍārabah* contracts

Variable	Mean	Std dev.
RESRALCT: to ensure efficient allocation	1.00	0.00
COMPLIAN: to ensure compliance with terms	1.00	0.00
VALDTYFR: to ensure information's validity	0.91	0.29
MAXEFRT: to maximize the agent's effort	0.74	0.45
SINGINFM: to get information signals	0.65	0.49
EXPOSURE: to improve the exposure to risks	0.43	0.51

Panel K: Descriptive statistics of the importance of areas of activity to be monitored in *muḍārabah* contracts

Variable	Mean	Std dev.	Minimum	Maximum
MONTPROD: monitoring the production	1.22	0.60	1	3
MONTFINC: financial performance	1.43	0.59	1	3
MONTDEFT: the probability of default	1.48	0.59	1	3
MONTABLT: the agent's ability	1.57	0.66	1	3
MONTINVS: investment	1.74	0.86	1	3
MONTPRKS: the agent's personal benefits	2.30	1.15	1	4

the appropriate rate of return for each *muḍārabah* contract. This finding is consistent with the conventional doctrine of portfolio theory with respect to the relationship between risk and expected return.

5.1.2 The restrictiveness of the *muḍārabah* contract

Panel D of Table 4.1 displays a clear picture of the extent to which the *muḍārabah* contract is likely to contain restrictions on the entrepreneur's decisions regarding the project's policies and the accounting policy choice. It is shown that the restrictions imposed by the bank on the agent's ability to dispose of all or part of the assets of the project (RSTDSPS), obtain additional finance (RFINANCE), and participate in mergers (RSTMRGE), represent the highest-rated constraints (96 per cent, 83 per cent, and 78 per cent, respectively). Restriction on maintenance of working capital (RSTWCAP) scores a moderate level, while restriction on purchasing securities (RSTSECRT) and restriction on payment of dividends (RDIVDIND) are accorded a low level of importance.

One explanation for these results relates to the main features of the *muḍārabah* contract. Given that the whole fund for the project is contributed by the bank on the one hand, and the entire losses are borne by the bank on the other, accordingly, and analogous to debt contracts, constraints should be imposed on the agent's capacity regarding the activities represented by the variables reported above. Restriction on disposition of the assets, or the asset substitution agency problem as in Jensen and Meckling (1976), is identified as the most important activity to be constrained.

Panel E of Table 4.1 exhibits descriptive statistics of the agent's discretionary power concerning the activities of the project. It is shown that the entrepreneur in a *muḍārabah* contract is assigned almost total responsibility in respect of production decisions, PRODDECN (98 per cent with 0.10 standard deviation), while a substantial level of discretion over investment decisions (INVSTDES) is granted to him. Discretion regarding the financing decisions (FINCDESN) emerges with an expectedly low score (26 per cent) but with high variance distribution. These results can be interpreted as a response to the nature of the role of the agent in *muḍārabah* contracts. Given that the main contribution of the agent in *muḍārabah* contracts is his managerial and entrepreneurial role, it seems reasonable to assign production and investment decisions to the agent. Further, it may be expected that the agent's discretion in relation to financing decisions is limited since he has a zero finance contribution. In general, these results show some consistency with the results reported in Panel D, particularly for the financing decisions.[7]

Based on the findings from the descriptive statistics of Table 4.1 (Panels A–E), it is reasonable to assume that *muḍārabah* contracts can be regarded as discretionary contracts, particularly in relation to production and investment activities. Accounting-based contractual restrictions may be lower than in other financial contracts, especially debt contracts.

5.1.3 The incidence of agency problems in *muḍārabah* contracts

Jensen and Meckling (1976) and Jensen (1986), among others, argue that agency problems of financial contracts, particularly overinvestment and the incentive to consume perquisites, are likely to be high when there is a greater proportion of outside capital and a full discretion assigned to the agent. We apply this proposition to the *muḍārabah* contract. As Panel F of Table 4.1 indicates, overinvestment agency (OVRINVST) problems scored high (rated 82 per cent with 0.39 standard deviation), overconsumption of the agent by personal benefits (PRSNLPF) scored 73 per cent, while the incentive to consume more perks (PERKS) than other financial contracts scored a moderate level (59 per cent).

Other agency problems, such as reduction of effort by agents (REDEFFRT), or shirking, and underinvestment (UNDRINVS) appear but with low levels (36 per cent and 18 per cent, respectively).

With reference to the premises of agency theory, these results can be interpreted as a reflection of the salient features of the *muḍārabah* contract, particularly the 'discretionary power' characteristic and 'zero liability of the agent towards normal losses', in addition to the condition that the whole fund of the project should be provided by the outside party. These features may motivate the agent in the *muḍārabah* contract to invest in projects with low or negative net present values and may create incentives for the agent to consume unnecessary perquisites. On the other hand, the diminishing (reduction) of underinvestment and shirking agency problems may be attributed to the extreme linearity feature of *muḍārabah* contracts.

Panel G displays the descriptive statistics of a controversial feature of *muḍārabah* contracts, namely: which party should bear the losses in the event of the project resulting in a negative outcome? It is shown that the bank mainly bears the normal losses which result from the normal practice of the agent (LOSSBANK). It is also shown that the agent is liable to bear losses to the same extent as the bank (83 per cent), if it is proved that the losses resulted from the incompetence of the agent (PERFORM). The above results are consistent with those reported in Panel H. It is shown that 91 per cent of the banks admit that losses should be borne by the agent if it is proved that these losses are linked directly to the agent's breach of the terms of agreement (BREACH), or as a consequence of the negligence of the agent (NEGLIGNC).

5.1.4 Monitoring and the contractual governance of *muḍārabah* contracts

It was earlier argued that a complex governance structure might be needed to guide the contractual relationship of *muḍārabah* contracts. The results of the descriptive statistical analysis suggest that monitoring and managing the incentive of the agent, through an appropriate contractual governance structure, appears to be of great significance in controlling and overcoming agency problems of *muḍārabah* contracts.

Panel I presents the magnitude of the importance of different mechanisms that are used to take an active role in monitoring *muḍārabah* contracts. Periodic management reports on project performance (PREPORT) and making available help and advice on how to manage the project (ADVICE) score the high-rated mean (1.48 and 1.78, respectively, with more or less the same variation). This result is consistent with one feature of the *muḍārabah* contract, namely that the agent enjoys the right to control and manage the project (having relinquished ownership of it). Representation on the company board (REPBOARD) and direct involvement in decisions affecting strategic policies (DINVOLVE) show a moderate level of importance (2.30 mean with 1.29 standard deviation, and

2.35 mean with 1.27 standard deviation, respectively). The extreme cases of not playing any role in project management (NOROLE) and providing management staff to the project (MANGSTAF) score low levels.

Panel J of Table 4.1 displays the descriptive statistics relating to the aims of the monitoring system in *muḍārabah* contracts. The three main aims are: to ensure that resources are allocated to their most profitable uses (RESRALCT); to ensure compliance with contractual agreement (COMPLIAN); and to ascertain the validity of the information reported by the agent (VALDTYFR). The results show that RESRALCT and COMPLIAN receive 100 per cent scores, while VALDTYFR has a mean of 0.91. The aim of providing incentives for maximum effort from the agent (MAXEFRT) and the aim of getting information signals about project progress and eventual outcome (SINGINFM) show a moderate level of importance.

These results can be interpreted as a reflection of the allocation of control rights in *muḍārabah* contracts. Since the agent in *muḍārabah* contracts is assigned great control rights (discretionary investment power) over the assets of the project, it is to be expected that the bank places emphasis on: the efficiency of the allocation of the resources in the project; the extent to which the agent is compliant with the contract's terms; and verification of the faithfulness of the agent.

The results above, therefore, suggest that the important areas of activity to be addressed in *muḍārabah* contracts include monitoring of production, financial performance, the probability of default, the agent's ability and the investment. Panel K presents descriptive statistics of these areas. It is shown that MONTPROD, MONTFINC, MONTDEFT, MONTABLT and MONTINVS are the most important areas for monitoring in a *muḍārabah* setting, according to respondents. It is found that less importance (2.30 score) is placed on monitoring the agent's potential for pursuing personal benefits (MONTPRKS). This result suggests that the agent is required to obey and adhere to religious norms to avoid certain opportunistic behaviour; we refer to this as a voluntary self-constraint agent.

5.2 Results from Bivariate Analysis

We report below the results from the bivariate analysis in terms of cross-tabulation of the variables that represent the incidence of agency problems, on the one hand, and each of the following, on the other: the risk of misreporting by the agent (MISREPT); lack of control rights (NOCONTRL); the high costs required for monitoring (HMONTCST); and the disadvantage in access to information (INFORMT). In each case, the incidence of agency problems is represented by overinvestment (OVERINST), underinvestment (UNDRINVS), personal benefits (PRSNLPFT), reduction of effect (REDEFFRT) and perquisites (PERKS).

5.2.1 Cross-tabulation analysis: the relationship between the risk of misreporting by the agent and the incidence of agency problems in *muḍārabah* contracts

Table 4.2 (Panels A–E) provides a simple contingency table (cross-tabulation) of two variables: the risk of misreporting (MISREPT) by the agent and the incidence of agency problems (overinvestment, underinvestment, personal benefit, reduction of effort, and perks) in *muḍārabah* contracts. All the reported correlation statistics are low, the largest (0.28 rounded down for rho) being the correlation between MISREPT and reduction of effort (REDEFFRT). This result suggests that banks' concern about misreporting is associated with a perception of shirking. In addition, it is shown that there is no relationship between MISREPT, on the one hand, and OVERINVST, PRSNLPFT or REDEFFRT, on the other.

Table 4.2 Contingency table for the relationship between the risk of misreporting by the agent and the incidence of agency problems in muḍārabah *contracts*

Panel A: Contingency table for overinvestment by misreporting of outcome

	MISREPT	
OVERINVST	No (%)	Yes (%)
No	0	20
Yes	100	80
Number	2	20
Chi-square	0.48889	0.48444
Spearman correlation	−0.14907	0.50799

Panel B: Contingency table for underinvestment by misreporting of outcome

	MISREPT	
UNDRINVST	No (%)	Yes (%)
No	0	90
Yes	100	10
Number	2	20
Chi-square	4.774	0.02597
Spearman Correlation	−0.67082	0.00063

Table 4.2 (continued)

Panel C: Overconsumption for personal benefits by misreporting of outcome

	MISREPT	
PRSNLPFT	No (%)	Yes (%)
No	0	30
Yes	100	70
Number	2	20
Chi-square	0.82500	0.36372
Spearman correlation	−0.19365	0.38787

Panel D: Contingency table for reduction of effort by misreporting of outcome

	MISREPT	
REDEFFRT	No (%)	Yes (%)
No	100	60
Yes	0	40
Number	2	20
Chi-square	1.25714	0.26219
Spearman correlation	0.23905	0.28399

Panel E: Contingency table for perks incentive by misreporting of outcome

	MISREPT	
PERKS	No (%)	Yes (%)
No	100	35
Yes	0	65
Number	2	20
Chi-square	3.17778	0.07465
Spearman correlation	0.38006	0.08103

In contrast, the contingency table presented in Panel B generates a chi-square value of 4.774, which is significant at the 5 per cent level, implying that we should have confidence in a relationship between the two variables in the population. Also, the Spearman correlation coefficient indicates a strong negative correlation (−0.67082), with statistical significance at the 5 per cent level, between MISREPT and UNDRINVST. Again, concerns about misreporting were associated with the underinvestment agency problem. This result is consistent with the theoretical expectations and Myers and Majluf (1984). Of the other variables, the one that is closest to being significant at the 10 per cent level is the PERKS variable. Panel E shows that there is a weak relationship (0.380) between the risk of misreporting and the incentive of the agent to consume perks in *muḍārabah* contracts.

5.2.2 Cross-tabulation analysis: the relationship between lack of control rights and the incidence of agency problems in *muḍārabah* contracts

Table 4.3 (Panels A–E) suggests that there is hardly any relationship between the lack of rights of control of the project (NOCONTRL) variable and each of OVRINVST, UNDRNVST, PRSLPFT, REDEFFRT and PERKS variables. Although in Panel B the respective column percentages are 73.3 per cent and 26.7 per cent, the chi-square value is not sufficiently large (2.281) for us to be confident that the relationship could not have arisen by chance, since as many as 13 per cent of sample outcomes failed to provide a relationship.

Table 4.3 Contingency table for the relationship between lack of control rights by the agent and the incidence of agency problems in muḍārabah *contracts*

Panel A: Contingency table for overinvestment by lack of control rights

	NOCONTRL	
OVRINVST	No (%)	Yes (%)
No	20	14.3
Yes	80	85.7
Number	15	7
Chi-square	0.10476	0.74619
Spearman correlation	0.06901	0.76026

Panel B: Contingency table for underinvestment by lack of control rights

	NOCONTRL	
UNDRINVST	No (%)	Yes (%)
No	73.3	100
Yes	26.7	0
Number	15	7
Chi-square	2.28148	0.13093
Spearman correlation	−0.32203	0.14386

Table 4.3 (continued)

Panel C: Overconsuming personal benefits by lack of control rights

	NOCONTRL	
PRSNLPFT	No (%)	Yes (%)
No	26.7	28.6
Yes	73.3	71.4
Number	15	7
Chi-square	0.00873	0.92556
Spearman correlation	−0.01992	0.92988

Panel D: Contingency table for reduction of effort by lack of control rights

	NOCONTRL	
REDEFFRT	No (%)	Yes (%)
No	60	71.4
Yes	40	28.6
Number	15	7
Chi-square	0.26939	0.60374
Spearman correlation	−0.11066	0.62396

Panel E: Contingency table for perks by lack of control rights

	NOCONTRL	
PERKS	No (%)	Yes (%)
No	46.7	28.6
Yes	53.3	71.4
Number	15	7
Chi-square	0.64648	0.42137
Spearman correlation	0.17142	0.44560

One explanation which may be used to justify the above findings is that since in *muḍārabah* contracts the major contribution of the agent is the managerial role, the allocation of control rights to the agent is expected to increase the value of the firm rather than to cause agency problems.[8]

5.2.3 Cross-tabulation analysis: the association between the high costs required for monitoring and the incidence of agency problems in *muḍārabah* contracts

Table 4.4 (Panels A–E) suggests that there is only a relationship between the high monitoring cost variable (HMONTCST) and the incentive to consume more perks variable (PERKS). Panel E shows that the distribution of the values of HMONTCST is associated with the distribution of the values of PERKS (respective column percentages are 25 and 75). In other words, a positive relationship between the two variables may exist as the chi-square (tau's) test of statistical significance generates a value (3.9663) with a significance level of 0.05, and a Spearman correlation coefficient of 0.528. Again, this result supports the expectation that monitoring costs will increase with expectations of perquisite consumption, resulting in high agency costs.

Table 4.4 Contingency table for the relationship between high monitoring cost by the agent and the incidence of agency problems in muḍārabah *contracts*

Panel A: Contingency table for overinvestment by high monitoring cost

	HMONTCST	
OVRINVST	No (%)	Yes (%)
No	16.7	18.8
Yes	83.3	81.2
Number	6	16
Chi-square	0.01273	0.910160
Spearman correlation	−0.02406	0.91537

Panel B: Contingency table for underinvestment by high monitoring cost

	HMONTCST	
UNDRINVST	No (%)	Yes (%)
No	100	75
Yes	0	15
Number	6	16
Chi-square	1.83333	0.17573
Spearman correlation	0.28868	0.19260

Table 4.4 (continued)

Panel C: Contingency table for personal benefit by high monitoring cost

	HMONTCST	
PRSNLPFT	No (%)	Yes (%)
No	50	18.7
Yes	50	81.3
Number	6	16
Chi-square	2.14844	0.14272
Spearman correlation	0.31250	0.15679

Panel D: Contingency table for reduction of effort by high monitoring cost

	HMONTCST	
REDEFFRT	No (%)	Yes (%)
No	83.3	56.3
Yes	16.7	43.7
Number	6	16
Chi-square	1.38318	0.23956
Spearman correlation	0.25074	0.26036

Panel E: Contingency table for perks by high monitoring cost

	HMONTCST	
PERKS	No (%)	Yes (%)
No	83.3	25
Yes	16.7	75
Number	6	16
Chi-square (Yates's correction)	3.9663	0.02308
Spearman correlation	0.52840	0.01147

All the correlation coefficients reported in the other panels of Table 4.4 (Panels A–D) appear to be very weak, and suggest that it is unlikely that there is a relationship among these variables.

5.2.4 Cross-tabulation analysis: the relation between the disadvantage in access to information and the incidence of agency problems

The correlation coefficients and the relative percentages in Table 4.5 (Panels A–E) suggest that there is no substantial association between the INFORMT variable and each of OVERINST, UNDRINVS, PRSNLPFT, REDEFFRT and PERKS variables. However, Panel E presents a reasonable Spearman's rho (0.3699) value, but since the statistical significance is larger than 0.05, we conclude that there is no substantial correlation between INFORMT and PERKS. These results, however, do not establish a relationship between the disadvantage in access to information and the incidence of agency problems in a *muḍārabah* contract.

Table 4.5 Contingency table for the relationship between disadvantage in access to information by the agent and the incidence of agency problems in muḍārabah *contracts*

Panel A: Contingency table for overinvestment by no access to information

	INFORMT	
OVRINVST	No (%)	Yes (%)
No	13.3	28.6
Yes	86.7	71.4
Number	15	7
Chi-square	0.74497	0.38807
Spearman correlation	−0.18402	0.41235

Panel B: Contingency table for underinvestment by no access to information

	INFORMT	
UNDRINVST	No (%)	Yes (%)
No	86.7	71.4
Yes	13.3	28.6
Number	15	7
Chi-square	0.74497	0.38807
Spearman correlation	0.18402	0.41235

Table 4.5 (continued)

Panel C: Contingency table for personal benefit by no access to information		
	INFORMT	
PRSNLPFT	No (%)	Yes (%)
No	20	42.9
Yes	80	57.1
Number	15	7
Chi-square	1.25714	0.26219
Spearman correlation	−0.23905	0.28399

Panel D: Contingency table for reduction of effort by no access to information		
	INFORMT	
REDEFFRT	No (%)	Yes (%)
No	66.7	57.1
Yes	33.3	42.9
Number	15	7
Chi-square	0.18707	0.66536
Spearman correlation	0.09221	0.68317

Panel E: Contingency table for perks by no access to information		
	INFORMT	
PERKS	No (%)	Yes (%)
No	53.3	14.3
Yes	46.7	85.7
Number	15	7
Chi-square (Yates's correction)	1.6117	0.20425
Spearman correlation	0.36991	0.09018

5.3 Correlation Test Results for Selected Ordinal Variables

It is expected that, according to the prediction of the agency contractual paradigm, the type of the agent and the characteristics of the project will have a substantial effect on the construction and the shaping of the contractual governance of financial contracts. We discuss the association between selected pairs of ordinal variables, pointing out the relationship between the characteristics of the agent and the project, the devices used in monitoring, and the areas to be monitored in *muḍārabah* contracts.

5.3.1 The relationship between the characteristics of the agent and the project and the devices utilised in monitoring *muḍārabah* contracts

Table 4.6 presents Spearman[9] rank order correlation matrix for the association between the characteristics of the agent and the project on the one hand, and the importance of the devices used in monitoring on the other. The former is represented by nine variables (omitting a reputation variable due to the absence of variation in its scores). The importance of means is represented by six variables used in monitoring *muḍārabah* contracts. The statistical correlation results in Table 4.6 can be summarized in three groups.

The first group of results indicates that there are significant relationships among the devices utilized in monitoring the *muḍārabah* contract. For example, the results show that banks place emphasis on giving advice on how to manage the project (ADVICE). The banks also require submission of periodical management reports (PREPORT): these serve to support and monitor the implementation of the advice given in the first place. In addition, it appears intuitively rational to find that direct involvement in decisions affecting the strategic policies of the project (DINVOLVE) is positively associated with the device for monitoring the management staff of the project [MANGSTAF, (0.57)], and with the representation on the board of the company [REPBOARD, (0.641)]. However, such involvement has a negative association with not playing any role in the project management itself [NOROLE (–0.429)]. This result also explains the negative relationship between MANGSTAF and NOROLE (–0.439) and that between PREPORT and REPBOARD (–0.583), as well as the positive correlation between MANGSTAF and REPBOARD (0.496). It can therefore be concluded that the mechanism of involvement has an impact on the form of devices used in monitoring a *muḍārabah* contract.

The second group of results shows that there is a positive relationship between social, safety and environmental considerations (SOCIALLY) and ADVICE; and between NOROLE and the expected profitability of the project (PRFPRJCT). The first relationship can be interpreted to suggest that social matters in *muḍārabah* contracts can be emphasized through providing advice to the management (agent) of the project. This relationship reflects the need to communicate social considerations through direct contact rather than through formal channels, the latter being less capable of conveying these issues. The link between not playing any role in the project and the profitability of the project can be regarded as a reflection of one of the features of *muḍārabah* contracts, in which the bank is prepared to take no role in controlling the project where

Table 4.6 Spearman correlation matrix for the monitoring devices and the characteristics of the agent and the project in mudārabah *contracts*

Variables	ADVICE	CREDWRTH	DINVOLVE	EXPRNCE	FNLRCRD	ISLMRULE	MANGTAF	NOROLE	PREPORT2	PRFPRJCT	REPBOARD	SOCIALLY
CREDWRTH	−0.163											
	(0.458)											
DINVOLVE	−0.132	0.082										
	(0.548)	(0.711)										
EXPRNCE	0.0778	0.227	0.084									
	(0.725)	(0.298)	(0.702)									
FNLRCRD	−0.150	0.318	−0.011	0.258								
	(0.494)	(0.139)	(0.958)	(0.234)								
ISLMRULE	0.073	−0.227	−0.327	−0.119	0.376							
	(0.740)	(0.297)	(0.127)	(0.588)	(0.077)							
MANGSTAF	0.157	0.059	0.570	0.037	0.120	−0.083						
	(0.474)	(0.790)	(0.005)	(0.866)	(0.584)	(0.706)						
NOROLE	−0.290	−0.025	−0.429	−0.201	0.342	0.252	−0.439					
	(0.179)	(0.910)	(0.041)	(0.357)	(0.111)	(0.246)	(0.036)					
PREPORT2	0.440	−0.308	−0.303	0.178	−0.273	−0.202	−0.241	0.092				
	(0.036)	(0.153)	(0.160)	(0.417)	(0.206)	(0.355)	(0.267)	(0.676)				
PRFPRJCT	−0.083	0.117	−0.270	0.168	0.176	0.370	0.048	0.388	−0.041			
	(0.706)	(0.597)	(0.212)	(0.443)	(0.421)	(0.082)	(0.828)	(0.068)	(0.851)			
REPBOARD	−0.153	−0.086	0.641	−0.061	0.096	−0.205	0.496	−0.253	−0.583	−0.205		
	(0.485)	(0.698)	(0.001)	(0.781)	(0.662)	(0.348)	(0.016)	(0.244)	(0.003)	(0.348)		
SOCIALLY	0.363	0.224	−0.102	0.025	−0.033	0.029	0.008	−0.259	0.063	−0.432	−0.213	
	(0.089)	(0.304)	(0.642)	(0.910)	(0.880)	(0.894)	(0.972)	(0.233)	(0.776)	(0.040)	(0.328)	
SECURITY	0.093	0.312	−0.082	−0.194	0.213	−0.040	−0.194	−0.052	−0.278	−0.273	0.041	0.234
	(0.672)	(0.148)	(0.707)	(0.373)	(0.329)	(0.855)	(0.374)	(0.816)	(0.200)	(0.207)	(0.854)	(0.283)
TIMPROFT	0.299	−0.136	−0.159	−0.234	0.145	0.000	−0.027	0.172	0.000	0.000	−0.042	0.389
	(0.166)	(0.537)	(0.469)	(0.283)	(0.509)	(1.00)	(0.904)	(0.432)	(1.00)	(1.00)	(0.849)	(0.067)
UNCTPRJT	−0.326	0.275	0.059	0.147	0.352	0.008	−0.082	0.017	−0.243	0.034	0.113	−0.131
	(0.130)	(0.204)	(0.791)	(0.503)	(0.099)	(0.970)	(0.709)	(0.938)	(0.265)	(0.876)	(0.607)	(0.552)

Notes:
Number of observations = 23.
Significance is given in parentheses.
The Spearman's rho figures are rounded to three decimal places.

it hopes to gain high profit from the superior knowledge of the agent and their capability to choose and implement an economically sound project.

Although not all the relationships are statistically significant, some interesting findings can be extracted from the third group of results. We summarize the important findings below.

It is shown that ADVICE is correlated positively with the time horizons for realization of profits (TIMPROFT), and negatively with UNCTPRJT. This result suggests that when the maturity of the contract is long (and a bridge of trust has been established between the bank and agent), providing help and advice may play an active role in monitoring the contract. However, if the degree of uncertainty of the project is high, providing advice only may not be sufficient for monitoring the agent.

Further, a negative relationship exists between current financial position and creditworthiness (CREDWRTH) and PREPORT (–0.308). This can be interpreted as an indication of the importance of the creditworthiness of the agent in assuring banks, consequently reducing the requirement for periodical management reports about the agent's performance.

The negative association between DINVOLVE and PRFPRJCT (–0.270) is consistent with the features of a *muḍārabah* contract and may offer weak support for the positive relationship between NOROLE and PRFPRJCT. It is common in *muḍārabah* contracts for the bank to relinquish the ownership and control rights of the project to the agent (NOROLE). Nevertheless, this status is conditional on the profitability of the project and the competence of the agent. Therefore, in the case of projects with marginal profitability, it is rational for the bank to be involved closely in monitoring and managing the project through direct involvement.

The positive relationship between the financial track records of the agent (FNLRCRD) and the tendency of the bank not to play any role in the management of the project (NOROLE) provides further support for the expectation that the agent's type may have an impact on the extent of monitoring in *muḍārabah* contracts. Banks confident about the agent because of high-rated financial records will consider it less necessary to play any role in the project management. Consistent with the proposition by Diamond (1991), good financial records may facilitate monitoring of the financial contract; hence FNLRCRD is negatively correlated with PREPORT.

Compliance with the Islamic *Sharīʿah* (ISLMRULE) is reported to be weakly but positively correlated with NOROLE (0.252), and negatively associated with REPBOARD (–0.205) and DINVOLVE (–0.327). These results can be interpreted as an indication of the strict adoption of the spirit of the *Sharīʿah*: the aim of the *Sharīʿah* is to overcome the main hurdle faced by small businesses, namely, financing and encouraging economically sound projects operated by high-quality agents by granting the control rights of the project to the agent (who has relatively superior knowledge) to gain benefits from this superiority at micro and macro levels.

NOROLE and SOCIALLY show a negative relationship (–0.259). This result is consistent with the link between social considerations and advice. Again the limits of formal reporting are being addressed by closer involvement, using this as a means to raise considerations other than profit.

The negative relationship between SECURTY and PREPORT contrasts with the negative relationship between UNCTPRJT and PREPORT (–0.278 and –0.243, respectively). When the security offered by the assets of the project is high, this gives some assurance about the funds provided under the contract. Consequently, the tendency of banks to monitor the project periodically becomes less important. However, when uncertainty of the cash flow is high, emphasis on the receipt of periodical management reports may be expected. In practice, this may not be sufficient to satisfy the banks. In this context, therefore, other methods may be demanded to cope with this uncertainty, and the relationship with previous track records (FNLRCRD) takes on greater importance, since this may indicate the reliability of the agent.

Overall, the evidence in Table 4.6 suggests that agency explanations are important in justifying the practice of *muḍārabah* contracts.

5.3.2 The areas of activity to be monitored in *muḍārabah* contracts and the relationship between the agent and project features

Table 4.7 presents the Spearman correlation coefficients for nine variables (three in relation to the agent, and six representing the project's characteristics) and six variables (MONTABLT, MONTFINC, MONTINVS, MONTPRKS, MONTPROD and MONTDEFT) which depict the activities to be monitored in *muḍārabah* contracts.

The results show that the experience and qualification of the agent (EXPRNCE) have a moderate positive relationship (0.358 with statistical significance at the 0.10 level) with monitoring production activities (MONTPROD). A weak correlation (0.260) is also reported between EXPRNCE and monitoring the ability of the agent (MONABLT). These findings reflect the significance of the agent's experience in constructing and pricing the *muḍārabah* contract. A surprising negative (–0.2806) relationship is shown between EXPRNCE and the importance of monitoring investment activities (MONINVS) in *muḍārabah* contracts. This result suggests that the use of highly experienced and qualified agents may reduce the need for rigorous monitoring of investment activity. The result is therefore consistent with the findings by Demski et al. (1984).

In addition, the financial track record of the agent (FNLCRD) shows weak and mixed signs of correlation with other variables. A negative relationship is shown between FNLCRD and each of the variables for monitoring the financing

Table 4.7 Spearman correlation coefficients for activities to be monitored and the characteristics of the agent and the project in mudārabah *contracts*

Variables	MONTABLT	MONTFINC	MONTINVS	MONTPRKS	MONTPROD	MONTDEFT
MONTFINC	0.4088					
	(0.053)					
MONTINVS	0.3440	0.0623				
	(0.108)	(0.778)				
MONTPRKS	0.3015	0.3159	0.4951			
	(0.162)	(0.142)	(0.016)			
MONTPROD	−0.1204	0.1819	−0.0792	−0.2428		
	(0.584)	(0.406)	(0.720)	(0.264)		
MONTDEFT	−0.0697	0.0284	0.1367	0.4651	0.1452	
	(0.752)	(0.898)	(0.534)	(0.025)	(0.509)	
EXPRNCE	0.2603	0.0543	−0.2806	−0.0848	0.3578	0.0267
	(0.230)	(0.806)	(0.195)	(0.700)	(0.094)	(0.904)
FNLRCRD	0.2721	−0.1854	0.1328	0.2387	−0.2022	−0.0456
	(0.209)	(0.397)	(0.546)	(0.273)	(0.355)	(0.836)
ISLMRULE	0.1922	0.0301	0.2190	−0.1166	−0.1494	−0.3340
	(0.380)	(0.892)	(0.315)	(0.596)	(0.496)	(0.119)
SOCIALLY	0.3800	0.1646	0.2176	0.1014	0.2455	0.0425
	(0.074)	(0.453)	(0.319)	(0.645)	(0.259)	(0.847)
SECURITY	−0.2169	−0.2997	0.0533	0.1034	−0.0305	0.2377
	(0.320)	(0.165)	(0.809)	(0.639)	(0.890)	(0.275)
UNCTPRJT	0.2254	0.1838	0.4325	0.3899	−0.0976	0.2502
	(0.301)	(0.401)	(0.039)	(0.066)	(0.658)	(0.250)
TIMPOFT	0.2335	0.1277	0.0600	0.0518	0.2039	−0.1254
	(0.283)	(0.562)	(0.786)	(0.814)	(0.531)	(0.569)
CREDWRTH	0.0205	−0.0698	−0.1659	0.0462	−0.2273	−0.1193
	(0.926)	(0.752)	(0.449)	(0.834)	(0.297)	(0.588)
PRFPRJCT	−0.1086	−0.0087	−0.3110	−0.4277	−0.2296	−0.5134
	(0.622)	(0.969)	(0.149)	(0.042)	(0.292)	(0.012)

Notes:
N = 23 observations.
The significance is given in parentheses.

activity [MONTFINC (–0.185), and with MONTPROD (–0.202)]. The variable for monitoring the agent's ability (MONTABLT) and monitoring the agent's potential for pursuing personal benefits (MONTPRKS) show a positive relationship with FNLCRD (0.272 and 0.239, respectively).

We interpret these results by relying on the premises of agency theory and the features of the *muḍārabah* contract. Accordingly, the results suggest that the financial track record of the agent gives an indication of his financial history and the probability of default. Consequently, there is more confidence in the success of a project managed by an agent with a good track record. However, there is also some emphasis on monitoring the agent's tendency to consume more perks, as suggested by Jensen and Meckling (1976). Notwithstanding the weak correlations between some of the variables, the results indicate the probable existence of a monotonic relationship between the characteristics of the agent and the project being monitored in *muḍārabah* contracts.

6. EVIDENCE FROM HYPOTHESIS TESTING

We report here the results from the deductive hypothesis testing (hypothetico-deductive) procedure, for each of the three hypotheses in this chapter.

6.1 Project Attributes

In H1 (section 3), it was hypothesized that Islamic banks will give high ranking to the specific attributes of the project in accepting or rejecting a *muḍārabah* contract *ex ante*. Differences between the banks' scores are considered in relation to their assessment as 'very important' (V), 'reasonably important' (R), 'important' (I) and 'neutral' (N) categories. The 'unimportant' category is omitted since no score was reported at all for this category across any of the variables of the project's attributes (UNCTPRJT, PRFPRJCT, SOCIALLY, TIMPROFT, SECURITY, and ISLMRULE). Thus, the null hypothesis (H_0) is:

$$H_0: V = R = I = N,$$

that is, the rating of importance is uniform for all the four rankings. The alternative hypothesis (H_1) is:

$$H_1: V \neq R \neq I \neq N.$$

This implies that the ranking is not uniform for the variable. In particular, using the one-tailed test, the alternative hypothesis considered is that 'very important' and 'reasonably important' are given higher rankings, indicating the importance attributed to the variable by the banks.

Table 4.8 Evidence from chi-square (one-tailed) tests for hypotheses on project attributes, entrepreneur attributes and religious considerations

Panel A: Chi-square (one-tailed) test for project attributes hypothesis

Variable	Chi-square	DF	Significance
ISLMRULE	47.4348	3	0.0000*
PRFPRJCT	33.5217	3	0.0000*
UNCTPRJT	18.9130	3	0.0003
TIMPROFT	15.0870	3	0.0017
SOCIALLY	8.4783	3	0.0371
SECURITY	3.6087	3	0.3069

Panel B: Chi-square (one-tailed) test for entrepreneur attributes hypothesis

Variable	Chi-square	DF	Significance
EXPRNCE	54.3914	3	0.0000**
FNLRCRD	35.6087	3	0.0000**
CREDWRTH	30.7391	3	0.0000**

Panel C: Chi-square (one-tailed) test for religious considerations hypothesis

Variable	Chi-square	DF	Significance
ISLMRULE	47.4348	3	0.0000
ADHRISLM	15.6957	1	0.0001

Note: DF = degrees of freedom.
* The statistical significance of ISLMRULE as well as PRFPRJCT is very small and does not appear because the values are presented to four decimal places only.
** The statistical significance of these variables is very small and does not appear due to presenting values to four decimal places only.

In Panel A of Table 4.8 the observed frequencies of ISLMRULE, UNCTPRJT, PRFPRJCT and TIMPROFT show highly significant differences ($p < 0.001$) from the expectation under the null of there being an equal number of responses in each of the four rankings. SOCIALLY shows a difference at the 5 per cent level of significance. In other words, since the probability of obtaining this result is low (1 out of 1000 – or for the SOCIALLY 5 out of 100), the null hypothesis is rejected. We conclude that there is a significant difference among the rank ordering of categories of these variables. The chi-square test results can be used descriptively to show the order of importance placed by the banks on project attributes. It is shown that 72 responses out of 138 are directed to the 'very important' category; the 'reasonably important' category scores 43, while 'important' and 'neutral' categories score only 20 and 30, respectively.

These test results generally support hypothesis 1. They suggest that project attributes are most likely to have a significant impact on accepting or rejecting the *muḍārabah* financing contract.

6.2 Entrepreneur Attributes

It was earlier hypothesized (H2, section 3) that banks will give high ranking to the specific attributes of the entrepreneur, in accepting or rejecting a *muḍārabah* contract *ex ante*. Hence

$$H_0: V = R = I = N,$$

that is, the four scales give equal ranking of importance of the CREDWRTH, EXPRNCE and FNLRCRD variables, and the four categories remaining after omitting 'unimportant' as a category are expected to contain the same frequencies.

$$H_1: V \neq R \neq I \neq N,$$

that is, the overall ranking of the four scales differs significantly.

The results of this test, reported in Panel B of Table 4.8, indicate that the null hypothesis is rejected and the alternative hypothesis is accepted at the 1 per cent level of significance.

These results are interesting from two main points of view. First, in each case the chi-square statistic is sufficiently large for us to be confident that the observed frequencies could not have arisen by chance, ranging in value from 54.3914 (with three degrees of freedom, significant at the 1 per cent level) to 30.7391 (with three degrees of freedom, significant at the 1 per cent level). In particular, the reputation and the experience of the entrepreneur are regarded as indispensable requirements for the bank to enter and establish such contracts. Second, these results support the conventional wisdom of agency contracting theory regarding agent's type and its impact on constructing and facilitating the financial agreement. In sum, the evidence is conclusive that the agent's quality is considered by Islamic banks to be a crucial element in constructing *muḍārabah* contracts.

6.3 Religious Considerations

It was earlier hypothesized (H3 in section 3) that compliance with *Sharīʿah* norms is a significant requirement for accepting or rejecting *muḍārabah* contract decisions *ex ante*. Panel C of Table 4.8 reports that the observed frequencies are significantly different ($p < 0.0001$) from those predicted by the null hypothesis of there being an equal number of subjects in each of four categories of ISLMRULE or two categories of ADHRISLM. The probability of obtaining this result by chance is highly unlikely with $p = 0.0001$. Consequently, the statistical and hypothesized outcomes are interpreted as being statistically different, and therefore the null hypothesis is rejected. It can be concluded that compliance of the project with Islamic rule, and the adherence of the agent to the *Sharīʿah* norms regarding their behaviour (honesty, trust and so on), play a significant role in *muḍārabah* decisions and represent distinct features of such contracts.

7. CONCLUDING REMARKS

This chapter has undertaken a systematic investigation of the agency characteristics of the *muḍārabah* financing contract between the Islamic bank and the entrepreneur. Key elements of agency theory are called upon in order to identify the main variables that capture the agency characteristics of the *muḍārabah* contract. After using questionnaire survey methods to collect primary data on Islamic banking practices, univariate and bivariate analyses as well as non-parametric methods are used to isolate the main variables that underpin the agency characteristics of the *muḍārabah* contract. Additional quantitative and qualitative analyses are adopted to circumvent the limitations of the questionnaire used. The chi-square (one-tailed) test is utilized to test the main three hypotheses of this study in order to determine the incidence of agency problems in *muḍārabah* contracts.

The results of the three hypotheses support the inductive findings and are consistent with the theoretical expectations. It is found that project attributes, the quality of the entrepreneur (or agent), and religious (*Sharīʿah*) considerations are the three most important agency contractual problems in *muḍārabah* financing practices by Islamic banks. These results have important policy implications for managers of Islamic banks, entrepreneurs dealing in *muḍārabah* contracts, and central banks that are charged with the regulation of Islamic banks. Bank managers may use the results in order to design strategies for reducing agency problems; for example, that is, to identify good projects and credible entrepreneurs, and acknowledge the *Sharīʿah* factor. Entrepreneurs have to pay attention to maintaining their credibility. Bank regulators should enforce the vigilance of the *Sharīʿah* boards in Islamic banks. In general, however, further research is needed to fully qualify these implications.

NOTES

1. The agent may be tempted to exploit this aspect in order to overconsume perquisites, avoid risk or to shirk on effort.
2. The hypotheses are intended to guide the structure of the empirical tests and to make the interpretation of the statistical results of this study meaningful.
3. It was also decided that the questionnaire would be supplemented by a limited in-depth interview contingent upon some initial analysis of the questionnaire data. The results of the interview fall outside the scope of this chapter.
4. As clearly stated by Bryman and Cramer (1994, p. 165), 'unlike chi-square, measures of correlation indicate both the strength and the direction of the relationship between a pair of variables'.
5. See, among others, Fama (1980) and Diamond (1991).
6. This allows us to test the significance of the differences between observed frequencies and expected (or theoretical) distributions.
7. It is shown that 83 per cent of the banks place constraints on financing decisions. In contrast, 26 per cent of banks allocate discretion to the agent regarding the financing decisions.
8. Outside the focus on *muḍārabah* contracts, Demski et al. (1984) reach similar findings in agency-contractual problems.
9. Spearman's rank order correlation or rho (ρ) is more commonly used by researchers in social science and is the most appropriate measure for determining the correlation for ordinal data (see, Bryman and Cramer, 1994).

REFERENCES

Bryman, A. and D. Cramer (1994), *Quantitative Data Analysis for Social Scientist*, London: Routledge.

Demski, J., J. Patell and M. Wolfson (1984), 'Decentralized Choice of Monitoring Systems', *The Accounting Review*, **LIX** (1), 16–34.

Diamond, D. (1989), 'Reputation Acquisition in Debt Markets', *Journal of Political Economy*, **97** (4), 828–61.

Diamond, D. (1991), 'Monitoring and Reputation: The Choice Between Bank Loans and Directly Placed Debts', *Journal of Political Economy*, **99** (4), 689–721.

Fama, E. (1980), 'Agency Problems and Theory of the Firm', *Journal of Political Economy*, **88** (2), 288–307.

Fama, E. (1990), 'Contract Costs and Financing Decisions', *Journal of Business*, **63** (1), 71–91.

Grossman, S. and O. Hart (1988), 'One Share One Vote and the Market for Corporate Control', *Journal of Financial Economics*, **20**, 175–202.

Holmstrom, B. (1989), 'Agency Costs and Innovation', *Journal of Economic Behaviour and Organization*, **12**, 305–27.

Jensen, M. (1986), 'Agency Costs of Free Cash Flow, Corporate Finance, and Takeovers', *American Economics Review*, **76** (2), 323–9.

Jensen, M. and W. Meckling (1976), 'Theory of the Firm: Managerial Behaviour, Agency Costs and Ownership Structure', *Journal of Financial Economics*, **3**, 305–60.

Jensen, M. and W. Meckling (1992), 'Specific and General Knowledge, and Organizational Structure' in L. Werin and H. Wijkander (eds), *Contract Economics*, Cambridge, MA: Blackwell.

Jensen, M. and J. Warner (1988), 'The Distribution of Power Among Corporate Managers, Shareholders, and Directors', *Journal of Financial Economics*, **20**, 3–24.

Khan, M. Fahim (1995), *Essays in Islamic Economics*, Leicester, UK: The Islamic Foundation.

Lang, L., A. Poulsen and R. Stulz (1995), 'Asset Sales, Firm Performance, and the Agency Costs of Managerial Discretion', *Journal of Financial Economics*, **37**, 3–37.

Libby, R. and M. Lipe (1992), 'Incentives, Effort, and the Cognitive Processes Involved in Accounting-related Judgements', *Journal of Accounting Research*, **30** (2), 249–73.

Mehran, H. (1995), 'Executive Compensation Structure, Ownership, and Firm Performance', *Journal of Financial Economics*, **38**, 163–84.

Myers, S. and N. Majluf (1984), 'Corporate Financing and Investment Decisions when Firms have Information that Investors do not have', *Journal of Financial Economics*, **13**, 187–221.

Penno, M. (1990a), 'Accounting Systems, Participation in Budgeting, and Performance Evaluation', *The Accounting Review*, **65** (2), 303–14.

Penno, M. (1990b), 'Auditing for Performance Evaluation', *The Accounting Review*, **65**, 520–36.

Ross, S. (1973), 'The Economic Theory of Agency: The Principal's Problem', *American Economic Review*, **63** (2), 134–9.

Siddiqi, M.N. (1991), 'Some Economic Aspects of *Muḍārabah*', *Review of Islamic Economics*, **1** (2), 21–33.

Smith, M. (1996), 'Shareholder Activism by Institutional Investors: Evidence from calPERS', *The Journal of Finance*, **LI** (1), 227–52.

Stulz, R. (1990), 'Managerial Discretion and Optimal Financing Policies', *Journal of Financial Economics*, **26**, 3–27.

Watts, R. and J. Zimmerman (1983), 'Agency Problems, Auditing, and the Theory of the Firm: Some Evidence', *Journal of Law and Economics*, **XXVL** (3), 613–33.

Watts, R. and J. Zimmerman (1990), 'Positive Accounting Theory: A Ten Year Perspective', *The Accounting Review*, **65** (1), 131–56.

Williamson, O. (1996), *The Mechanisms of Governance*, New York: Oxford University Press.

Zou, L. (1992), 'Ownership Structure and Efficiency: An Incentive Mechanism Approach', *Journal of Comparative Economics*, **16**, 399–431.

COMMENTS

Abdel-hameed Bashir

This chapter is an empirical attempt to explain the behaviour of Islamic banks. Since empirical work on Islamic banking and finance is scarce, such attempts are welcome and should be encouraged. The chapter starts by analysing the *muḍārabah* contract as a principal–agent relationship. Three main features of the *muḍārabah* contract are discussed: risk, linearity and control rights. Moreover, the project attributes, entrepreneur's qualities and the *Sharīʿah* requirements are highlighted as the most important features of the contract. The chapter also states that the agency problem is more severe in *muḍārabah* than in the standard debt contract. The authors emphasize the important implications of auditing and accounting standards in evaluating, monitoring, and facilitating the *muḍārabah* contract.

The authors also attempt to test their results empirically. For this purpose, they have formulated three hypotheses concerning the practical aspects of the contract. In particular, they emphasize the role of asymmetric information in deriving the terms of the contract between the two parties. Agency cost is considered the sole determinant of whether the contract will be signed or not.

I have following comments on the chapter:

1. It is written so that it stands on its own. No previous work in the field is cited, nor is any literature review on the theory of the firm given.
2. In their description of the *muḍārabah* contract, the authors state that the bank (principal) is passive, without sufficient power to control the project. This is hardly new, because this is the basis of the agency problem. However, in an ownership structure where one or more shareholders own a large share of stocks, this ownership can serve as a check on management. The shareholder (bank) may choose to assume an active role by securing a seat on the board of directors, providing direct monitoring, and possibly influencing management decision-making (see Schranz, 1993).
3. The authors claim that the linearity of the *muḍārabah* contract makes the compensation scheme for the agent a purely concave function of the outcome. This statement is not true, because by the nature of the *muḍārabah* contract, the agent is risk-neutral. Therefore, linearity of the compensation makes the contract convex (risk-neutral) rather than concave (risk-averse).
4. The chapter claims that linearity of the contract will align the interest of the two parties and induce appropriate incentives for the agent, without mentioning how this would be achieved. For the interests of the two parties to be aligned, the contract must be incentive compatible.

5. How do the personal qualities of the entrepreneur affect contracting? Since personal qualities are unobservable, adverse selection problems will arise, and therefore, the contract will be second best. This will further raise the cost of screening (a dead-weight loss).
6. The chapter claims that incorporating the Islamic code of behaviour will reduce the agency problem without mentioning how these codes will be incorporated. Can it be implemented through the court system or through the institution of *ḥisbah*? (See Bashir, 1998, Gambling and Karim, 1991.)
7. The data used are qualitative (binary). Therefore, the results are not very conclusive and may be misleading.
8. One of the hypotheses states that the relationship between agency problem and the magnitude of asymmetric information is positive. This is a known fact rather than a hypothesis to be tested. It is well known that when information is asymmetric, agency costs arise.
9. The way the hypotheses are set is very confusing. For example, H1 and H2 contradict each other. Furthermore, H3 does not specify what to accept and what to reject.

REFERENCES

Bashir, A. (1998), 'Ethical Norms and Enforcement Mechanism in Profit-Sharing Arrangements', *The Mid-Atlantic Journal of Business*, **34** (3), 255–71.

Gambling, T. and R. Karim (1991), *Business and Accounting Ethics in Islam*, London: Mansell Publishing Company.

Schranz, B.K. (1993), 'The Use of Equity Positions by Banks: The Japanese Experience', *Economic Review*, **4**, Federal Reserve Bank of San Francisco.

5. Incentive-compatible constraints for Islamic banking: some lessons from Bank Muamalat

Adiwarman A. Karim

1. INTRODUCTION

Presley and Sessions (1994) draw a comparison between a *ribā* contract[1] and a *muḍārabah* contract under symmetric and asymmetric information. The key assumption is asymmetric information. The manager is assumed to have superior information to investors in two respects: first, having signed a contract with investors, the manager is able to observe the demand or productivity conditions affecting the project before committing to production decisions; and second, he alone observes his personal level of effort. Such asymmetric information is not unusual and, indeed, rationalizes the manager's involvement in the project. But while the manager's relative informational expertise suggests that he should be delegated some authority over production decisions, the exploitation of this expertise is problematic. Since effort is private information, the manager cannot be compensated directly for its provision. A revelation problem, therefore, arises with the manager's preferences over productive inputs only coinciding with those of investors if he personally bears the entire risk of adverse shocks.

If the manager is risk-averse then such a policy, while productively efficient, is sub-optimal (see Holstrom and Weiss, 1985). Furthermore, a policy of paying the manager a fixed return independent of the outcome is also inefficient because there is no incentive for him to supply more effort when its marginal product is high.

One way out of this dilemma is to design an incentive-compatible contract, which ensures that the cost of misinformation by the manager is sufficiently high so as to make honesty his best policy. To obtain such incentive compatibility with minimum loss in efficiency requires the contract to specify inefficiently low levels of productive inputs in particular states of the world (see Hart, 1983; Hart and Holstrom, 1987).

This chapter surveys several contributions on the subject of incentive-compatible constraints and evaluates the practices of the Bank Muamalat, Indonesia, in their light. There are four groups of constraints which are of our concern: higher stake in net worth; high operating risk firms have higher leverage; lower fraction of unobservable cash flow; and lower fraction of non-controllable costs. The need for a higher stake in net worth is discussed by Ross (1977), and Harris and Raviv (1990); high operating risk firms having higher leverage is discussed by Kim and Sorensen (1986); lower fraction of unobservable cash flow is discussed by Chang (1987); and lower fraction of non-controllable costs is discussed by Suh (1988). In order not to prejudge these models, we first summarize them below.

2. SUPERIORITY OF ISLAMIC MARK-UP-BASED FINANCING

According to available information, all Islamic banks are heavily involved in mark-up-based transactions on a predetermined rate of return.[2] Preference for mark-up-based transactions over profit/loss-sharing is not without reasons.

Under asymmetric information, Gale and Hellwig (1985) show that the standard debt contract is the optimal contract. Williamson (1986) develops a similar model, in which monitoring is done *ex post*. Still, debt contract is the optimal one. Neither Gale and Hellwig (1985) nor Williamson (1986) get the first-best solution for their models. They come up with second-best solutions. Unlike Gale and Hellwig or Williamson, Diamond (1984) develops a model in which monitoring is *ex ante* and there are financial intermediaries. The result is the same: the debt contract is optimal. Here Diamond gets the first-best solution for his model.

The term ‘standard debt contract’ or ‘debt contract’ is somehow misleading because the definition used does not capture all the features of interest-based contracts such as penalty interest and compounding interest for due obligations, which could happen without bankruptcy. The Islamic mark-up-based scheme has some features similar to an interest-based debt contract in terms of its predetermined fixed rate of return (mark-up). But it has several differences which make it uniquely Islamic: (i) it is commodity-based financing; (ii) there is no penalty mark-up for past-due obligations; (iii) there is no compounding of mark-up for past-due obligations; (iv) there is no floating mark-up rate during the whole period of contract; and (v) in the case of bankruptcy, only the initial debt (including the mark-up) is recovered.

Constraint (i) is to ensure that the money is used for buying real assets. Constraints (ii) and (iii) are applied in case the customer is unable to pay. However, if the customer is unwilling to pay, the bank may charge him penalties. Constraints (iv) and (v) are consequences of the Islamic mark-up-based scheme. In this scheme, let us say that the customer does not have the necessary cash for a car available at $10 000 cash. The bank will buy the car for the customer for cash and, in turn, sell it to the customer, say, for $10 800 with deferred payment within 12 months (that is, 8 per cent mark-up). Hence the customer has a debt of $10 800.

The mark-up-based scheme has similar features to the 'standard debt contract', and hence has the advantages of being an optimal contract. If an Islamic bank has to choose one or the other, clearly it will choose the mark-up-based scheme.

Bashir and Darrat (1992) show that if a borrower knows that he is being monitored, he can predict what actions will be taken by the borrower, given the monitoring process undertaken by the lender. In other words, each player's utility depends on the other player's action. They may play cooperative or non-cooperative games. A *mushārakah* contract can be modelled as a two-person, two-period partnership game. Each player's utility depends on the other player's action through a commonly observed consequence (profit), which is itself a function of both players' action and an exogenous stochastic environment. The game is thus one of decentralized decision-making in which individual optimizers select their decisions so as to maximize their lifetime utilities. The game's outcome depends on these decisions. Studies show that profit-sharing investment can enhance the level of investment.

Furthermore, Presley and Sessions (1994) show that if the necessary incentive-compatible constraint is applied to ensure truthfulness, the profit-sharing contract may permit a more efficient revelation of any informational asymmetries between the lender and the borrower.

The experience of Bank Muamalat shows that the proportion of profit-sharing financing significantly increased in 1998 after the bank launched its pilot project based on an incentive-compatible profit-sharing contract. Although the data cover only a very short period of time, some lessons can be learnt.

3. INCENTIVE-COMPATIBLE CONSTRAINTS

For profit-sharing, an incentive-compatible constraint is crucial to ensure that the cost of misconduct and negligence is sufficiently high to make honesty the best policy of the agent. Some relevant factors discussed in the literature are summarized in this section; the experience of Bank Muamalat based on these factors is reviewed in section 4.

3.1 Higher Stake in Net Worth

When an entrepreneur has a higher stake in his net worth, his incentive to be dishonest will be significantly reduced because he has a great deal to lose. With a lower net worth, since he has a little to lose the entrepreneur tends to make riskier investments. Ross (1977), using an asymmetric information model, and Harris and Raviv (1990), using an agency model, conclude that leverage is positively correlated with default probability.

An Islamic bank may also require the entrepreneur to maintain minimum holdings of certain assets relative to the business size, thus keeping its net worth high. If this is not done, the entrepreneur tends to increase his debt as the value of the firm increases. In financial contracting theory there are many theoretical and empirical studies which conclude that leverage is positively correlated with firm value.[3]

Another way is to ask for collateral. In Islamic law, collateral is not compulsory for *muḍārabah* and *mushārakah* contracts. Any loss is to be borne by the provider of funds (Islamic bank) except if it is due to misconduct, negligence or violation of the conditions of the contract. Therefore, collateral is important to protect the Islamic bank from any misconduct.

3.1.1 Asymmetric information model

Ross (1977) develops the following model where managers know the true distribution of the firm's returns, but investors do not. It is assumed that the firm's return distributions are ordered by first-order stochastic dominance. Managers benefit if the firm's securities are more highly valued by the market but are penalized if the firm goes bankrupt. Investors take larger debt levels as a signal of higher quality. Since lower-quality firms have higher marginal expected bankruptcy costs for any debt level, managers of low-quality firms do not imitate higher-quality firms by issuing more debt.

Suppose that the date-one returns, x, of a firm of type t are distributed uniformly $[0,t]$. The manager is privately informed about t. He chooses the face value of debt, D, to maximize a weighted average of the market value of the firm at date zero and the expected value at date one, net of a penalty, L, for bankruptcy. Let $V_o(D)$ be the value assigned to the firm at date zero by the market if the debt level is D. The manager's objective function is then:

$$(1-\gamma)\,V_o(D)+\gamma\,(t/2-LD/t) \tag{5.1}$$

where γ is a weight; $t/2$ is the expected payoff at date one given the manager's information, D/t is the probability of bankruptcy. If investors infer that $t = a(D)$ when the manager issues debt of face value D, then: $V_o(D) = a(D)/2$.

Substituting this into the objective function and taking the derivative with respect to D gives the first-order condition. In equilibrium, investors correctly infer t from D, that is, if $D(t)$ is the manager's optimal choice of debt level as a function of firm type t, then $a(D(t)) \equiv t$. Using this in the first-order condition and solving the resulting differential equation gives: $D(t) = ct/L + b$, where c and b are constants.

It is easily seen from the above formula that increases in the bankruptcy penalty, other things being equal, reduce the debt level and the probability of bankruptcy. Ross also shows that this probability is increasing in firm type t. Thus firm value, debt level, and bankruptcy probability are all positively related in this model.

3.1.2 Agency model

Harris and Raviv (1990) develop a model where managers and investors disagree over an operating decision. Managers are assumed always to want to continue the firm's current operations even if investors prefer liquidation of the firm. The model predicts that firms with higher liquidation values, for example, those with tangible assets, and/or firms with lower investigation costs will have more debt, will be more likely to default, but will have higher market values than similar firms with lower liquidation values and/or higher investigation costs. The intuition for the higher debt level is that increases in the liquidation value make it more likely that liquidation is the best strategy. Therefore, information is more useful and a higher debt level is called for. Similarly, decreases in investigation costs also increase the value of default, resulting in more debt.

Payments to stockholders discounted to date one consist of (a) the amount debt-holders pay for their claim, (b) in the case of default, first-period income minus default costs, and the payment to debt-holders, plus the larger of the liquidation value or the present value of second-period income, and (c) in the absence of default, the present value of the firm's income over periods one and two net of the promised payment to debt-holders.

In this model, if the firm defaults in period one, then the probability that it will reorganize is independent of default costs and its debt level, and decreases with increases in the liquidation value function. If the liquidation value function is not increasing in current income, then the probability of reorganization depends on current income and firm scale, only through the ratio of current income to firm scale. The optimal debt level decreases with increases in default costs and increases with increases in liquidation value. The expected debt coverage ratio moves in the opposite direction from the debt level with changes in default cost and liquidation value. Moreover, under the constant returns to scale assumption, the debt level is proportional to firm scale and the expected debt coverage ratio is independent of firm scale. Debt level and default probability move in the same direction with shifts in default costs and liquidation value. Under the constant returns to scale assumption, default probability is independent of firm scale.

3.2 High Operating Risk Firms Have Higher Leverage

Kim and Sorensen (1986) develop a model to test empirically for the presence of agency costs and their relation to the debt policy of corporations. Assuming that each firm makes some efforts to resolve the agency cost of debt by adding some kinds of bind covenants, the effectiveness of agency cost-resolving covenants may be a function of ownership structure. As the cost to insider shareholders of violating covenants increases, the probability of wealth transfer declines. Moreover, many of the standard bond covenants (such as call provisions, sinking bonds and so on) are designed to transfer *ex post* agency costs back to shareholders. The more shares insiders own, the greater the amount of the agency cost that will be borne by insiders.

Kim and Sorenson show that the presence of agency cost-resolving covenants is more effective and disciplinary when the contracts are written by firms with high inside ownership. Since the cost of violating covenants will be borne by the shareholders, costs to insiders who are directly involved in major corporate decisions of high α firms[4] will exceed costs to insiders of low α firms. This implies that high α firms face lower residual agency costs than do their low α counterparts.

Kim and Sorensen (1986) then develop a regression model to explain the determination of long-term borrowing by examining the effects of insider ownership in the presence of other important factors.

Their results tend to refute the traditional notion that firms with high business risk have lower 'debt capacity'. Moreover, they support Myers's (1977) argument that, in the presence of growth-induced agency problems, high operating variance may reduce the agency cost of debt, rather than increase it. Other conclusions are: high-growth firms use less debt rather than more debt, high operating risk firms use more debt rather than less debt, and firm size appears to be uncorrelated to the level of debt.

3.3 Lower Fraction of Unobservable Cash Flow

Islamic banks may reduce the unobservable portions of entrepreneurs' cash flows, and thus the degree of asymmetric information. It has been shown that leverage increases with the fraction of cash flow that is unobservable. A business with a higher portion of cash flow gives ample opportunity for the entrepreneur to understate his profit, and it will be difficult for the bank to verify the true amount of the profit.

Chang (1987) develops an agency model in which contracts may not depend directly on the value of the firm's assets. He assumes that verification is possible at a cost, and that one component of a firm's income can be included in the contract without cost, and the existence of an asset or return that can be contractually allocated to outsiders. He shows that the optimal contract with investors involves debt, and that the entire contractable component of a firm's income in excess of what is required to pay debt-holders is assigned to outside investors. The manager keeps that part of the non-contractable component not used to pay debt-holders.

He also shows that more profitable firms have less debt. If returns are stochastically larger, debt becomes safer, and the promised payment on the debt can be reduced. This reduces the verification region.

Last but not least, an increase in the fraction of income that is observable, holding the distribution of total income constant, also reduces the debt level. This is not surprising since such an increase also increases the expected payout, *ceteris paribus*.

3.4 Lower Fraction of Non-controllable Costs

Suh (1988) addresses the issue of why it could be optimal to allocate apparently non-controllable costs for management control purposes in a multi-agent, sequential department setting. In every business there are unpredictable costs, for example escalation of input price or new regulation on minimum wage level. These non-controllable costs will reduce the entrepreneur's profit and thus the profit sharing for the Islamic bank.

Suh shows that if there is no noise in the quality-generating process, then: (a) the optimal contract for the final product division manager is a non-trivial function of revenue alone. That is, there will be no demand for revenue allocating non-controllable intermediate costs to the final product division for performance evaluation purposes; and (b) the optimal contract for the intermediate division manager is a non-trivial function of both revenue and intermediate product costs.

It is likely that the quality of intermediate products, which is not observable in general, is the outcome of a random process influenced by the intermediate product division manager's quality-raising effort. Noise in the quality-generating process of the intermediate division then becomes one source of common uncertainty faced by both divisions.

The common uncertainty, which arises from the sequential departmental structure of the model, induces a positive environmental correlation such that the optimal contract for the final division manager is decreasing in intermediate costs. For, by the monotone likelihood ratio property, if a more (less) costly situation is observed, it is likely to imply, other things being equal, a higher (lower) quality of intermediate products, which implies a more (less) productive state for the final product division.

4. APPLICATION OF INCENTIVE-COMPATIBLE CONSTRAINTS

Bank Muamalat[5] has assigned its Bandung Branch as a pilot project for implementation of *muḍārabah* and *mushārakah* in West Java province. At the practitioner's level, especially *muḍārabah* and *mushārakah* financing for small and medium entrepreneurs, a short-term contract is preferred. Being small, they do not want to take greater risks by putting their money into long-term projects, which may also create liquidity problems for them. What they really need is short-term *muḍārabah* financing. Why? Again, being small, they need another party to share their business risks, should something unexpected happen.

Small entrepreneurs usually have no barriers to enter new business. Thus it is logical for them to diversify their type of business, since every business has its own risk. Therefore, profit-sharing financing should be arranged by projects on a short-term basis.

Short-term profit-sharing by job order is offered[6] to reduce the risk of products/services not demanded. For example, an entrepreneur who already has an order to carry out a certain project but has no working capital to start with may ask an Islamic bank to provide profit-sharing financing. The Islamic bank knows beforehand the value of the project and is able to determine the profit-sharing ratio given the risks involved. By doing this, the Islamic bank distributes the risk to the entrepreneur (performance risk) and to the job-order issuer (credit risk). The small entrepreneur has no financial liability to carry the burden of credit risks. He will be responsible for ensuring his obligations and performance as agreed. On the other hand, the Islamic bank, through bank-checking mechanisms provided by the central bank, ensures that the credit record of the job-order issuer is in good standing, a task which can be done easily by a bank, but is impossible for small entrepreneurs.

A longer-term profit-sharing, which is now being offered,[7] is profit-sharing by purchase contract. It is designed to reduce the risk of unmatched product specification, and is targeted at small entrepreneurs who get sub-contracts from bigger companies. For example, an entrepreneur who already has a two-year contract to supply leather to a shoe factory with deferred payment at the end of every month, and the entrepreneur has no working capital to do so, may ask the Islamic bank to provide profit-sharing financing. In this scheme the entrepreneur's cash flow is observable, and the Islamic bank determines its profit-sharing ratio based on the payment schedule as stated in the contract. Unlike profit-sharing by job order, which will take two to six months to get the job done, purchase contracts may take two years. The examples show how an Islamic bank may reduce the unobservable portion of the entrepreneur's cash flow, and thus the degree of asymmetric information.

For an entrepreneur with a higher degree of unobservable cash flow but relatively stable revenue, the Islamic bank may offer revenue-sharing to reduce the problem of cost disputes, for example uncontrollable costs.[8] Unlike profit-sharing, in a revenue-sharing scheme all expenses are borne by the entrepreneur. Such a scheme is based on the empirical evidence found by Kim and Sorensen (1986) that leverage increases with increases in operating risk.

4.1 Cooperative Financing

Cooperative financing is provided for the working capital needs of cooperatives. This is a special-purpose financing, that is, working capital for staple foods trading. A minimum of 25 per cent fixed asset collateral is required, while another 75 per cent is covered by *kafālah* (guarantee) provided by a third party. *Kafālah* is assumed as intangible net worth, that is, trust and reputation of the cooperative. If the cooperative cannot find any third party willing to give a guarantee for his/her reputation, this can be a bad signal for the bank. The importance of trust and reputation is emphasized by many studies.[9] The third party is responsible for the risk of cheating, the fixed asset collateral is to avoid any business misconduct, while as required by the nature of *muḍārabah*, the bank is responsible for business risk. Since this *muḍārabah* fund can only be used for certain types of business as agreed in the contract, the bank does not apply leverage as an incentive-compatible constraint, nor maximum ratio of operating costs to operating income. *Ḥawālah* (right to get paid from the cooperative's receivables) is not relevant because the bank requires the cooperative to sell on cash only. For prudent investment, a maximum ratio of fixed asset to total asset is applied.

Cooperatives are required to sell the staple food with a profit margin of 10 per cent. Sales turnover is assumed to be twice a month at the minimum. If this assumption is achieved, then the bank will get 2.4 per cent profit, while the cooperative will get 17.6 per cent profit monthly. Thus the cumulative amount of a cooperative's profit at the end of the year would be enough to repay the *muḍārabah* fund (100 per cent) and to replace it with his own equity (another 100 per cent). The profit-sharing ratio is 12 per cent for the bank and 88 per cent for the cooperative.

4.2 Cooperative's Members Financing

The Cooperative's members financing is provided for the investment and working capital needs of the cooperative's members for their businesses. This is two-step financing, where *muḍārabah* is applied between Bank Muamalat and the cooperative, and a variety of Islamic contracts, for example *salam*, *murābaḥah*, *ijārah*, *muḍārabah*, are applied between the cooperative and its members. A minimum of 25 per cent fixed asset collateral is required, while another 75 per cent is covered by *kafālah* provided by the cooperative and another third party. Cooperatives are required to achieve an expected weighted average minimum return of 16 per cent per annum. Uncontrollable costs and unobservable cash flow are minimized by applying revenue-sharing, rather than profit-sharing. In special cases where uncontrollable costs and unobservable cash flow are insignificant, profit-sharing may also be applied. As in cooperative financing, it would be too expensive to exercise periodic monitoring or to ask for audited financial statements. However, stochastic monitoring is applied. To avoid overinvestment, a maximum ratio of fixed assets to total assets is applied. The revenue-sharing ratio is 12.5 per cent for the bank and 87.5 per cent for the cooperative member from the realized weighted average return.

4.3 Islamic Rural Bank Financing

Islamic rural bank financing is provided for working capital needs of Islamic rural ranks. There are 78 Islamic rural banks in Indonesia, with 16 of them in West Java province. This is two-step financing, where *muḍārabah* is applied between Bank Muamalat and the Islamic rural bank, and a full range of Islamic banking products are applied between the rural banks and their clients. Fixed assets collateral is required although there is no minimum requirement. The facility is covered by *kafālah* provided by the shareholders' of the Islamic rural bank, and *ḥawālah* of the Islamic rural banks from their customers to Bank Muamalat. Audited financial statements are required, as well as a maximum ratio of operating cost to operating income, to avoid misreporting and operating inefficiency respectively.

To be eligible, Islamic rural banks are required to achieve an expected weighted average minimum return of 36 per cent per annum. Revenue-sharing is applied with the ratio of 58 per cent for Bank Muamalat and 42 per cent for the Islamic rural banks.

4.4 Other Commercial Financing

These *muḍārabah* and *mushārakah* facilities are provided for those who cannot fit into the three financing schemes outlined above. Each and every facility is specifically designed and structured to fit a certain business. There is no standard profit-sharing ratio, nor standard collateral ratio requirements. In any case, incentive-compatible constraints are always applied with four general guidelines: a higher stake in net worth and/or collateral; lower operating risks; a lower fraction of unobservable cash flow; and a lower fraction of non-controllable costs. (See Table 5.1.)

Table 5.1 Incentive-compatible constraints introduced in profit-sharing contracts

	Muḍārabah and *mushārakah* financing			
	Cooperative financing	Cooperative's member financing	Islamic rural bank financing	Other commercial financing
Net worth				
Leverage ratio	No	No	Yes	No
Fixed assets collateral	Yes	Yes	No	Yes
Kafālah	Yes	Yes	Yes	Yes
Ḥawālah	No	No	Yes	Yes
High operating risks				
Max. fixed assets to total assets ratio	Yes	Yes	No	Yes
Max. op. costs to income ratio	No	No	Yes	Y/N
Unobservable cash flow				
Stochastic monitoring	Yes	Yes	No	Y/N
Periodic monitoring	No	No	Yes	Y/N
Audited financial statement	No	No	Yes	Y/N
Non-controllable costs				
Revenue sharing	Yes	Yes	Yes	Yes
Min. profit margin	Yes	Yes	Yes	Yes

5. GROWTH AND PROFITABILITY OF *MUḌĀRABAH* AND *MUSHĀRAKAH*

The pilot project for implementation of *muḍārabah* and *mushārakah* financing began in June 1998. *Murābaḥah* contracts are also applied for cooperative financing and cooperative's members financing, if the purpose is to acquire commodities. *Salam* financing is also categorized as *murābaḥah.*

Significant growth in *muḍārabah* shows the success of implementation. It also enjoys a high profitability. Not all *muḍārabah* financings experienced positive profits, as is their nature. Loss was experienced in cooperative financings. (See Table 5.2 for the figures.) This was due to government intervention in the staple food market such that prices dropped, and the profit margin reduced significantly. Since the cooperatives are required to sell with a profit margin of 10 per cent, sales turnover decreased, unsold commodities increased, and inventory costs increased.

Compared to *murābaḥah*, *mushārakah* yielded a slightly higher profitability. The insignificant negative growth of *mushārakah* is due to the decreasing participation of the bank.

Table 5.2 Performance of incentive-compatible profit-sharing contracts

	1998		1999		Growth outstanding (%)
	Outstanding ('000s rupiah)	Return (%)	Outstanding ('000s rupiah)	Return (%)	
Murābaḥah	**24 153.97**	**17.16**	**12 408.0**	**16.86**	**–49**
Cooperative	Nil	Nil	550.00	0.21	n.a.
Cooperative's member	2 047.6	2.68	1 240.2	20.70	–39
Other commercial	22 106.3	18.50	10 617.8	17.27	–52
Muḍārabah	**2 415.7**	**18.94**	**27 708.5**	**248.29**	**1 047**
Cooperative	Nil	Nil	1 186.1	–0.62	n.a.
Cooperative's member	Nil	Nil	6 949.9	9.66	–0.03
Other commercial	709.1	25.04	17 924.4	221.73	2 427
Mushārakah	**4 922.67**	**15.60**	**4 843.5**	**17.42**	**–0.01**

6. CONCLUDING REMARKS

Muḍārabah and *mushārakah* financing are indeed viable modes of financing. The crucial point is to design and structure these kinds of financing with incentive-compatible constraints.

As identified by many studies and adopted by Bank Muamalat, there are four general guidelines for incentive compatible constraints: a higher stake in net worth and/or collateral; lower operating risks; a lower fraction of unobservable cash flow; and a lower fraction of non-controllable costs.

Bank Muamalat began its pilot project in the Bandung Branch in June 1998 for the implementation of *muḍārabah* and *mushārakah* financings with incentive-compatible constraints. So far, the results have been quite promising in terms of growth and profitability.

NOTES

1. The term '*ribā* contract' is misleading. It is defined as a contract with a predetermined fixed rate of return. This definition applies to Islamic mark-up-based financing with some conditions.
2. See, for example, Iqbal et al. (1998).
3. See for example, Harris and Raviv (1990), and Stulz (1991). These studies are also supported by many empirical studies such as Lys and Sivaramakrishnan (1988); Cornett and Travlos (1989) and Dan et al. (1989).
4. The symbol α is the ratio of the number of shares owned by corporate insiders to the total number of common shares outstanding.
5. Bank Muamalat is the first Islamic bank in Indonesia, established in 1992.
6. Bank Muamalat (1997).
7. Ibid
8. Ibid; Suh (1988).
9. See, for example, Burchell and Wilkinson (1997).

REFERENCES

Bank Muamalat (1997), *Manual For PLS Financing*.

Bashir, A.M. and A.F. Darrat (1992), 'Equity Participation Contracts and Investment: Some Theoretical and Empirical Results', *The American Journal of Islamic Social Sciences*, **9** (2), 219–32.

Burchell, Brendan and Franke Wilkinson (1997), 'Trust, Business Relationships and the Contractual Environment', *Cambridge Journal of Economics*, **21**, 217–37.

Chang, Chun (1987), *Capital Structure as Optimal Contract*, Working Paper, Carlson School of Management, University of Minnesota.

Cornett, Marcia and Nicolas Travlos (1989), 'Information Effects Associated with Debt-for-Equity and Equity-for-Debt Exchange Offers', *Journal of Finance*, **44**, 451–68.

Dan, Larry, Ronald Masulis and David Mayers (1989), *Repurchase Tender Offers and Earnings Information*, Working Paper, University of Oregon.

Diamond, D.W. (1984), 'Financial Intermediation and Delegated Monitoring', *Review of Economic Studies*, **51**, 394–414.

Gale, D. and M. Hellwig (1985), 'Incentive-compatible Debt Contracts: The One-period Problem', *Review of Economic Studies*, **52**, 647–63.

Harris, Milton and Arthur Raviv (1988), 'Corporate Control Contests and Capital Structure', *Journal of Financial Economics*, **20**, 55–86.

Harris, Milton and Arthur Raviv (1990), 'Capital Structure and Informational Role of Debt', *Journal of Finance*, **45**, 321–49.

Hart, O. (1983), 'Optimal Labour Contracts Under Asymmetric Information: An Introduction', *Review of Economic Studies*, **50**, 3–35.

Hart, O. and B. Holstrom (1987), 'The Theory of Contracts', in T. Bewely (ed.), *Advances in Economic Theory: Fifth World Congress*, Cambridge, UK: Cambridge University Press.

Holstrom, B. and L. Weiss (1985), 'Managerial Incentives, Investments, and Aggregate Implications: Scale Effects', *Review of Economic Studies*, **52**, 403–26.

Iqbal, Munawar, Ausaf Ahmad and Tariqullah Khan (1998), *Challenges Facing Islamic Banking*, Occasional Paper No. 2, Jeddah, Saudi Arabia: Islamic Research and Training Institute, Islamic Development Bank.

Kim, Saeng Wi and Eric Sorensen (1986), 'Evidence on the Impact of the Agency Costs of Debt on Corporate Debt Policy', *Journal of Financial and Quantitative Analysis*, **21** (2), 131–44.

Lys, Thomas and Konduru Sivaramakrishnan (1988), 'Earning Expectations and Capital Restructuring: The case of Equity-for-Debt Swaps', *Journal of Accounting Research*, **26**, 273–99.

Myers, Stewart C. (1977), 'Determinants of Corporate Borrowing', *Journal of Financial Economics*, **5**, 147–75.

Presley, J.R. and J.G. Sessions (1994), 'Islamic Economics: The Emergence of a New Paradigm', *The Economic Journal*, **104**, 584–96.

Ross, Stephen (1977), 'The Determination of Financial Structure: The Incentive Signalling Approach', *Bell Journal of Economics*, **8**, 23–40.

Stulz, Rene M. (1991), 'Managerial Discretion and Optimal Financing Policies', *Journal of Financial Economics*, **26**, 3–27.

Suh, Yoon (1988), 'Noncontrollable Costs and Optimal Performance Measurement', *Journal of Accounting Research*, **26** (1), 154–68.

Williamson, S.D. (1986), 'Costly Monitoring, Financial Intermediation, and Equilibrium Credit Rationing', *Journal of Monetary Economics*, **18**, 159–79.

COMMENTS

Muhammad Nejatullah Siddiqi

Since the advent of Islamic banking theory a number of issues have been raised regarding the compatibility of the basic model – the two-tier *muḍārabah* – with incentives (Khan, 1985, pp. 49, 85, 105; Kazarian, 1991, pp. 118–20, 123, 131, 239–40, 247–8).

The advent of *murābaḥah* and its predominance in the practice of Islamic banking has done little to mitigate the situation. Rather it has evoked fresh, though different, reservations (Muhammad, 1996; Attiyah, 1407H).

Thus far Islamic economists have dealt with this issue largely theoretically (Haque and Mirakhor, 1987, pp. 144–61; Siddiqui and Fardmanesh, 1992).

It is, therefore, very refreshing to find Adiwarman Karim arguing that Bank Muamalat Indonesia is successfully introducing constraints which make the *muḍārabah* contract incentive-compatible.

Karim recognizes that the incentive problem is not peculiar to Islamic banking models since asymmetric information is a universal feature of agency and investment management. He surveys the recent contributions on the subject.

Literature on four groups of constraints is noted: higher stake in net worth; high leverage; lower fraction of unobservable cash flow; and lower fraction of non-controllable cost. The chapter is built around these four points. He also notes that Islamic mark-up has certain features similar to the 'standard debt contact' which is considered optimal in certain conditions. He then quotes recent papers by Bashir and Darrat and Presley and Sessions to the effect that profit-sharing contracts would be more efficient subject to certain provisos. But the writer himself offers little by way of endorsement.

Relying on recent studies, Karim concludes that 'high-growth firms use less debt rather than more debt, high operating risk firms use more debt rather than less debt, and firm size appears to be uncorrelated to the level of debt'.

Useful information about Bank Muamalat financing of small business is provided in section 4. It would be instructive to make a comparative study of Islamic banks' financing of small business in the Gulf, which tends to be mostly in *murābaḥah*, pure and simple. The variety of contracts reported by Karim could enrich Islamic banking practice in its heartland.

The conclusion '*muḍārabah* and *mushārakah* financing are indeed viable modes of financing. The crucial point is to design and structure these kinds of financing with incentive-compatible constraints' is duly supported by evidence from Bank Muamalat pilot project launched in 1998. The thinness of data calls for further research covering a wider time span and, possibly, larger geographical area.

We also recommend paying greater attention to the problems raised by Kazarian (1991) and others so as to make the design of profit-sharing contracts more robust and capable of application to longer-term and larger financing. Could it be possible, for example, to have a progressive scale of the ratio in which profits are shared, the profit share of *muḍārib*/entrepreneur increasing in the end slabs of profits earned, once the profits exceed a certain amount? Such questions are worth serious thought.

REFERENCES

Attiyah, Jamaluddin (1407H), *Al-Bunūk al-Islamiyyah Bain al-Ḥurriyyah wal Tanẓīm, al-Taqlīd wal Ijtehād, al-Naẓariyyah wal Taṭbīq*, Doha, Qatar: Kitab al Ummah.

Haque, Nadeem ul- and Abbas Mirakhor (1987), 'Optimal Profit-Sharing Contracts and Investment in an Interest Free Economy', in Mohsin S. Khan and Abbas Mirakhor, *Theoretical Studies in Islamic Banking and Finance*, Houston, TX: The Institute For Research and Islamic Studies.

Kazarian, Elias (1991), *Finance and Economic Development, Islamic Banking in Egypt*, Lund, Sweden: University of Lund.

Khan, Waqar Masood (1985), *Towards an Interest Free Economic System*, Leicester, UK: The Islamic Foundation.

Muhammad, Yusuf Kamal (1996), *Al-Maṣrafiyyah al-Islamiyyah, al-Aẓmeh wal Makhraj*, Cairo, Egypt: Dar Nashr li'l Jamiat al-Miṣriyyah.

Siddiqui, Shamim Ahmad and Mohsen Fardmanesh (1992), 'Saving and investment under *Muḍārabah* Finance', *Review of Islamic Economics*, **2** (1), 31–51.

6. How informal risk capital investors manage asymmetric information in profit/loss-sharing contracts

Mohammad Abalkhail and John R. Presley

1. INTRODUCTION

Islamic banks have existed for almost 30 years but the use of profit/loss-sharing methods is not yet widely established. The constraints on the development of these methods are believed to be caused not only by the asymmetric information that the contract involves but also by the nature of banks as short-term finance institutions.

It is argued here that the practices of profit/loss-sharing (PLS) contracts in the informal markets could provide lessons for the application of these contracts in Islamic financial institutions. Recently, informal venture capital investors have been recognized as an important source of finance for small and medium-sized enterprises (SMEs) through the application of venture capital financing. Unfortunately, very little research, if any, has been devoted to understanding how these investors fund particular investments in Muslim countries.

In the conventional paradigm, capital markets are perfect. Individuals and firms are assumed to be able to obtain as much funding as they want at the market interest rate. The theory also often assumes that capital markets are informational efficient, when prices perfectly reflect all the available information (Stiglitz, 1985).

Fama (1970) introduced a model of capital markets in which he assumed the existence of three types of efficiency: strong form, semi-strong form and weak form. The strong form exists when the value of a firm is a reflection of all information about it, no matter what is its source. A semi-strong form exists when the value of a firm is a reflection of all the publicly available information about it. A weak form exists when the value of a firm is a reflection of only historically available information.

Information seems to be a very important element of the efficiency of financial markets. Copeland and Weston (1988) concluded that most research supports Fama's semi-strong form. However, the problem that faces research when testing venture capital markets (formal and informal) against these forms is the diminished flow of investment information. This market is characterized by information asymmetry. Poindexter (1976) argues that compared with other capital markets, this limited flow of information is mainly due to the relative scarcity of market intermediaries.

Thus the main function of the venture capital market intermediary is to ensure that both supply and demand in the market get as much accurate information as possible upon which to base their investment decision (Fiet, 1991). However, intermediaries find it very difficult to exist in venture capital markets, as Fiet (1991) argues, because it is difficult to support themselves financially. Thus, this characteristic of the market complicates the decision to invest in the market and creates high asymmetric information between investors and entrepreneurs after funds are made available to the venture.

It is argued here that the asymmetric information in the risk capital market can be divided into two levels: pre-investment and post-investment. In the pre-investment stage, asymmetric information is very high. Investors face difficulty finding opportunities and this gives rise to search costs. Also, when an investor meets an entrepreneur, knowledge differences between them create asymmetric information. Entrepreneurs usually know their own collateral, industriousness, moral character and business prospects better than venture capitalists. In essence, entrepreneurs possess inside information about the enterprise for which they are seeking financing (Leland and Pyle, 1977). Investors would benefit from knowing the true characteristics of entrepreneurs and the quality of their proposed ventures (Jensen and Meckling, 1978).

Because of the lack of information transfer, investors face the risk of adverse selection (information concerning the characteristics of a venture) and moral hazard (information concerning the true characteristics of an individual entrepreneur).

Without information transfer, the market may perform poorly. Akerlof (1970) argues that under asymmetric information, average quality price will be offered in the market which will lead to a reduction in the supply of good-quality projects. Investors take different mechanisms into account in their decision-making and evaluation criteria in order to reduce the risk of asymmetric information.

This chapter presents a detailed investigation in Saudi Arabia of informal investors' decision-making behaviour across the full investment process, including pre-investment as well as post-investment periods. A theoretical framework, based on the asymmetric information, principal–agent analysis and incomplete contracts that characterize this market is used. Based on existing literature, five hypotheses are formulated and tested to see how informal investors in Saudi Arabia behave to reduce the inefficiencies and risks associated with the asymmetric information problem that is believed to exist in PLS contracts.

In the informal sector, the main difficulty is the identification of investors. Their market transactions are held privately and very little (if any) information is publicly available (Wetzel, 1983; Wetzel and Seymour, 1981; Mason et al., 1991; Fiet, 1991). Wetzel states, 'the total population of informal investors is unknown and probably unknowable' (1983, p. 26). So, researchers investigating informal risk capital investors have had to rely on non-conventional methods to reach investors. Pioneer studies utilized a snowball sample. Baty (1964), Hofman (1972) and Fiet (1991) studied different regions in the United States, and Mason et al. (1991) in the UK by using a snowball technique to reach informal venture capital investors.[1] This study used the same techniques to identify a sample group of 150 informal investors in Saudi Arabia.

2. FORMULATION OF HYPOTHESES

The lack of intermediary function increases the cost of finding opportunities. Investors and entrepreneurs find it very difficult to identify each other. This gives rise to search costs. Search costs can be identified as part of the transaction cost (Coase, 1960). The asymmetric information that characterizes the risk capital market will lead to an increase in search costs. Investors in this market face a very poorly defined environment within which to find good prospective deals. The typical investment prospect is too small a company to be identifiable as a potential customer (Tyebjee and Bruno, 1984). The search by a venture for an investor, and the search by an investor for an opportunity can be an expensive, time-consuming business. The search is compounded by pitfalls and dead-ends that often end in failure and frustration (Gaston, 1989). For this reason, we could expect that various players may act as important matching intermediaries. Informal investors often rely on friends and associates and so on to find investment opportunities. Investors create referral networks that deals pass through. These networks will reduce the search costs and provide a first gate to control risk. How informal investors deal with this issue is tested through hypothesis 1, which states:

Given the absence of intermediaries, investors rely on friends more than on other sources of information for finding investment opportunities.

When an opportunity reaches an investor, he uses different criteria to minimize the fear of being caught in a bad deal. These criteria evaluate all the aspects of the venture. The lack of previous research on the investment decision process of informal investors required this study to develop a general decision process, which can be accepted on a logical basis. Mason and Rogers (1996) indicate that the business angels' investment decision takes two stages of evaluation: the initial screening stage, where investors reach a decision about the proposal within an average of 10.7 minutes; and the evaluation stage, where investors do further research and collect more information about the opportunity. Boocock and Woods (1997) indicate that in the decision process in formal venture capital the exact number of stages differs, but there is a general agreement that the investment cycle takes at least two stages: screening and evaluation. In the initial screening stage investors use specific criteria to test if the venture meets the investors' minimum objectives. Riding et al. (1993) and Mason and Rogers (1996) found that the potential of the product or service in the market place was the most important aspect of the deal that investors were concerned about at this stage, followed by the entrepreneur/management team and financial criteria.

However, the initial screening stage does not satisfy investors about the quality of chosen projects. Asymmetric information will affect the ability of investors to distinguish good-quality ventures. Moral hazard prevents direct information transfer. Under these assumptions, adverse selection may exist. In order to prevent the adverse selection problem, investors invest in specific information. Rational investors would only invest if they expected to earn a return with a positive net present value more than any other project with the same level of risk. Because specific information is specialized, it is of little or no value for reducing risk in more than one deal (Barney and Ouchi, 1986). The literature illustrates that different criteria have different weights of influence at various stages of the investment process (Riding et al., 1993; Mason and Rogers, 1996). Unfortunately, investigating evaluation criteria in a time line requires an observation of the decision when it is being made. Getting such access is difficult and not possible on a large scale.

To evaluate a deal, investors direct their resources towards gathering information about the deal (Fiet, 1991, p. 18). What criteria investors use to reduce market risks, distinguish good projects and prevent adverse selection on the venture quality is checked through hypothesis 2, which states:

Informal investors depend on specific criteria to prevent the selection of low-quality entrepreneurs. However, investors consider the entrepreneur's track record as the most important criterion.

In addition to checking the quality of the entrepreneurs, investors also use some criteria to reduce the risk of adverse selection with respect to the quality of the venture. This is the subject of hypothesis 3, which states:

Informal investors use specific criteria to prevent investment in a low-quality venture. However, investors consider the product's market as the most important criterion.

While investors gather information about the venture and its entrepreneur from different sources, they usually rely on their expertise and intuition to make their decision. In general, they may prefer syndication to assure themselves that other investors approve their evaluation and agreement to invest in the project. Another venture capitalist's willingness to invest in the firm may be an important factor in the lead venture investor's decision to invest (Pence, 1982; Lerner, 1994). The syndication is a chance to check out investors' own thinking against other knowledgeable sources (Lerner, 1994; Aram, 1989).

In addition, investors may co-invest to improve their network. Offering opportunities to other investors will enhance the relationship and improve the size of the network. This clearly can be true if investors co-invest with investors not already in the existing network. In order to check the motives of co-investing we use hypothesis 4, which states:

Investors co-invest in order to improve network size.

After making the financial investment, investors apply different strategies to monitor the projects. In order to monitor venture quality and the entrepreneurs' behaviour, investors use different methods in the post-investment stage. Staging capital is considered a powerful mechanism to control risks associated with the venture and reduce monitoring costs. As Sahlman (1990) notes, staged capital infusions are the most potent control mechanisms a venture capitalist can employ. Gompers (1995) states that entrepreneurs may have private benefits from managing the firms they establish which may not be perfectly correlated with investors' monetary returns. Entrepreneurs may have incentives to continue projects which should be abandoned. Entrepreneurs may also invest in projects that generate high personal benefits but low monetary returns for investors. To check the importance of staging we formulate hypothesis 5, which states:

Investors use staging of finance to reduce monitoring costs.

3. RESULTS

The investigation outlined in this chapter is part of the first ever detailed investigation to build a better understanding of Saudi informal investors' characteristics and decision-making behaviour across the full investment process. This section presents the results of testing the hypotheses developed in the previous section. Investors' decision-making behaviour will be analysed to see how investors minimize the asymmetric information and control problems that are associated with it.

3.1 Information Sources

Informal investors operate in a very difficult environment where information is extremely rare. As search costs increase, investors will not find it profitable to invest. In this poorly defined environment, rational investors may find it in their interest to connect themselves to informal networks to share information about opportunities (Rubenstein, 1958).

The Saudi informal venture capital market is expected to be even less efficient than the same markets in developed countries, especially after the introduction of matching services in developed countries. Consequently, the reliance on the available information sources should be evident to Saudi informal investors. Against this background we test the following null hypothesis:

H_0: *Information sources are equally important to Saudi informal investors.*

Eight sources of information were developed from the literature and the preliminary interviews with Saudi informal investors. Respondents were asked to state the actual use of these sources in obtaining information about investment opportunities.

Table 6.1 ranks the information sources by using the Friedman two-way ANOVA test. It is clear that the difference in the importance of information sources is statistically significant, which implies the rejection of the null hypothesis. Saudi investors attached different importance levels to their use of the available information sources. In contrast to the literature, active personal search is at the forefront of the sources of investment opportunities. Informal networks, such as friends and business associates, came second and third respectively. On the other hand, formal information sources, such as banks, real-estate agencies and chambers of commerce are the least used.

Research in the US (Wetzel and Seymour, 1981; Haar et al., 1988; Fiet, 1991), the UK (Mason et al., 1991) and Sweden (Landström, 1993) finds that business associates and friends are the most important providers of investment information. If this is the case in developed markets, why do Saudi investors insist on searching for investments themselves, clearly introducing higher search costs? There are two explanations for this. First, the number of investment opportunities that are circulated in the informal network may be low and does not satisfy investors' available funds. Second, Saudi investors may hold a conservative view about market risks (which are due to unforeseen competitive conditions) and agency risks (which are caused by the separate and possibly divergent interests of investors and entrepreneurs) and this leads to a personal search for a venture that they know and an entrepreneur that they can trust.

Table 6.1 Friedman two-way ANOVA test to rank the importance of the information sources

Information source	Importance rank
Active personal search	6.25
Friends	5.46
Business associates	4.82
Entrepreneurs	4.71
Consultation agencies	4.01
Chambers of commerce	3.81
Banks	3.53
Real-estate agencies	3.41
Test statistics:	
N	153
Chi-square	204.021
DF	7
Asymp. sig.	0.000

3.2 Overall Evaluation

Informal investors receive many opportunities but invest only in a very small number of them. This indicates that they are looking for a specific project and a unique entrepreneur to commit their funds for a long-term equity investment in an unquoted firm. These criteria are very important in seeing how these investors manage to control the agency and market risks that are involved in risk capital financing. They also provide some insights into the emphasis that investors attach to *ex ante* and *ex post* investment criteria.

In this section an overall evaluation of the investment criteria is undertaken. As this study adopted the large-scale questionnaire, it concentrated on an overall evaluation of the factors influencing the decision to invest. It employs the same technique used by two of the most cited UK criteria articles in the literature (Macmillan et al., 1985 and 1987). This technique was also employed in a recent and most extensive study on informal investors in the UK (Osnabrugge, 1998).

3.2.1 Ranking of investment criteria

Asymmetric information that existed in the risk capital market will affect the ability of investors to distinguish good-quality ventures and entrepreneurs. Moral hazard prevents direct information transfer. Under these assumptions, adverse selection may exist. The owners of low-quality projects will foist these upon an unformed market. Investors, on the other hand, will assign average project and entrepreneur value. This will drive out the good-quality projects or entrepreneurs from the market, leading either to bad proposals or failure of the market to exist, much as Akerlof's (1970) market for used cars will result in only 'lemons' for sale.

In order to prevent investment in a low-quality venture or entrepreneur, investors direct their sources to gather information about the deal (Fiet, 1991, p. 18). Therefore, the ranking of these criteria should reflect the risks that investors fear from involvement in risk capital financing. Also, the ranking of these criteria will give insights into the importance of each criterion to reduce the risks that are associated with it.

Table 6.2 presents an overall ranking of criteria that evaluate different aspects of the deal, entrepreneur, product, market, financial issues and other attributes of the business. Also, the table demonstrates the heterogeneity within the whole group of informal investors. The standard deviation scores explain the agreement between investors on the ranking of a specific criterion. It is clear that, overall, the entrepreneur is the criterion that most attracted informal investors to the investment opportunities that were actually funded. Five of the first ten criteria have to do with the entrepreneurs. Investors will not back ventures unless the entrepreneur has a good track record as a founder of previous ventures, has established a reputation for trustworthiness evaluates well and reacts to risk, is familiar with the venture's market and is capable of sustained effort. The second criterion is the product's market, and thus concerned with financial factors. Although most past studies on informal investors have not used such detailed criteria for each criteria group, they do support the overall relative importance of the different groups identified in this study (Mason et al., 1995; 1996; Stevenson and Coveney, 1994).

However, Osnabrugge's (1998) study of UK informal investors clearly supports the results of this study where the entrepreneur fundamentally determines whether the investor will place a fund or not. This is clearly noted by Macmillan et al. (1985).

3.2.2 Selection of entrepreneur

The most important investment criteria identified by the informal investors were the characteristics of the entrepreneur. In this section, analysis of the ranking of the criteria relating to the entrepreneur will be discussed. Factor analysis will be applied to provide more insight into the most important aspect

Table 6.2 Overall ranking of criteria

Variables	*N*	Mean*	Std dev.
Entrepreneur has a good track record as a founder of previous ventures	156	4.71	0.53
Product stimulates existing market	156	4.56	0.82
Trustworthiness/honesty of the entrepreneur	156	4.48	0.77
Entrepreneur is familiar with the market	154	4.42	0.66
Market has high growth rate	153	4.35	0.65
Appropriate return	156	4.35	0.65
Entrepreneur evaluates risk well	155	4.29	0.63
Entrepreneur is capable of sustained effort	156	4.08	0.76
Well-established distribution channels	156	4.04	0.90
Amount of finance sought	156	4.00	1.00
Investor is familiar with the industry	156	3.83	1.00
Entrepreneur provided some equity	156	3.81	1.06
Entrepreneur was recommended to the investor by a trustworthy source	156	3.79	0.84
Low threat of early competition	156	3.71	0.97
Entrepreneur has an ability to articulate when discussing venture	156	3.55	0.98
Entrepreneur has a good track record as an employee in other companies	156	3.54	0.97
Investment could easily be made liquid	156	3.37	1.13
Geographical area of the project	156	3.31	1.14
Industrial sector of the project	156	3.31	1.09
Protection of product	156	3.17	1.21
Entrepreneur has a family or friendship link with the investor	156	2.38	1.29
Government is a customer for the product	156	2.29	1.14
Entrepreneur comes from acceptable social class or family name	156	2.21	1.17
Entrepreneur's father is a successful businessman	156	1.83	1.02

* The differences between means are statistically significant at the 5 per cent level.

(factor) of the entrepreneur as seen by informal investors. In order to do that we state the null hypothesis as:

H_0: *Informal investors depend on specific criteria to prevent the selection of low-quality entrepreneurs. However, they assign the same importance to different criteria related to the entrepreneur's characteristics.*

Table 6.3 presents the key factors affecting the investment decision. The reputation of the entrepreneur is ranked as the first criterion. Investors are highly motivated by a real previous success. This was well documented in the few interviews that were performed at an earlier stage of this study. According to these investors, the entrepreneur will find it much easier to raise funds if he has a good reputation from a previous venture. This clearly shows how serious informal investors are about controlling agency problems. Adverse selection is one of the two primary agency problems. It refers to the misrepresentation by the entrepreneur of his abilities. The entrepreneur may falsify claims to have certain skills when he is hired. By ranking previous success as a founder of a previous venture at one and previous success as an employee in other companies at eight, it can be argued that investors are trying to reduce adverse selection risks in relation to entrepreneur skills.

Table 6.3 Rank factors affecting the investment decision

Variables	Mean rank	Factor
1. Entrepreneur has a good track record as a founder of previous ventures	9.68	Reputation
2. Trustworthiness/honesty of the entrepreneur	8.97	Reputation
3. Entrepreneur is familiar with the market	8.74	Skills
4. Entrepreneur evaluates risk well	8.30	Skills
5. Entrepreneur is capable of sustained effort	7.49	Skills
6. Entrepreneur was recommended by a trustworthy source	6.89	Reputation
7. Entrepreneur provided some equity	6.66	Reputation
8. Entrepreneur has an ability to articulate when discussing venture	6.02	Skills
9. Entrepreneur has a good track record as an employee in other companies	5.89	Reputation
10. Entrepreneur has a family or friendship link with the investor	3.71	Origins
11. Entrepreneur comes from acceptable social class or family name	3.13	Origins
12. Entrepreneur's father is a successful businessman	2.51	Origins

The other aspect of the reputation factor is the trustworthiness/honesty of the entrepreneur. This also reflects the investor's fear of the second primary source of agency problems, moral hazard. Moral hazard occurs when the entrepreneur does not fulfil the target originally agreed upon in the contract or the entrepreneur prevents the transfer of crucial information to the investor. Pettit and Singer (1985) claim that this problem may be more crucial in a smaller firm since the management team is usually dominated by one individual.

The second factor that ranked highly in the investor's decision was the skill of the entrepreneur. Although the origins of the entrepreneur were ranked at the bottom, this study anticipated that origins might be placed in a higher position, especially in a culture such as that of Saudi Arabia. Investors appear to be interested in the quality/trustworthiness of the entrepreneur regardless of his origins. However, ranking the references of the entrepreneur as number six may indicate that Saudi informal investors prefer to know the entrepreneur personally. Indeed, this is another mechanism to reduce asymmetric information but it may contribute strongly to the inefficiency of the market owing to the fact that investors will only know a limited number of entrepreneurs.

Controlling agency problems The literature has identified two primary approaches which may be applied by investors to reduce agency problems. The first, the principal–agent approach, is essentially 'classical' agency theory and is primarily concerned with determining the optimal contract between principal and agent (Hart, 1995; Jensen and Meckling, 1978). The second is the incomplete contract approach which relies on the idea that contracts can be complete. So, when dealing with the potential effects of moral hazard or adverse selection, the principals can limit divergences from their interests by incurring screening costs to reduce asymmetric information between them and agents. More comprehensive contracts can then be formulated to influence the agent's behaviour (Pettit and Singer, 1985). These contracts can either be behaviour or outcome-based (Ross, 1977; Hart, 1995).

The principal–agent stream of research is clearly concerned with determining the optimal contract, behaviour versus outcome, between the principal and the agent whilst placing more emphasis on an *ex ante* rather than on an *ex post* stage. In contrast, the incomplete contract approach puts more emphasis on an *ex post* control. So, both provide a risk reduction at every stage of the investment process, but each places more emphasis on different stages.

According to Hart and Holmstorm (1987), because contracts are not complete and cannot specify each party's obligations in every contingency, it is the *ex post* allocation of power and control that matters. So, to control the agency problem and exert power over the investment, informal investors become more involved in it. This creates an active inside investor, not a sleeping partner.

In this section, the first approach will be discussed because it is viewed as an *ex ante* mechanism to manage the risks associated with agency problems. The importance of the *ex ante* approach can best be explained and analysed after reviewing the literature about the ability of informal investors to control entrepreneurs in the post-investment stage. It is well documented that many formal venture capital firms in the UK and the US are not afraid to replace the entrepreneurial team if the venture is not performing up to expectations (Kanellos, 1996; Gorman and Sahlman, 1989; Macmillan et al., 1988). In fact, in his UK study, Hall (1988) found that 73 per cent of the venture capitalists interviewed had replaced management where necessary, while in the US, Carter and Van Auken (1994) found that 28.86 per cent of venture capital investment had required a change of management.

In contrast, informal investors replace management infrequently and, therefore, place greater emphasis on finding a competent entrepreneur in the initial appraisal of the investment (Mason et al., 1995).

Table 6.4 Friedman test to rank monitoring methods

Variables	Mean rank
1. Provide incentives if certain goals achieved	3.67
2. Investor participates in the board of directors	3.49
3. Entrepreneur provides some of the capital	3.44
4. No monitoring because I trust him	2.27
5. No monitoring because we have the same interests	2.13

Table 6.4 shows that Saudi informal investors are still concerned about the behaviour of entrepreneurs even if they have found a trustworthy entrepreneur. This is clearly indicated by the high ranking of the monitoring methods and the low ranking of 'not taking any monitoring actions'.

When dealing with the potential effects of agency problems, the informal investors limit divergences from their own interests by extensive evaluation to reduce the asymmetries of information between them and the entrepreneur. At this level of knowledge about the venture and the entrepreneur, Saudi informal investors write comprehensive contracts to influence the entrepreneur's behaviour.

These contracts can either be behaviour- or outcome-based, as implied by the principal–agent approach (Sappington, 1991; Jensen and Meckling, 1976). Saudi informal investors apply this approach as follows:

(a) Outcome-based contracts

1. Provide incentives if certain goals are achieved (Rank 1).
2. Entrepreneur provides some of the capital (Rank 3).

Both provide motives for entrepreneurs on outcomes (profitability). These methods of contracting shift some of the risks and uncertainty to the entrepreneur and so lead to a reduction in the cost of monitoring.

(b) Behaviour-based contracts

1. Monitoring (Board of Directors) (Rank 2).

One way of monitoring is to monitor/observe the behaviour of the entrepreneur to ensure that he is working to the best interest of both parties. Table 6.4 clearly indicates that Saudi informal investors prefer the outcome-based to the behaviour-based method. The cost of monitoring may be the main reason for this difference. Also, entrepreneurs' behaviour in small firms may not be easily observed.

3.2.3 Selection of venture

If the entrepreneur was cited as the most important aspect, other aspects of the business were also ranked highly in the informal investor's decision. Table 6.2 showed that market issues are also a serious concern among the other attributes of the business. This section examines the ranking of criteria related to the business and its market. Specifically, we test the null hypothesis:

H_0: *Informal investors depend on specific criteria to prevent the selection of low-quality ventures. However, they assign the same importance to different criteria related to the venture characteristics.*

Table 6.5 shows the statistical significance of the ranking of market criteria. This implies that the null hypothesis must be rejected. Three out of the first four primary requirements for Saudi informal investors about the business are related to market considerations. The business under evaluation should stimulate the existing market with a good potential growth rate and well-established distribution channels. Second, investors are attracted by the appropriate return that the venture is promising.

The low ranking of the protection of the product and the fact that government is the main consumer of the product may be explained by the nature of the Saudi economy. High-technology products, which have a patent production, are considered a minority among small and medium enterprises (SMEs). The government's role as a big consumer in the economy decreased after the completion of the infrastructure of the country and the decrease in its expenditures since the late 1980s.

Table 6.5 Friedman test to rank criteria related to other attributes of the business

Variables	Mean rank	Arith. mean	Std dev.	Median
1. Product stimulates existing market	9.20	4.56	0.82	5.00
2. Market has high growth rate	8.59	4.35	0.65	4.00
3. Appropriate return	8.40	4.35	0.65	4.00
4. Well-established distribution channels	7.69	4.04	0.90	4.00
5. Amount of finance sought	7.44	4.00	1.00	4.00
6. Investor is familiar with the industry	6.73	3.83	1.00	4.00
7. Low threat of early competition	6.25	3.71	0.97	4.00
8. Investment could be easily made liquid	5.57	3.37	1.13	3.00
9. Geographical area of the project	5.14	3.31	1.14	3.00
10. Industrial sector of the project	5.11	3.31	1.09	3.00
11. Protection of product	4.96	3.17	1.21	3.00
12. Government is a customer for the product	2.94	2.29	1.14	2.00

Most of the informal investor literature in the US and UK also supports these findings to a certain degree. Some studies found that informal investors prefer unique products (Osnabrugge, 1998; Mason and Harrison, 1992; Mason et al., 1996; Landström, 1995) in a niche market (Drake, 1995), have little interest in the 'proprietary nature of the product or service, or knowing the industry in which the venture will compete' (Haar et al., 1988, p. 21), and that unlike formal venture capital firms, informal investors are 'not interested in competitive insulation' (ibid., p. 11), although the literature on informal investors supports the importance of the market growth potential (Osnabrugge, 1998; Mason et al., 1991).

3.3 Co-investing

An important aspect of the deal origination is co-investing. According to Bygrave (1987), 'where there was more uncertainty, there was more co-investing' (p. 151). Hence, co-investing may be practised in this stage of the decision process to share information and expertise about investment opportunities, which implies better networking. In our survey, investors were asked how frequently they co-invested and the reasons that motivated them.

Table 6.6 presents the frequency of co-investing. A third of the sample is very active and nearly 50 per cent are sometimes co-investors. This means that more than 80 per cent of Saudi informal investors frequently co-invest. Only 10 per cent have never practised co-investment.

Table 6.6 The use of co-investing

	Never	Rarely	Sometimes	Often	Total
Frequency	15	12	72	54	153
Percentage	9.6	7.7	46.2	34.6	98.1
Valid percentage	9.8	7.8	47.1	35.3	100.0
Cumulative percentage	9.8	17.6	64.7	100.0	
Mean*	3.08	Std dev.	91	Median	3

* On a scale from 1–4, 4 being often.

This result may raise some misinterpretations when compared to the literature because frequency categories are not presented. According to Harrison and Mason (1992), UK informal investors are operating more independently: only 44 per cent have used syndication, compared with the US situation, where no more than 9 per cent of informal investors operate individually. On the other hand, Saudi investors usually co-invest with those who are well known to them, mostly friends (mean 3.69) or family members (mean 3.20); other formal organizations are less frequently reported.

Since Saudi informal investors co-invest frequently, the question that may be asked here is why this method is popular. The discussion with Saudi informal investors and the theoretical literature offer reasons that motivate informal investors to co-invested finance. The importance of the various reasons for co-investment is ranked in the case of Saudi Arabia in Table 6.7.

On the basis of these data, we test the following null hypothesis:

H_0: *Saudi investors give equal importance to the different reasons for co-investment.*

Table 6.7 indicates that Saudi investors co-invest mostly because they want to reduce the risk of adverse selection. Venture capitalists, upon finding an attractive venture, typically do not make a binding commitment to provide funds (Lerner, 1994). Rather, they send the proposal to other investors for their review. Another venture capitalist's interest in financing the firm may be an important factor for the lead investor to invest. Surprisingly, it is rare that investors co-invest to improve their relationship with their networks. This may be due to the fact that investors always co-invest with investors who are already known to them. Consequently, as the ranking of the reasons is statistically significant, the null hypothesis must be rejected.

Table 6.7 Friedman two-way ANOVA test to rank the importance of reason for co-investing

Reasons to syndicate	Arithmetic mean	Importance rank
To reduce the risk of choosing a low-quality venture	4.33	2.43
To provide different expertise to the venture	4.20	2.40
To improve the relationship to the investor's network	2.38	1.17

Test statistics:

N	135
Chi-square	172.28
DF	2
Asymp. sig.	0.000

3.4 Post-Investment Behaviour

In reality the problem regarding asymmetric information cannot be overcome, though time may help to clear up some of the unanswered questions about entrepreneurs and ventures. Investors may be unable to predict future events in order to write complete contracts that specify each party's obligations in all contingencies. So, investors are assumed to apply different methods in the *ex post* stage to provide sufficient flexibility so that re-negotiation may be obtained.

Three causes are found in the literature for the incompleteness of contracts: first, the transaction cost cause, which argues that the costs of contracting for unlikely events may well outweigh the benefits; second, the bounded rationality cause, which argues that agents either have only limited ability to evaluate elaborate contingencies or are not able to foresee unlikely contingencies. A third explanation is asymmetric information, which argues that a person may refrain from including a certain clause in a contract in order to signal his type (Spier, 1992; Hart and Holmstorm, 1987).

With this theoretical background in mind, investors' behaviour is examined at the post-investment stage to investigate how they control entrepreneurs' behaviour and re-negotiate contracts when new information arises. In this section two methods of post-investment activities among Saudi informal investors will be analysed:

1. Staging of finance.
2. Involvement with the venture.

3.4.1 Staging of finance

An important mechanism in post-investment relations between informal investors and entrepreneurs is staging of finance (Gompers, 1995). Sahlman (1990) notes that staged capital infusions are the most potent control mechanisms a venture capitalist can employ. Prospects for the firm are periodically re-evaluated. The shorter the duration of an individual round of financing, the more frequently the venture capitalist monitors the entrepreneur's progress and the greater the need to gather information. Sahlman also notes that staging of finance will provide the strongest possible incentive for the entrepreneur to work at least as hard as was projected. If the project succeeds in the first round, the price of the share will be higher for the second round, which will provide good motivation for the entrepreneur (Sahlman, 1988). This may also indicate that staging of finance will be an incentive for high-quality entrepreneurs and projects to accept venture capital financing. This will reduce adverse selection problems that investors may face in the first round due to the difficulty of knowing the true quality of the entrepreneur and the venture.

Informal Saudi investors' behaviour about staging of finance is discussed below.

Frequency of staging of finance Table 6.8 presents the frequency of staging of finance. Nearly 80 per cent are frequent users of staging. Only 11 per cent have never practised staging. This clearly indicates that staging is a popular method among Saudi informal investors.

In the literature in the case of the UK investors, Mason et al. (1995) found that 21 per cent of informal investors staged initial investments whilst Coveney

(1996) found that 55 per cent of his sample provided additional rounds of finance after the initial investment. This is also investigated by Osnabrugge's (1998) study, which found that 21 per cent of informal investors staged their investments with more frequency in the earlier stages of a venture. Unfortunately, no such research has been conducted on informal investors in the US.

Table 6.8 The use of staging of finance

	Never	Rarely	Sometimes	Often	Total
Frequency	18	12	81	45	156
Percentage	11.5	7.7	51.9	28.8	100.0
Valid percentage	11.5	7.7	51.9	28.8	100.0
Cumulative percentage	11.5	19.2	71.2	0.0	100.0
Mean*	2.98	Std dev.	0.9	Median	3

* On a scale from 1 to 4, 4 being often.

Motivations to stage finance It is important to discover why Saudi informal investors staged finance. Discussion with Saudi informal investors and the theoretical literature offer few reasons that motivate informal investors to stage finance. Saudi informal investors were asked to rank the importance of these reasons. To check the relative importance of different reasons, we formulate the null hypothesis as:

H_0: *Saudi informal investors give equal importance to different reasons to stage finance.*

Table 6.9 indicates that Saudi informal investors stage finance mostly to assess the quality of the venture and then to assess the quality of the entrepreneur. Consequently, as the ranking of the reasons is statistically significant, the null hypothesis must be rejected.

Uncertainty associated with venture quality criteria requires informal investors to look for mechanisms to reduce the risk of investing in a bad venture. The explanation for ranking second for the reason 'assess the quality of the entrepreneur' may be due to the fact that investors are very serious about wanting to be sure about the quality of the entrepreneur before making any commitment to the deal. This view was very clear when discussing overall ranking of all criteria in the previous section.

However, the results in Table 6.9 indicate some variation in the ranking of these reasons, which may imply that different groups among informal investors can be identified.

Table 6.9 Friedman test to rank the importance of the reasons for staging of finance

Reasons that drive staging of finance	Importance rank	Arithmetic mean	S.D.
Assess the quality of the venture	2.40	4.07	1.10
Assess the quality of the entrepreneur	2.11	3.83	1.05
Create an incentive and reduce monitoring costs	1.49	3.18	0.99

Test statistics:

N	132
Chi-square	70.77
DF	2
Asymp. sig.	0.000

3.4.2 Involvement with the venture

The involvement of informal investors in the ventures that they funded is expected to provide two benefits to the venture. First, informal investors' involvement plays an important role in devoting their management and technical experience to the venture. This creates the added value that is well known in such contracts. Second, informal investors' involvement with the venture creates a controlling and monitoring mechanism that helps informal investors to reduce the asymmetric information that exists in such relations.

Ranking of involvement methods Table 6.10 presents the ranking of the actual use of the methods of Saudi informal investors' involvement in their investee firms. It clearly indicates that Saudi informal investors are rarely involved in daily operations and rarely work on a full-time basis. Also, working on a part-time basis seems not to be practised regularly by informal investors. On the other hand, informal investors keep in contact with the investee firms through other involvement methods. They place more importance on involvement through consulting the venture as and when needed, monitoring periodic reports, and monitoring the firm from within the board of directors. Also, investors may contact the firm to provide consultation but in reality this will give them more access to the firm. So consultation may be viewed as an important mechanism to gain more control and monitoring.

The international informal investors' literature documents well the active, hands-on involvement of informal investors in their investee firms (Mason and Harrison, 1992; Mason et al., 1991; Freear et al., 1990, 1991, 1993; Wetzel,

1983; Landström, 1993; Coveney, 1996; Osnabrugge, 1998). However, the literature has shown informal investors to be active in the running of the business instead of more strategic and passive roles such as monitoring financial statements and involvement in the board of directors. This does not mean, however, that informal investors are involved in the daily operations (Osnabrugge, 1998).

Table 6.10 Friedman two-way ANOVA test to rank the actual use of involvement methods

Methods of involvement	Frequent use rank	Arithmetic mean
Consulting as needed	5.09	4.33
Review periodic reports and general meeting	5.05	4.29
Board of directors	4.24	3.50
Work part-time with the firm	2.54	2.06
No involvement	2.24	1.77
Work full-time with the firm	1.85	1.38

Test statistics:

N	156
Chi-square	532.914
DF	5
Asymp. sig.	0.000

Staged finance and involvement in the investee firms are seen to provide an important mechanism to reduce the asymmetric information that is clearly associated with this kind of finance and also to support the added value that investors may provide to the investee firm. Providing capital to the venture through the staging method is considered by most informal investors as an important approach to reducing asymmetric information surrounding the entrepreneur and the venture quality. Also, it creates an incentive for the entrepreneur to work harder. This will lead to a better re-evaluation in the second-stage financing, which the entrepreneur will appreciate. Involvement of investors in the operations of the venture is also practised widely among Saudi informal investors. However, involvement does not mean that investors are involved in the daily running of the business. Instead, they monitor the business through consultation and participation in the board of directors. Saudi informal investors are more involved in those monitoring activities which do not require active hands-on involvement.

NOTE

1. According to Kadushin (1968), 'A snowball is a device for obtaining an open-ended sociometric starting with a given list, usually a sample of some universe, each respondent is asked to name several others who are then interviewed and so on' (in Hofman, 1972, p. 77). However, this study utilized the mailing and snowball methods, which resulted in a sample of 150 informal investors who were approached and studied.

REFERENCES

Akerlof, G. (1970), 'The Market for "Lemons": Quality, Uncertainty and the Market Mechanism', *Quarterly Journal of Economics*, **84**, 488–500.

Aram, J.D. (1989), 'Attitudes and Behaviours of Informal Investors Toward Early-Stage Investments, Technology Based Ventures and Coinvestors', *Journal of Business Venturing*, **4**, 333–47.

Barney, J.B. and W.G. Ouchi (1986), *Organizational Economics*, San Francisco, CA: Jossey-Bass.

Baty, G.B. (1964), 'The Initial Financing of the New Research-based Enterprises in New England', Boston, MA: Federal Reserve Bank of Boston.

Boocock, G. and M. Woods (1997), 'The Evaluation Criteria used by Venture Capitalists: Evidence from a UK Venture Fund', *International Business Journal*, **16** (1), 36–57.

Bygrave, W.D. (1987), 'Syndicated Investments By Venture Capital Firms: A Networking Perspective', *Journal of Business Venturing*, **2**, 139–54.

Carter, R.B. and H.E. Van Auken (1994), 'Venture Capital Firms' Preferences for Projects in Particular Stages of Development', *Journal of Small Business Management*, January. Cited in Mark Osnabrugge (1998), 'The Financing of Entrepreneurial Firms in the UK: A Comparison of Business Angels and Venture Capitalist Investment Procedures', unpublished PhD thesis, Oxford University, UK.

Coase, R.H. (1960), 'The Problem of Social Cost', *Journal of Law and Economics*, **3**, 1–44.

Copeland, T. and J.F. Weston (1988), *Financial Theory and Corporate Policy*, 3rd edn, Reading, MA: Addison-Wesley.

Coveney, P. (1996), 'Informal Investment in Britain: An Examination of the Behaviours, Characteristics, Motives and Preferences of British Business Angels', Oxford University, unpublished doctoral thesis. Cited in Mark Osnabrugge (1998), 'The Financing of Entrepreneurial Firms in the UK: A Comparison of Business Angels and Venture Capitalist Investment Procedures', unpublished PhD thesis, Oxford University, UK.

Drake, T. (1995), 'An Investor's Check List', *Venture Capital Report*, October.

Fama, E.F. (1970), 'Efficient Capital Markets: A Review of Theory and Empirical Evidence', *Journal of Finance*, **25**, 383–417.

Fiet, J.O. (1991), 'Managing Investments in Specific Information: A Comparison of Business Angels and Venture Capital Firms', unpublished PhD thesis, Texas A and M University.

Freear, J., J. Sohl and W. Wetzel (1990), 'Raising Venture Capital: Entrepreneurs' View of the Process', *Frontiers of Entrepreneurship Research*, Wellesley, MA: Babson College.

Freear, J., J. Sohl and W. Wetzel (1991), 'Raising Venture Capital to Ginance Growth', *Frontiers of Entrepreneurship Research*, Wellesley, MA: Babson College.

Freear, J., J. Sohl and W. Wetzel (1993), 'Summary: Angel Profiles: A Longitudinal Study', *Frontiers of Entrepreneurship Research*, Wellesley, MA: Babson College.

Gaston, R.J. (1989), *Finding Private Venture Capital for Your Firm: A Complete Guide*, New York: Wiley.

Gompers, P. (1995), 'Optimal Investment, Monitoring, and the Staging of Venture Capital', *Journal of Finance*, December, 1461–89.

Gorman, M. and W.A. Sahlman (1989), 'What Do Venture Capitalist Do?', *Journal of Business Venturing*, **4**, 231–48.

Haar, E., J. Starr and I. Macmillan (1988), 'Informal Risk Capital Investors: Investment Patterns on The East Coast of The USA', *Journal of Business Venturing*, **3**, 11–29.

Hall, P. (1988), 'Investment Evaluation in UK Venture Capital Funds: the Appraisal of Risk and Return', unpublished MBA thesis, London: City College.

Harrison, T. and C. Mason (1992), 'International Perspectives on The Supply of Informal Venture Capital', *Journal of Business Venturing*, **7**, 459–75.

Hart, O. (1995), *Firms Contracts, and Financial Structures*, Oxford, UK: Oxford University Press.

Hart, O. and B. Holmstorm (1987), 'The Theory of Contracts', Chapter 3 in T.F. Bewley (ed.), *Advances in Economics Theory, Fifth World Congress*, Cambridge, MA: Cambridge University Press.

Hofman, C.A. (1972), 'The Venture Capital Investment Process: A Particular Aspect of Regional Economic Development', unpublished PhD thesis, University of Texas at Austin.

Jensen, M.C. and W.H. Meckling (1976), 'Theory of the Firm: Managerial Behaviour, Agency Costs and Ownership Structure', *Journal of Financial Economics*, **3**, 305–60.

Kadushin, C. (1968), 'Power, Influence and Social Circles: A New Methodology for Studying Opinion-Makers', *American Sociological Review*, **33** (5), October.

Kanellos, M. (1996), 'Finding Venture Capital is no Easy Road', *Computer Reseller News*, **702**, 145–46. Cited in Mark Osnabrugge (1998), op. cit.

Landström, H. (1993), 'Informal Risk Capital in Sweden and Some International Comparisons', *Journal of Business Venturing*, **8**, 525–40.

Landström, H. (1995), 'A Pilot Study of the Investment Decision-Making Behaviour of Informal Investors in Sweden', *Journal of Small Business Management*, July.

Leland, H. and D. Pyle (1977), 'Information Asymmetries, Financial Structure, and Financial Intermediation', *Journal of Finance*, **32**, 371–87.

Lerner, J. (1994), 'The Syndication of Venture Capital Investments', *Financial Management*, **23** (3), Autumn, 16–27.

Macmillan, I., R. Siegel and S. Narasimha (1985), 'Criteria Used by Venture Capitalists', *Journal of Business Venturing*, **1** (1), 119–28.

Macmillan, I., L. Zemann and Subbanarasimha (1987), 'Criteria Distinguishing Successful from Unsuccessful Ventures in the Venture Screening Process', *Journal of Business Venturing*, **2** (2), 123–37.

Macmillan, I.C., D.M. Kulow and R. Khoylian (1988), 'Venture Capitalists' Involvement in their Investments: Extent and Performance', *Journal of Business Venturing*, **4**, 27–47.

Mason, C.M., R.T. Harrison and J. Chaloner (1991), *Informal Risk Capital in the UK: A Study of Investors Characteristics, Investment Preferences and Investment Decision-*

Making, Venture Finance Project, Working Paper No. 2, University of Southampton, UK, and University of Ulster, NI, Business School.

Mason, C.M. and R.T. Harrison (1992), 'The Supply of Equity Finance in the UK: A Strategy for Closing the Equity Gap', *Entrepreneurship and Regional Development*, **4**, 357–80.

Mason, C.M. and R.T. Harrison (1993), 'Strategies for Expanding the Informal Venture Capital: An Evaluation of a British Initiative', *Frontiers of Entrepreneurship Research*, Wellesley, MA: Babson College.

Mason, C.M. and R.T. Harrison (1996), 'Why Business Angels Say No: A Case Study of Opportunities Rejected by Informal Investor Syndicate', *International Small Business Journal*, **14** (2), March, 35–51.

Mason, C.M. and A. Rogers (1996), *Understanding the Business Angels' Investment Decision*, Venture Finance Research Project, Working Paper No. 14, University of Southampton, UK and University of Ulster, NI, Business School.

Mason, C.M., R.T. Harrison and P. Allen (1995), *Informal Venture Capital: A Study of the Investment Process, the Post-Investment Experience and Investment Performance*, Venture Finance Research Project, Working Paper No. 12, University of Southampton, UK and University of Ulster, NI, Business School.

Osnabrugge, Mark (1998), 'The Financing of Entrepreneurial Firms in the UK: A Comparison of Business Angels and Venture Capitalist Investment Procedures', unpublished PhD thesis, Oxford University, UK.

Pence, C.C. (1982), *How Venture Capitalists Make Investment Decisions*, Ann Arbor, MI: UMI Research Press.

Pettit R.R. and R.F. Singer (1985), 'Small Business Finance: A Research Agenda', *Financial Management*, **14** (3), 47–59.

Poindexter, J.B. (1976), 'The Efficiency of Financial Markets: The Venture Capital Case', unpublished PhD thesis, New York University.

Riding, A., P. Dalcin, L. Duxburg, G. Haines and R. Safrata (1993), *Informal Investor in Canada: The Identification of Salient Characteristics*, Ottawa, Canada: Carleton University.

Ross, S. (1977), 'The Determination of Financial Structure: The Incentive Signaling Approach', *Bell Journal of Economics*, **8**, 23–40.

Rubenstein, A.H. (1958), 'Problem of Financing and Managing New Research-Based Enterprises in New England', Babson, MA: Federal Reserve Bank of Boston. Cited in W.E. Wetzel (1987), 'The Informal Venture Capital Market: Aspects of Scale and Market Efficiency', *Journal of Business Venturing*, **2**, 299–313.

Sahlman, W.A. (1988), 'Aspects of Financial Contracting in Venture Capital', *Journal of Applied Corporate Finance*, **1** (2), 23–36.

Sahlman, W.A. (1990), 'The Structure and Governance of Venture-Capital Organisations', *Journal of Financial Economics*, **27**, 473–521.

Sappington, D.E. (1991), 'Incentives in Principal–Agent Relationships', *Journal of Economic Perspectives*, **5** (2), 45–66.

Spier, K.E. (1992), 'Incomplete Contracts and Signalling', *Rand Journal of Economics*, **23** (3), 432–43.

Stevenson, H. and P. Coveney (1994), 'Survey of Business Angels: Fallacies Corrected and Six Distinct Types of Angel', Henley-on-Thames, UK: Venture Capital Report Ltd. Cited in Mark Osnabrugge (1998), op. cit.

Stiglitz, J. (1985), 'Information and Economic Analysis: A Perspective', *Economic Journal*, **95**, 21–41.

Tyebjee, T. and A. Bruno (1984), 'A Model of Venture Capital Investment Activity', *Management Science*, **30** (9), September, 1051–67.

Wetzel, W.E. (1983), 'Angels and Informal Risk Capital', *Sloan Management Review*, Summer, 23–34.

Wetzel, J and. C. Seymour (1981), *Informal Risk Capital in New England*, USA: Centre for industrial and Institutional Development, University of New Hampshire, USA.

COMMENTS

Sultan Abou-Ali

The chapter deals with one of the very important issues in Islamic economics from both the theoretical and practical points of view. I believe that the abolition of usury (*ribā*) has to do more with the equity of income distribution than any other measure (such as the allocation of resources or the efficiency of capital utilization). Hence the investigation into the behaviour of the informal risk capital investor, especially with regard to the problem of asymmetry of information in profit/loss-sharing (PLS) contracts sheds important light on the determinants of this investment.

As the chapter points out, the PLS contracts are not, at present, widely used in Islamic banking. This, in my opinion, is due to several reasons, of which three are particularly important. First, the administration of ventures under PLS requires special skills not yet available on a wide scale to commercial banks. Second, banking laws enforce rules and controls on some banking activities and on the allocation of bank's funds in direct investment unless they are merchant banks. These rules of control and supervision were developed for regular banking practices. Islamic banking requires revision of these rules to be adequate for its proper functioning. Third, and most important, PLS requires the existence of two parties ready to execute the deal on the same basis. Experience shows that depositors in Islamic banks are ready to deal on the basis of PLS. Therefore, the supply of funds is relatively abundant. The majority of the users of funds (the demand side), on the other hand, do not accept this way of doing business. They prefer to know the cost of funds in advance. The result is that Islamic banks had to resort to techniques other than PLS (for example mark-up) in order properly to utilize the available deposits. In all cases, the problem of the asymmetry of information will arise whenever the supplier and user of funds are different from each other, regardless of the mode of investment (loans, PLS, and so on). Most of the non-performing loans in ordinary banks are caused by the problems of adverse selection and/or moral hazard associated with the asymmetry of information. It is, thus, interesting to investigate the nature and consequences of this problem in the case of informal risk capital investors. This is the subject of the chapter with application to Saudi Arabia.

1. Sources of Data

The sample size used in the chapter comprises 156 observations. The population size, however, is not mentioned. Similarly, the way the sample was drawn is not explained. The appropriate size of the sample is not assessed. This information is important and necessary to evaluate the reliability of the results of the analysis.

The tabulation of the results shows that the number of respondents varies between 135 and 156, a difference which amounts to about 13 per cent of the sample size. The reasons for non-responding and the effect of the variation warrant an explanation.

2. Definition of the Informal Investor

The chapter does not explicitly define what is meant by 'informal risk capital investors' in the Saudi Arabian case. I take it that the term 'informal' is used in contrast to 'formal' or 'institutional' investors. If this is so, 'informal' investors would include a very wide range of individuals and firms. It might include those persons who are self-employed and do not engage a *muḍārib* (an entrepreneur) as well as those who would employ one. It is evident that in the first case the problem of asymmetry of information will not arise and should thus be excluded. Also the cases where the informal investors invest in portfolio selection are different from the cases of direct investment. Both, none the less, might be liable to the risks of asymmetric information, albeit in a different way.

Grouping the informal investors in one category may be misleading. It is normal to expect that the behaviour of the investors would be affected by several variables, such as level of education, size of wealth, location of residence (urban, rural), availability of formal financial institutions (banks, stock exchange, non-banking financial intermediaries), attitudes towards risk, and the like. The chapter dealt with the traits of the entrepreneur chosen by the investors, but did not explicitly deal with the differences in the characteristics of the informal investor himself. It would have been interesting to analyse the results in a double classification, that is, by type of both investor and entrepreneur. This suggestion would also apply to the other attributes of the venture such as product market, return, liquidity of investment, industrial sector, and so on. The results would have been enriched by breaking down informal investors according to their attitudes and characteristics.

3. The Results

The chapter tests five main hypotheses. We discuss these hypotheses and their results one by one.

(a) The first (null) hypothesis: 'Information sources are equally important to Saudi informal investors.' Eight sources of information are identified. These are: active personal search; friends; business associates; banks; real-estate agencies; entrepreneurs; consultation agencies; and chambers of commerce. It was found that active personal search is the most important source and that the value of the chi-square (about 204) leads to rejecting the null hypothesis. In addition to the two explanations given by the authors (low number of available investment opportunities and the conservative view of Saudi investors towards risk), a third one may be provided. That is, Saudi informal investors decide to invest in the areas of their own preference and then substantiate that from other sources. That is to say, that they may have a prior idea of the type of investment suitable to their preferences regardless of the availability of information about investment opportunities or market and agency risks they might face.

As shown in Table 6.1, the values of the median and the arithmetic mean need verification. The same would apply to Table 6.3. Furthermore, the third explanation for the low quality of ventures that are seeking equity finance (crowding out businesses that are looking for financing) seems to be unlikely in view of the relative abundance of funds in Saudi Arabia.

(b) The second (null) hypothesis: 'Informal investors depend on specific criteria to prevent the selection of low-quality entrepreneurs. However, they assign the same importance to different criteria related to the entrepreneur's characteristics.' The analysis of the questionnaires led to the rejection of the null hypothesis. It finds that the track record of the entrepreneur is the top priority in evaluating his performance. This is an expected outcome.

(c) The third (null) hypothesis: 'Informal investors depend on specific criteria to prevent the selection of low-quality ventures. However, they assign the same importance to different criteria related to the venture characteristics.' The test of statistical significance shows that those informal investors do not use specific criteria to avoid adverse selection. Consequently, the null hypothesis is rejected. It was found that the investors consider the product market as the most important criterion. Furthermore, the most important elements related to the product market are: stimulating the existing market, high rate of growth of the market and the appropriate return on investment. This conclusion is again in conformity with the theory of rational investment.

(d) The fourth (null) hypothesis: 'Saudi investors give equal importance to the different reasons for co-investment.' The authors reject this null hypothesis and find that co-investing is done to reduce the risk of adverse selection. This result seems to be expected and conforms to the previous observation regarding the availability of financial resources in Saudi Arabia.

(e) The fifth (null) hypothesis relates to using staging of finance as a method for obtaining new information about the venture. The other method dealt with is the degree of involvement in the venture. This hypothesis tries to assess the methods of safeguarding against the asymmetry of information at the post-investment stage. It is found that the most important factors are: assessment of the quality of the venture, followed by the assessment of the quality of the entrepreneur. These seem to be plausible and expected results.

Involvement with the venture might have two purposes, namely: increasing the value added; and controlling and monitoring the venture as a means of reducing the consequences of asymmetric information. The chapter does not indicate the purpose of involvement in the venture in the case of Saudi informal investors. However, it points to the various methods of involvement. The method which obtained the highest rank is 'consulting as needed'. This actually means that the investor is not strongly involved with the venture, since he would not express any view if he were not consulted. The highest involvement with the venture would be 'work full-time with the firm'. This class acquired the lowest rank (Table 6.10). It is also reasonable to assume that 'review periodic reports and general meetings' does not constitute strong involvement with the firm. Therefore, the methods of involvement with the venture which might hedge against the asymmetry of information are: member of the board of directors; and work part- or full-time with the firm. The total of the ranks of these three methods is 8.15 out of 21, that is, 39 per cent. This makes it hard to believe that Saudi informal investors use the method of involvement with the venture as a technique to avoid the risks of the asymmetry of information. In view of these comments, further research on the methods by which Saudi informal investors solve the problem of the asymmetry of information in the post-investment stage is required.

4. Conclusion

The chapter investigated an important issue in Islamic economics. It further sharpened the understanding of the behaviour of Saudi informal investors towards the problem of the asymmetry of information. It shows that this problem exists in Muslim communities as elsewhere, contrary to what some researchers might claim. Holding some information from the other party in PLS contracts seems to be a common feature of human behaviour regardless of religion and culture. The chapter is commended for using questionnaires to test the various hypotheses. More intensive use of this method in economics would make this science more realistic and account for cultural variations. However, the value of the chapter would be enhanced by including a section on the implications and consequences of its findings for Islamic economics.

7. Choice between debt and equity contracts and asymmetrical information: some empirical evidence

Kazem Sadr and Zamir Iqbal*

1. INTRODUCTION

Although an Islamic financial system offers a combination of both equity- and non-equity-based instruments, the system's preference for equity contracts often raises concerns regarding its efficiency and stability.[1] It has been asserted that prohibition of debt contracts creates an incentive for Islamic banks to concentrate their asset portfolios on low-risk trade financing instruments when faced with asymmetric information.[2] This chapter presents empirical evidence based on the last 15 years of data from the Agricultural Bank of Iran (ABI) which demonstrates that reduction in information asymmetry and increased direct participation by the financier led to a preference for equity participation over lower-risk short-term instruments, thus improving efficiency.

The conclusions drawn in the chapter are significant for (i) the choice of contract in a world with enhanced information and monitoring, (ii) the importance of high returns to investment in information-gathering and monitoring for reducing information asymmetry and thus improving the efficiency and viability of a financial intermediary operating on Islamic principles, and (iii) optimal portfolio composition of an Islamic bank.[3] Section 2 discusses the theoretical foundations of financial intermediation with asymmetric information and its relevance to Islamic finance. Section 3 analyses procedural and policy changes undertaken by the Agricultural Bank of Iran to reduce information asymmetry and its impact on the composition of its portfolio. Finally, a summary of results and conclusion is given in section 4.

* The views expressed in this chapter are of the authors only and do not reflect the views of their institutions.

2. ASYMMETRIC INFORMATION AND PORTFOLIO CHOICES

It is critical to understand why conventional banks exist, why they prefer to enter into debt contracts, and what disadvantages as well as advantages are associated with such contracts. Traditionally, the existence of banks in an economic system is considered to be justified because of their ability to intermediate between the preference of lenders (investors/depositors) for short-term liquid assets and the preference of borrowers (entrepreneurs) for long-term illiquid liabilities by transforming maturities and doing so at a reduced aggregate cost of gathering and monitoring information on borrowers. Within a risky and uncertain environment, information-gathering is necessary to improve the quality of decision-making as well as to optimize the effects of actions of economic agents. Although financial intermediaries specialize in information collection to reduce this uncertainty to some extent, such reduction is always incomplete because information production involves costs such as the cost of searching, administrating, monitoring, screening, verifying, and so on. Specialization in information production involves economies of scale and/or scope in case of non-convexities in the cost structure of financial intermediaries.[4]

Furthermore, banks play the crucial role of acting as a screening device for lending and the allocation of credit. Asymmetric information literature suggests that banks, as intermediaries, not only save on duplicated monitoring costs, but also on indirect costs of transmitting information through signals. By diversifying risks across assets, banks are able to provide signals at lower costs. Ascertaining and monitoring that an entrepreneur is creditworthy requires resources, and providing or guaranteeing credit entails risk-taking. Such monitoring is costly, especially if duplicated by individual investors. Diamond (1984) develops an explanation of financial intermediation which is based on minimizing the cost of monitoring. With asymmetric information, intermediation arises endogenously as part of an incentive-compatible contracting arrangement that economizes on monitoring costs.

The question of why banks prefer fixed-rate contracts has been much harder to explain.[5] An explanation of a role for debt is that it minimizes the information requirement of a financial contract when the performance of the project is not observable by the financial institution.[6] Diamond (1984, 1996) concludes that the best way to delegate monitoring is for the delegated monitor, that is, the bank, to issue unmonitored debt, which will be subject to liquidation costs. He demonstrates that the optimal unmonitored financial contract between a borrower and a lender is a debt contract that involves positive expected deadweight liquidation costs, which are necessary to provide incentives for repayment.[7] Whereas the lenders' capital is provided protection through bankruptcy laws, borrowers are encouraged to enter into debt contracts by granting tax deductibility for interest payments.

Both debt and equity contracts suffer from adverse selection and moral hazard problems under asymmetric information but to differing degrees.[8] Since Islamic modes of finance are primarily equity-based, it is often claimed by critics of the Islam system that under asymmetric information it will be subject to higher degree of adverse selection and moral hazard. In the case of the debt-based conventional system the debtor is obliged to pay back the principal and the interest, regardless of the outcome of the project, whereas in Islamic banking both parties share all the benefits and losses and, therefore, the negligence of one party affects the profitability of the whole venture.[9]

The degree of adverse selection and moral hazard is directly linked to the degree of information asymmetry and market completeness. Analytical work demonstrates that under perfect information and a high degree of market completeness, equity finance is subject to less adverse selection and moral hazard effects.[10] Suppose that the risk-neutral lenders (financiers) and potential shareholders (equity investors) have the same level of information on groups of firms, that is, about the characteristics of the firms, their industry, the record of payment, bank relations, and so on, but do not have information about the risk characteristics of individual members within groups. They can sort among groups of borrowers those whose expected productivities are the same but cannot sort them within groups according to their degrees of riskiness. Under these conditions, the lenders (financier/banks) will ration out borrowers with lower payoff and high variations even though they are the most productive. Banks, unlike equity investors, will avoid financing new, productive groups of borrowers who may be perceived to be risky even though the banks are risk-neutral. They may lower economic growth by reducing opportunities to innovate and impede industrial adjustment in developing countries.[11]

The choice of debt or equity contracts as part of a financial intermediary's asset portfolio is also determined by the degree of its risk aversion. Analytical work suggests that in the case of both risk aversion and risk neutrality, under perfect information it is inefficient to select a debt contract over equity. Under risk aversion, there is no straightforward dominance of the fixed-rate debt contract over an equity contract. Although a fixed-rate debt contract minimizes the monitoring costs, it does not spread the risk optimally. On the other hand, for a sufficiently high degree of risk aversion, an equity contract may dominate a debt contract.[12] Similar to risk aversion, if preferences are risk-neutral and the choice of risk level is unobservable, it would be an inefficient choice to sacrifice higher-mean asset payoffs.[13]

Therefore, reduction of information asymmetry is a prerequisite for the implementation of an equity-based system. A successful implementation will require financial institutions to invest additional resources in information-collecting activities.[14] Additional monitoring and supervision required to reduce information asymmetry come at an additional operating cost which is considered by some to be a deadweight cost without creating extra value and thus handicaps Islamic banks in competition with conventional banks.[15] Proponents of Islamic banking counter-argue that additional monitoring costs are offset by the benefits of supervision, which creates at least three advantages.[16] First, better monitoring and closer supervision can overcome moral hazard and adverse selection problems. Second, stronger supervision provides greater knowledge of the market conditions and environment under which the enterprise subject of the contract has to operate and this allows the supervisors greater ability to forecast further market developments. Finally, stronger supervision provides broader knowledge of comparative advantages of the industry, region or locality in which the resources are invested, which makes it possible to obtain better estimates of the return to further investment in the industry or region under consideration.

To summarize, a financial intermediary's decision to enter into a debt or an equity contract on its assets side is greatly influenced by the degree of information asymmetry. As information asymmetry is reduced, it will be more efficient to prefer equity to debt. The extra cost of information generation, supervision and monitoring is to be considered as an investment which entails selection of superior projects and efficient allocation of resources.

3. CASE STUDY: AGRICULTURAL BANK OF IRAN

The Agricultural Bank of Iran (ABI) supplies funds to the agricultural sector of the Islamic Republic of Iran through a wide range of instruments. Since the implementation of the Interest-Free Banking Law (IFBL) in 1983, ABI has switched from conventional modes of financing to instruments compatible with Islamic principles. ABI's asset portfolio contains a well-diversified mix of instruments ranging from low-risk products to high-risk equity participation. This bank enjoys a high recovery rate every year. In 1996, 80 per cent recovery rate of the total outstanding debt left over before and after implementation of the IFBL was reported. Recovery rate on Islamic contracts is impressive and ranges between 95 and 99 per cent.[17]

An examination of past balance sheets reveals very interesting facts which are relevant to the theory of Islamic finance. In the late 1980s and early 1990s, ABI's management decided to undertake several initiatives to improve its service, enhance efficiency and increase returns. These initiatives included investment in supervision and monitoring, a reduction in operating and processing costs, and investment in research and development. The results are remarkable, demonstrating that with increased information-sharing and monitoring, a permanent shift has taken place in the composition of the ABI's asset portfolio. The proportion of equity participation (*mushārakah*) in the ABI's asset portfolio has increased substantially.

Through continuous and frequent supervision, the ABI has established a very solid and trusting relationship with the partners. By investing in supervision, the bank seems to be able to learn about profitable investment opportunities in various agricultural regions and also about the entrepreneurial and moral characteristics of its partners. The bank uses this expertise to improve over time the allocation of its capital resources among the best alternative projects and also to the best-qualified farmers. The fact that the bank has continued monitoring of its customers over time, while effectively expanding the domain of its activities, reveals that it has enjoyed the benefits of close supervision, and that this monitoring has been a profitable investment in gaining new and better information.[18]

Effective and continuous supervision accompanied by the provision of technical assistance and monitoring enabled the ABI to gain up-to-date information and the expertise required to cope with uncertainties and asymmetric information problems that may be associated with Islamic contracts, particularly *mushārakah*. One indicator of 'proper selection' of the ABI from many potential entrepreneurs because of knowledge gained through supervision is the collection of dues in provinces that were destroyed by Iraqi troops during the eight-year war. The buildings and all the files and records of the ABI branches located in these provinces were destroyed. After the war, when those units resumed activity, they had no written claims over any of their partners. However, the latter all willingly submitted a copy of their own contracts to the bank and showed their own records, from which bank's claims could be worked out and collected. Enjoying such a trusting relationship with the partners, the ABI's managers could easily shift to profit/loss-sharing arrangements with them.

With the objectives of reducing operating costs, enhancing efficiency of processing contracts and improving monitoring and supervision, the ABI management also undertook the task of thoroughly revising the procedural codes of contracts with the help of a task force.[19] In designing new procedures, cost-cutting was not the only objective. An effort was also made to minimize the bank customer's time for preparing the necessary documents or visiting the bank. Time required to conclude a transaction or contract starts the moment a farmer approaches a branch of the bank and applies for finance and extends until the end of the period during which the application is processed in different departments of that branch. This process includes economic appraisal, payment of the fund, supervision, transfer of the venture to the applicant after its completion, and collection of dues. Long-term contracts are expected to take more time since the use of funds supplied is continuously supervised by the ABI to ensure that they are spent as specified in the contract.

Table 7.1 shows the number of steps that the ABI omitted from the codes of procedure of alternative Islamic modes of finance during 1990–95.[20] As can be noted, the main cost-saving and reduction in processing time is in the case of *mushārakah* financing, for which total time required to complete the contract has been reduced by 36 per cent, and by at least 20 per cent for other types of contracts.[21] Short-term contracts that are often used to provide the operating costs of farming are not usually supervised on site. This is why forward purchase, a short-term transaction, takes the least time for the ABI. *Mushārakah*, *juʿālah* and instalment sale of machinery are long-term contracts; among these *juʿālah* is the most time-consuming and therefore the most expensive method of finance for the bank.

Table 7.1 Number of steps and average time needed to conclude a contract

	Number of steps			Time consumed (minutes)		
Modes of finance	1990	1995	Saving (%)	1990	1995	Saving (%)
Forward purchase	229	135	41	557	406	27
Instalment sale of raw materials	272	182	33	668	506	24
Instalment sale of machinery	266	222	17	731	586	20
Mushārakah	339	201	41	1 171	749	36
Juʿālah	N/A	N/A	N/A	1 242	N/A	N/A

In addition to reductions in operating costs, the task force also undertook initiatives to re-engineer the process and code of procedures to enhance monitoring and to encourage equity contracts (*mushārakah*) with farmers. The task force (consisting of representatives from different departments in the ABI) benefited from the support of the board of directors and could contribute greatly to expanding the application of various contracts. In the past, the ABI has made substantial efforts to suit *juʿālah* to the credit needs of the agricultural sector but, due to its high associated transaction costs, the task force decided to investigate alternative instruments such as *mushārakah*.

Whereas Islamic finance offers a range of basic building blocks, each legitimate type of contract has certain characteristics and is suitable for a particular usage. A *mushārakah* arrangement is the most general and versatile form of contract that can be used for all productive and service activities in which the parties involved jointly share the benefits and costs of the enterprise.

The fact that the ABI could substitute *mushārakah* for *juʿālah* without any substantial effort demonstrates the point. An advantage of *mushārakah* over *juʿālah* and/or instalment contract between the ABI and its customers is that there are no third parties. For example, in the case of *juʿālah*, in addition to the bank and the farmer, it is necessary to have the consent of an agent who guarantees to carry out the job specified in the contract. Thus the agreement is signed by three parties, according to the required codes of procedure in the ABI. In the case of an instalment sale, a separate firm supplies the commodity being demanded. The bank buys it from the seller for the farmer. If, however, the seller is delinquent, the contract becomes vulnerable. This problem often occurs when the seller is a government agency, yet it will not prevent a *mushārakah* arrangement from being operational due to the nature and respective terms of the agreement in the deal. Here, the farmer is not only the receiver of the fund, but is also the sole decision-maker.

In 1990 an important proposal was put forward by the task force to reduce the transaction costs of *mushārakah*. It suggested the elimination of the registration of this contract in the Notary Public Office. This procedural change saved considerable time and expense for the bank's partners. More important, until 1990, *mushārakah* was used to finance long-term investments but, upon the task force's recommendation, it was extended to finance short-term activities and provide the operating costs of farmers. This is the most significant change for extending the applicability of *mushārakah*, making it the dominant method of finance in the ABI since 1990 (Table 7.2). In the meantime, the collateral requirement was further reduced. For applications under 1.5 billion rials a third-party guarantee is sufficient. For a larger sum, real estate is required as collateral. However, if the cash capital demanded exceeds the value of the farmer's estate, the difference can be secured by promissory notes. Furthermore, when an agreement is reached between the bank and a farmer, it can be renewed up to three times without any new or additional security. The original collateral presented is sufficient for up to three years or three renewals.

In relation to the significance of scientific research, ten research projects were completed in collaboration with different universities. Measures were also taken to launch new research projects, including analysis of rural financial markets, transaction costs of financial contracts for farmers, and optimal cash management. The last project helped to maintain the minimum amount of cash required at each branch at each period, in order to supply maximum credit within available resources.

The results of enhanced supervision, simplification of processes and research and development are reflected in the portfolio composition of the ABI. Table 7.2 lists the structure of the assets portfolio of the ABI for the last 15 years, giving clear evidence of increased share of *mushārakah* contracts since 1990 after the introduction of the measures mentioned above.

Table 7.2 Methods of finance in the Agricultural Bank of Iran (%)

	1984	1985	1986	1987	1988	1989	1990	1991	1992	1993	1994	1995	1996	1997	1998
Total funds supplied (billion rials	150.8	199.5	201.9	279.9	382.6	444.3	.626.4	956.9	1 076.4	1 752.1	2 363.7	3 361.9	3 695.2	5 288.2	6 791)
Qarḍ al-ḥasan	55.2	57.0	58.1	57.4	51.6	43.8	33.1	17.2	17.6	16.4	12.7	8.7	7.75	5.3	4.3
Instalment sale	35.4	30.7	28.5	28.4	30.8	33.6	36.5	42.4	25.7	21.7	20.6	17.1	16.7	23.9	28.3
Forward purchase	6.3	8.6	9.6	9.4	10.2	12.6	12.1	12.1	8.5	8.7	8.7	11.8	8.6	12.6	18.6
Juʿālah	1.3	2.8	3.3	4.2	6.0	8.3	7.3	2.3	0.6	0.1	0.1	0.1	–	0.1	0.1
Mushārakah	–	0.8	0.4	0.5	0.7	1.2	4.0	16.4	38.3	42.4	41.8	44.8	48.1	42.4	32.0
Muḍārabah	1.8	0.1	0.1	0.1	0.2	0.4	6.9	9.3	9.3	10.5	16.0	17.3	18.7	15.7	16.6
Hire purchase	–	–	–	–	0.5	0.1	0.1	0.3	–	0.2	0.1	0.2	0.2	–	0.1
TOTAL	100	100	100	100	100	100	100	100	100	100	100	100	100	100	100

Source: *Annual Reports* of the Agricultural Bank of Iran.

A review of the trend in the portfolio composition of the ABI shows a well-diversified portfolio encompassing a wide range of instruments. In its initial years after the Interest-Free Banking Law, few partnership arrangements such as civil partnership or *muḍārabah* were used. Instalment sale, the contract best known by the public, had the dominant role in financing agricultural activities at that stage. In a period of three years the share of *juʿālah* contracts in providing long-term credit became noticeable. Its share rose to 8 per cent in 1989. However, its growth soon declined and civil partnership or *mushārakah* arrangements took over its role. As of 1989, and due to changes made by the ABI authorities in the supply of funds procedure to small farmers and also the elimination of barriers to farmers' eligibility to acquire financial assistance, the share of *mushārakah* financing started to rise. In 1992, it exceeded that of instalment sale and in 1996 about 48 per cent of the total sum of the ABI funds were supplied through *mushārakah* partnership. Furthermore, monitoring also resulted in increased recovery rates of alternative modes of financing, which was the highest for *mushārakah* (92 per cent) contracts as compared to other modes (for example 84 per cent for forward purchase agreement) during the period 1990–94.[22] It is important to note that the ABI does not monitor very closely the forward purchase agreement and as a result a lower recovery rate is observed for this type of contract. Although an overall increase in the share of *mushārakah* is clearly evident from the data, a downward trend is observed starting in 1997. This was the result of a policy change by the management of the ABI to optimize the use of different instruments for short- and long-term funding in order to achieve a more balanced portfolio. It was recognized that the use of *mushārakah* for short-term financing was less efficient than using *salaf* or instalment sale or *muḍārabah*. As a result, the ABI portfolio is now considered more balanced with a major portion still allocated to equity financing.

For comparison purposes, Table 7.3 shows the structure of the assets portfolio of other Islamic banks operating in the Islamic Republic of Iran. There are clear differences in the composition of the ABI's portfolio and those of other Islamic banks where portfolio composition is fairly static for the same period of time.

The shift in the ABI's portfolio composition towards an increased share of *mushārakah* contracts cannot be attributed solely to increased monitoring and supervision. Although the ABI is a development finance institution, and monitoring and supervision has always been part of its practices before and after the introduction of Islamic banking, further enhancement and research was prompted by a strategic move to encourage the Islamic financial principle of equity participation and to achieve a well-diversified and efficient portfolio of assets. The shift in the portfolio composition was the result of the measures undertaken to increase the efficiency of banking operations through monitoring and to reduce information asymmetry. Other initiatives which contributed to

Table 7.3 Composition of outstanding facilities extended to non-public sector by Islamic banks (%)

Modes of transaction	1984–85	1985–86	1986–87	1987–88	1988–89	1989–90	1990–91	1991–92	1992–93	1993–94	1994–95	1995–96	1996–97
Instalment sales	34.0	32.6	35.7	42.7	47.1	46.8	49.0	47.0	46.5	45.0	45.8	45.0	43.4
Muḍārabah	18.5	15.6	15.5	12.6	11.0	10.7	10.2	9.7	8.5	7.5	7.3	6.8	6.7
Civil partnership	15.0	13.2	13.9	13.9	11.7	12.8	14.5	17.8	17.6	17.4	18.1	19.4	19.6
Qarḍ al-ḥasan	10.8	10.8	11.6	10.6	9.7	7.5	5.7	4.2	3.6	4.6	4.4	4.7	4.5
Hire-purchasing	1.8	0.9	0.8	0.8	0.8	0 .5	0.4	0.7	0.5	0.7	0.8	1.0	1.1
Forward deals	3.7	3.2	3.9	3.9	4.9	6.7	5.3	5.0	6.7	6.9	6.2	5.5	5.0
Equity participation	3.6	7.3	6.6	7.1	7.1	5.8	4.6	4.8	5.2	4.8	3.6	2.7	3.8
Direct investment	0.6	3.6	2.7	1.7	1.3	1.3	1.3	1.3	1.9	2.6	2.4	1.7	2.8
Juʿālah	0.3	1.4	1.4	1.8	2.8	5.1	6.6	7.0	6.0	6.0	6.6	7.0	6.6
Debt purchasing	11.7	10.1	6.4	3.1	0.1	0.6	0.3	0.1	0.1	0.1	0.1	0	0
Other	0.2	1.2	1.6	1.7	2.6	2.2	2.1	2.4	3.5	4.3	4.7	6.2	6.5

Source: Sadr (1999b).

increased equity participation include extension of *mushārakah* from a long-term financing vehicle to a short-term operating costs financing vehicle, elimination of the collateral requirement for small farmers, the substitution of the equity mode for *juʿālah* and instalment sale, and finally, a reduction in processing costs of *mushārakah* contracts. Therefore, one can infer that while close monitoring and increased supervision may not be necessary, it certainly was a sufficient, condition for shifting from fixed-income instruments to equity contracts.

4. CONCLUSIONS

The more incomplete the financial markets and the greater the information imperfection, the greater the need for banking institutions which prefer to lend on the basis of debt with minimum monitoring.[23] Such banking institutions become indispensable where capital markets do not exist or are very thin. With increased supervision and monitoring, information asymmetry is minimized and under such circumstances it is not efficient for the financial intermediary to lend on the basis of debt. Close monitoring and supervision should not be considered as an extra cost but should be viewed as an investment to build a knowledge base of superior quality entrepreneurs and projects.

Recent growth in equity markets of industrial countries has led to a phenomenal expansion of the mutual funds industry, which is providing efficient means of placing funds on profit/loss-sharing principles. This growth can be attributed to reduced informational asymmetry in capital markets. Technological advancements (such as the Internet) have further facilitated the dissemination of results of research and market sentiments to small investors.[24]

The case study of the ABI demonstrates that a financial intermediary operating in an Islamic financial system will (i) benefit from investing in supervision and monitoring, (ii) broaden its client base through process simplification, (iii) achieve a well-diversified assets portfolio containing debt-like (*murābaḥah, salam*, and so on) as well as equity (*mushārakah*) instruments, and (iv) finally, optimize its return by a combination of short- and long-term instruments.

NOTES

1. Equity-based instruments include *mushārakah* and *muḍārabah* whereas examples of non-equity-based instruments include sales contracts and *ijārah*. A non-equity-based contract is not a debt contract but its return profiles are very similar to those of a fixed-income debt contract. True description of non-equity-based contracts will be similar to asset-backed financial claims that are directly linked to a real asset.
2. Cobham (1993).

3. For a detailed analytical background on these points, please see Khan, W. (1987), Mirakhor (1987) and Haque and Mirakhor (1987).
4. Scholtens (1993).
5. For a detailed discussion, see Iqbal and Mirakhor (1999).
6. Khan, W. (1987).
7. Diamond (1996).
8. Adverse selection occurs in debt contracts when lower-quality borrowers are supplied credit beyond a certain level of interest rates, and the moral hazard occurs when applicants undertake greater risks in reaction to the contract. Adverse selection in equity contracts may occur before the contract, whereby potential entrepreneurs who are most likely to produce an undesirable outcome are the ones who most actively seek out a contract and are thus most likely to be selected. Equity contracts are subject to moral hazard after the contract takes place and refers to the hazard that the agent has the incentive to engage in activities that are undesirable, that is, against the contract.
9. Cobham (1993).
10. Cho (1986).
11. Ibid.
12. Khan, W. (1987).
13. Cho (1986).
14. Khan, W. (1987).
15. Cobham (1993).
16. Sadr (1999a).
17. Agricultural Bank of Iran annual reports.
18. Sadr (1999b).
19. Ansari et al. (1993) and Milani (1996).
20. Sadr (1999b).
21. Milani (1996).
22. Sadr (2000). The recovery rate is defined as the ratio of the actual receipt to what had been planned and agreed by each contracting party.
23. Markets are considered incomplete when the sources of uncertainty affecting the fundamental asset/security are not spanned by traded securities. In other words, a full set of contingent claims on basic assets is not available in the market.
24. Iqbal and Mirakhor (1999).

REFERENCES

Agricultural Bank of Iran, *Annual Reports*, various years.

Ansari, Behrukh, K. Sadr and A. Arabmazar (1993), 'Cost of Islamic Contracts in Interest Free Banking: The Case of Agricultural Bank of Iran', *Proceedings of the 4th Annual Islamic Banking Seminar*, Tehran, Iran: Banking Institute of Iran, Central Bank of Iran.

Central Bank of the Islamic Republic of Iran (1994/95–1996/97), *Economic Reports and Balance Sheets*.

Cho, Y.J. (1986), 'Inefficiencies From Financial Liberalization in the Absence of Well-Functioning Equity Markets', *Journal of Money, Credit and Banking* (18), 191–9.

Cobham, David (1993), 'Financial International', *Economia*, Società e Instituzioni, **5** (1), 1993.

Diamond, D.W. (1984), 'Financial Intermediation and Delegated Monitoring', *Review of Economic Studies*, **51** (3), 393–414.

Diamond, D.W. (1996), 'Financial Intermediation as Delegated Monitoring: A Simple Example', *Federal Reserve Bank of Richmond Economic Quarterly*, **82** (3), Summer, 51–66.

Haque, Nadeem ul- and Abbas Mirakhor (1987), 'Optimal Profit-Sharing Contracts and Investment in an Interest-Free Islamic Economy', in Mohsin Khan and Abbas Mirakhor (eds), *Theoretical Studies in Islamic Banking and Finance*, Texas: The Institute of Islamic Studies, pp. 141–61.

Iqbal, Zamir and Abbas Mirakhor (1999), 'Progress and Challenges of Islamic Banking', *Thunderbird International Business Review*, **41** (4/5), July–October, 381–405.

Khan, Waqar M. (1987), 'Towards an Interest-Free Islamic Economic System', in Mohsin Khan and Abbas Mirakhor (eds), *Theoretical Studies in Islamic Banking and Finance*, Texas: The Institute of Islamic Studies, pp. 75–106.

Milani, Ali (1996), 'Simplifying the Procedures and Modes of Finance in the Agricultural Bank of Iran', *Proceedings of the 7th Annual Islamic Banking Conference*, Tehran, Iran: Central Bank of Iran.

Mirakhor, Abbas (1987), 'Short-term Asset Concentration and Islamic Banking', in Mohsin Khan and Abbas Mirakhor (eds), *Theoretical Studies in Islamic Banking and Finance*, Texas: The Institute of Islamic Studies, pp. 185–200.

Sadr, Kazem (1999a), 'The Role of *Mushārakah* Financing in the Agricultural Bank of Iran', *Arab Law Quarterly*, 245–56.

Sadr, Kazem (1999b), 'A Review of the Performance of Interest Free Banking in Iran', paper presented at the International Conference on Islamic Economics in the 21st Century, Kuala Lumpur, Malaysia: International Islamic University.

Sadr, Kazem (2000), *Increasing the Efficiency of Equity Financing in the Agricultural Bank of Iran over the Period of 1990–94*, Research Report, Tehran, Iran: Agricultural Bank of Iran.

Samsami, H., K. Sadr, A. Arabmazar and B. Ansari (1996), 'A Model of Islamic Banking', *Eqteṣād* (4).

Scholtens, Lambertus J.R. (1993), 'On the Foundations of Financial Intermediation: A Review of the Literature', *Kredit und Kapital*, **26** (1), 112–41.

COMMENTS

Abdul Azim Islahi

The economics of information is one of the recent developments in the area of economic theory. Its use in the field of Islamic banking and finance is widely discussed. But there is still a lack of empirical studies. The authors should undoubtedly be commended for producing a thought-provoking chapter on the subject. They have presented empirical evidence from the experience of the Agricultural Bank of Iran (ABI) showing that a reduction in information asymmetry and increased monitoring by the ABI led to the preference of variable return instruments (VRIs) such as *mushārakah*, *muḍārabah* over the fixed return instruments (FRIs), like *murābaḥah*, *ijārah*, *bay*ʿ *al-salaf*, and so on. According to the authors, with increased supervision and monitoring, information asymmetry is minimized and under such circumstances it is not efficient for the financial intermediary to lend on the basis of debt. The extra cost of information generation, supervision and monitoring is to be considered an investment, which entails selection of superior projects and an efficient allocation of resources. The theoretical part of the chapter should not detain us long, as considerable discussion has already taken place on this issue and a good deal of literature has come out on financial intermediation and asymmetrical information. The importance of the chapter lies in its empirical evidence.

The authors seem to accept and strive to verify the thesis that banks prefer fixed return instruments (FRIs) because they minimize the information requirement of a financial contract when the performance of the project is not observable by the financial institution, and that reduction of information asymmetry is a prerequisite for implementation of an equity-based system (or variable return instruments, VRIs). But this assertion is contested by the classical example of the used-car market. Informational asymmetry in the used-car market, being a one-time relation between the buyer and seller, is much more prone to moral hazard than an equity contract. But the fact that the market for used cars exists should be enough to prove that mere informational asymmetry could not be an obstacle in the way of equity-based contracts. It may be noted that the seller of a used car is absolved of any obligation if any defect is found in the car after the sale, whereas the bank's client will be held responsible if it is discovered that the loss is his fault.

Coming to the empirical part of the chapter, the authors argue that the ABI achieved symmetric information through investment in supervision and monitoring and expenditure on research and development. Due to overcoming the problem of moral hazard through information-sharing and monitoring, the share of equity participation (*mushārakah*) in its portfolio increased substantially. They have attributed this to the decrease in the average number of steps and time that the ABI takes to conclude a contract (Table 7.1), a relative increase in the share of *mushārakah* over time (Table 7.2), and to the composition of outstanding facilities extended to the non-public-sector by Islamic banks (Table 7.3). I feel that the data given are not sufficient to substantiate the point that the authors wanted to make.

The authors have repeatedly emphasized that the ABI's investment in supervision and monitoring resulted in greater benefits. However, it is not clear what was the volume of investment for this purpose and as a result what benefits or returns it could derive. Had the authors shown the total costs in procurement of information and monitoring by ABI, and the resultant increase in its revenue, it would have been more convincing that these information costs were not a deadweight loss to society.

According to the authors, the major shift in the ABI's portfolio during the last 15 years was towards *mushārakah*, because of eliminating the problems of chances of moral hazard. But it should be noted that out of the two equity-based contracts, *mushārakah* and *muḍārabah*, the former is the least vulnerable to moral hazard as in this case both partners contribute both capital and labour and the bank has a right to interfere. At a later stage the authors themselves accept that the shift in the ABI's portfolio towards an increased share of *mushārakah* cannot be attributed solely to increased monitoring and supervision but also to a number of other factors. Had they argued that the increasing share of *muḍārabah* (pure equity participation) was due to achievement of more symmetric information, their argument might have been more convincing. But the chapter is silent on any 'procedural change about *muḍārabah* to save steps, time, and expense for the bank's partners'.

The chapter gives the impression that the dominance of mark-up and other fixed-return instruments in the early days of the ABI after implementation of the Interest Free Banking Law in 1983, and still in other commercial banks, has been due only to information asymmetry and fear of moral hazard. But that is probably not absolutely correct. It might have been due to their need for liquidity. The *muḍārabah* and *mushārakah* market is less liquid unless a secondary stock market also exists. Moreover, different Islamic instruments have their own characteristics and advantages. FRIs such as *murābaḥah*, *ijārah*, and *bay*ʿ *al-salam* have an advantage over VRIs such as *muḍārabah* and *mushārakah*, because the former can be utilized for meeting end-use purposes such as household consumption needs, the purchase of durable goods, machinery, tools, equipment and the like, whereas the latter cannot. The authors consider moral hazard as an inevitable consequence of asymmetric information. Many studies have shown that this is effective only when principals and agents have a one-time relation. In a permanent and perpetual contract, with a competition for scarce capital, it will be eliminated. Similarly, a small or one-man firm may capitalize on relative informational advantage. But this is less likely when a firm is a legal entity. It is for the same reason that moral hazard problems do not prevent people from depositing their savings with Islamic banks on a purely equity basis. It will be advisable to check whether there is any advantage from changing the condition of borrowers from small to big or from a one-time relation to a repetitive contractual relation in the changing capital structure of the ABI.

Another important factor that may eliminate the occurrence of moral hazard in spite of asymmetrical information is the prevalence of ethical values and moral commitments. If Islamic morality is fostered, the standard of expected behaviour will improve, covenants in the written contracts will be honoured, business records will be accurate, and monitoring costs will eventually fall. Thus developments of equity contracts in the ABI may not be wholly due to investment in control and supervision. It may be, to a great extent, due to prevalence of ethical atmosphere.

If we allow for an honest world, the moral hazard problem, which introduces the deadweight cost in the variable return instruments, may be eliminated. The fact that ethical and moral changes in the society led to the increasing participation by the ABI is clear from the authors' own statement that even after destruction of all records in the Iraq–Iran War, the farmers themselves provided such records and 'all willingly submitted a copy of their own contracts to the bank ... from which their debt could be worked out and collected'.

The authors claim that, along with investment in supervision and monitoring, the ABI also maintained a balanced and well-diversified portfolio encompassing a wide range of instruments. But Table 7.2 shows that more than two-thirds of capital was invested in *mushārakah* and *muḍārabah*. This cannot be considered to be a balanced portfolio. The other Islamic banks invested in ten types of instruments while the ABI was confined to seven. Interestingly, the instruments of *muzāraʿah* (sharecropping), and *musāqah* (fruit sharing), especially for the agriculture sector, do not figure in the ABI's portfolio at all.

8. Islamic banking contracts as enforced in Iran

Ali Yasseri*

1. INTRODUCTION

As from 21 March 1984, all Iranian banks drastically changed their methods of operation from interest-based to interest-free standards, in conformity with the Law for Usury (Interest)-Free Banking Operations, which had been passed six months earlier. This law, which had fundamentally altered banking operations from interest-based to interest-free practices, was not the only drastic transformation faced by the banking system of the country. Two major changes had also occurred a few years earlier: (1) on 7 June 1979, Iran had nationalized its entire banking and insurance systems, and (2) nationalization was accompanied, four months later, by the merger of 36 banks and 16 savings and loan associations into six commercial and three specialized banks, with thousands of branches scattered all over the country. In the past few years, one specialized bank was added to the list, while the Post-bank also received its charter from parliament and has been practising some form of banking functions in close collaboration with the country's postal network. With some 14 600 branches, the government-owned banking system has about 155 000 employees, 14 per cent of whom have university education.

Since Article 44 of the Iranian Constitution prohibits establishment of private-sector banks, the Iranian Central Bank in 1998 issued a licence to a private-sector non-bank credit institution to offer saving and investment services to the public and to undertake normal banking operations, except those related to current accounts. This step was taken in order to inject some form of competition into the system, while abiding by the constitutional prohibition against the formation of private-sector banks. Many such licences are in the pipeline.

In this chapter, an effort is made to describe the Islamic financing contracts as utilized by Iranian banks. Section 2 throws some light on various uses of

* The views and analyses contained in this chapter represent personal opinions of the author and are not attributable to any other source.

different Islamic financial contracts. Section 3 concentrates on details of the two most frequently used contracts in the Iranian banking system. These details will provide interesting insights into the operational aspects of Iranian banking. Section 4 discusses some implications of these contracts for the banking system. The approach taken in this chapter, although necessarily coloured by legal jargon, is not strictly speaking that of a lawyer's approach to the subject; rather, the implications of legal niceties will be considered from a practical banking angle.

2. USES OF ISLAMIC CONTRACTS IN IRAN

The Usury (Interest)-Free Banking Law (henceforth referred to as the Law) specifies that mobilization of monetary resources by Iranian banks shall be undertaken either through *qarḍ al-ḥasan* deposits (current and savings), or through term investment deposits.[1] *Qarḍ al-ḥasan* deposits are in the nature of loan contracts, and are based on the creditor–debtor relationship. These deposits become the banks' own assets under their total ownership, and should be repaid either on demand (in the case of sight deposits), or when they become due (in the case of time and savings deposits).

Term investment deposit accounts are opened by risk-prone depositors and are utilized by Iranian banks, which enjoy power of attorney, and are based on the attorney–client contract of *wakālah*, for which the banks are authorized to charge their clients appropriate legal fees. This is in contrast with the practice of some non-Iranian Islamic banks that mobilize financial resources through the investment accounts based on the *muḍārabah* contract. Term investment deposits, according to the same Article 3 of the aforementioned Law, may be used in joint ventures (*mushārakah*), *muḍārabah*, hire purchase, instalment transactions, *muzāraʿah*, *musāqah*, direct investment, forward dealings (*salaf*) and *juʿālah* transactions. The laws and regulations also permit utilization of *bayʿ al-dayn* (debt purchase)[2] and equity partnership as modes of transaction. *Muzāraʿah* and *musāqah*, which are exclusively used in agriculture, are no longer utilized by Iranian banks owing to limited applicability. Table 8.1 describes the Islamic contracts' various uses in the Iranian banking system. It is to be noted that *muḍārabah* as currently utilized in the Iranian banking system is exclusively employed as a mode of short-term trade financing. In addition, Article 9 of the Law prohibits Iranian banks from concluding *muḍārabah* contracts with the private sector for the purpose of importation.

The reasons behind the use of *muḍārabah* only for short-term trade financing or its prohibition in the case of private-sector imports are not quite clear; there does not seem to be any religious injunction against using this mode of financing in other sectors of the economy, or for longer-term investments and transactions. It seems more likely that both decisions are administrative in nature, taken at the time when Islamic banking operations were in their infancy and thus in need of utmost supervision and control, and also when private-sector activities, especially when they use scarce foreign exchange resources, had to be curbed because the country was in the midst of a costly and prolonged war.

Table 8.1 Islamic contracts' various uses in Iran's banks

Economic sectors		Short-term (one year and under) contracts	Medium to long-term (more than one year) contracts
Production	Industry Mines Agriculture	• *Mushārakah* • *Ju'ālah* • Instalment sales (raw materials, spare parts, tools) • *Qarḍ al-ḥasan* • Forward sales • *Muzāra'ah* (agriculture) • *Musāqah* (agriculture)	• *Mushārakah* • *Ju'ālah* • Instalment sales (machinery and equipment) • *Qarḍ al-ḥasan* • Hire purchase • Direct investment • Equity partnership
Trade	Domestic Imports Exports	• *Mushārakah* • *Murābaḥah* • *Ju'ālah*	• *Mushārakah* • *Ju'ālah* • Equity partnership
Services		• *Mushārakah* • *Ju'ālah*	• *Mushārakah* • *Ju'ālah* • Hire purchase • Instalment sales (machinery and equipment) • Equity partnership • *Qarḍ al-ḥasan*
Housing and construction		• *Mushārakah* • *Ju'ālah* • Instalment sales, (building raw materials)	• *Mushārakah* • *Ju'ālah* • Equity partnership • Direct investment • Instalment sales (housing and construction) • Hire purchase (housing and construction)

Source: *Bank Melli Iran*, monthly magazine, No. 52.

It can also be seen from Table 8.1 that two modes of financing, that is, *mushārakah* and *juʿālah*, are in fact multi-purpose contracts and are used in all sectors of the economy, for both short- and long-term transactions. Here again, the all-embracing nature of these two contracts is more a result of administrative arrangements rather than any single characteristic of the contracts themselves. Since, in Iran, *istiṣnāʿ* is not used as a mode of financing, *juʿālah* (commissioning) is utilized as a close substitute. Some *Sharīʿah* scholars believe that *istiṣnāʿ* is more akin to *salam* (in Iran called *salaf*) transactions, as payments are made in advance while the products are delivered in the future after the manufacturing process has been completed. However, in Iran, *juʿālah* as a multi-purpose financing vehicle is concluded with payment made in advance, with a down payment, or on an instalment basis according to the progress of work.

Table 8.2 shows the order of importance of each mode of financing in Iranian banks' asset portfolios. It is evident from the table that instalment sale, which is the Iranian version of *murābaḥah*, is the most important mode of financing in Iran. It is equally true that *murābaḥah* is also the most popular mode of Islamic financing in Islamic banks outside Iran. *Mushārakah*, equity partnership and *muḍārabah* are next in order of importance. These three models, together, account for almost 80 per cent of all the financing extended by the Iranian banks during the year 1377 (1998).

Table 8.2 Composition of financing modes used in granting credit facilities by the banking system (%)

Financing mode	1374[a] (1995)	1375 (1996)	1376 (1997)	1377 (1998)
Instalment sales	45.0	43.4	56.0	56.1
Musharākah (civil)	19.4	19.6	11.6	9.4
Equity partnership	2.7	3.8	4.7	6.9
Muḍārabah	6.8	6.7	6.4	6.3
Salaf	5.5	5.0	5.2	5.9
Qarḍ al-ḥasan	4.7	4.5	4.6	5.0
Direct investment	1.7	2.8	2.5	1.7
Juʿālah	7.0	6.6	1.6	1.5
Hire purchase	1.0	1.1	0.8	0.6
Bayʿ al-dayn	0	0	0	0
Others	6.2	6.5	6.6	6.4
Total	100.0	100.0	100.0	100.0

[a] Iranian year ending 20 March 1995.

Source: Central Bank of the Islamic Republic of Iran.

2.1 Legal Underpinnings

According to Article 15 of the Law, all Islamic banking modes of financing are considered binding legal documents, enforceable even without a court order. This characteristic is associated with all 'self-enforcing' legal documents, such as cheques, as opposed to 'court-enforcing' legal documents, such as promissory notes or bills of exchange. The self-enforcing nature of Islamic banking contracts makes it unnecessary for the banks, before foreclosing or taking other punitive actions, to seek court orders in cases of violation of the terms of the contract by the agent–entrepreneur. Instead, legal actions to seek redress or foreclosure can start immediately. These contracts are routinely drawn up and signed in the banks. When contracts represent transactions involving real estate, they should be drawn up and duly signed by both parties in notary public offices. All contracts signed in notary public offices are also self-enforcing.

The Iranian Civil Code also differentiates between irrevocable and revocable contracts.[3] An irrevocable contract is defined as a contract which cannot be revoked by either party to the contract. All contracts are considered as irrevocable unless explicitly declared to be revocable by law. Article 186 of the Iranian Civil Code defines revocable contracts as those according to which 'each party to the contract is able to revoke it at any time'. Examples of revocable contracts according to which each party to the contract may abrogate the contract unilaterally are *mushārakah* contracts, *wakālah* contracts and *muḍārabah* contracts.

In the case of *mushārakah* and *muḍārabah* contracts, both of which can be abrogated unilaterally, or each party to the contract can at any time ask for appropriation of the assets and profits of the partnership, banks protect their interests against this possibility by including in the contract a provision depriving the partner (in the case of *mushārakah*, or the agent, in the case of *muḍārabah*) of this right under the law.

Upon signing the contract, the partner or the agent willingly gives up his right under the law. This inclusion in the revocable contract, making it irrevocable for the bank's partner, has been judged not to be in contradiction with the *Sharīʿah*.

Generally speaking, for a contract to be legally sound and religiously valid, four conditions need to be fulfilled:

1. The bona fide intention and agreement of the parties to the contract to enter into a transaction must be ascertained.
2. The parties' soundness and maturity of mind and body should be established.
3. The conformity of the subject matter of the contract with the *Sharīʿah*, its practicality, specificity, availability and transferability need to be verified.

4. The purpose and motive involved in the transaction should not be contrary to the *Sharīʿah*.

The contracts are usually so worded that the conditions mentioned above are reflected in them. In addition, when the contracts are to be signed either in the notary public's offices or in the banks, both parties to the contract are made fully aware of all legal nuances and implications before they sign the contract. Bank officials and employees in the notary public offices make sure that the implications of the contracts are fully understood and appreciated by the parties.

For example, cancellation of a valid contract by mutual consent is a prerogative given by Article 283 of the Iranian Civil Code to both parties of a contract under certain conditions. Or under Article 396 of the same Code, both parties to the contract have several options to cancel a valid irrevocable contract when, for example, certain conditions under the contract are later found to have remained unfulfilled; or else when one party can prove that he was deceived, or the description of the commodities or services under the transaction was incorrect. Therefore, the contracts are worded in such a way that the bank clients in effect disclaim such options and renounce their rights to resort to such options during the term of the contract.

3. SAMPLE PROVISIONS OF SOME CONTRACTS

3.1 Instalment Sales

This is the most frequently used Islamic financing contract in Iran and, according to Table 8.2, represented 56.1 per cent of all bank financing extended by the Iranian banks in the Iranian year 1377 (ending 20 March 1998). It is both a short-term and medium- and long-term financing vehicle that is used in production, services, housing and construction, but not in trade financing. This is because of explicit references in Articles 10, 11 and 13 of the Law which refer to the use of the instalment sales contract in housing (Article 10), industry, mining, agriculture and services (Article 11) and raw materials and spare parts for productive units (Article 13, section A). As can be seen from Table 8.1, *muḍārabah*, *mushārakah* and *juʿālah* are employed in the financing of trade. The reasons for this division, however, seem to be administrative rather than *Sharīʿah*-related.

Accordingly, there are three separate bodies of rules and regulations pertaining to instalment sales transactions: (i) those employed in the financing of raw materials and spare parts and tools for manufacturing; (ii) those for financing machinery and equipment; and (iii) those for financing housing and construction. The differences between these three sets of regulations are, however, minor and reflect the different nature of transactions in each case. For example, in the case of instalment sales transactions used in housing finance, obtaining city planning permits from the Iranian Ministry of Housing and Town Planning is included, while rules and regulations for the other two cases do not include this proviso. Other minor differences in regulations and also in the exact wording of the three types of instalment sales contract reflect variations in the nature of each transaction.

The banking rules and regulations, in addition to the relevant articles of the Law, govern the wording and implications of the Islamic banking contracts. These regulations are both of a general nature and also certain sections of them relate to specific contracts. The general rules are applicable to all contracts and pertain to the general conditions of loans and facilities granted by the banks as well as all forms of deposits placed with the banks by their customers. Accordingly, financial facilities granted by the banks should be such that the banks would recover both the principal and the expected profit in due course. Banks should exercise supervision over the proper implementation and utilization of the contracts, should demand sufficient security to guarantee repayment of the loans and facilities, and should insure both the collateral and assets of the business once the contract has come into force.

The specific rules and regulations pertaining to instalment sales transactions define this mode of financing as 'the sale of an asset by one party to another at a fixed price in such a manner that the whole or part of the said price will be received in equal or unequal instalments at a specified future date or dates'.

Banks are authorized to buy the raw materials, spare parts, working tools and other essentials needed by the producers and manufacturers (upon their written request and on their undertaking to buy and utilize the above-mentioned items), and to sell them the same in instalments.

These rules and regulations clearly show that the law-makers were careful to confine banks to their roles as financial intermediaries; hence the inclusion in the rules of the necessity of a written request for financing from the clients before the banks can enter into the contract. Thus banks are not authorized to purchase items and sell them on credit on their own initiative and volition.

Whereas the spirit and purpose of Islamic banking is for banks to assume two roles: as an intermediary of funds; and also as an entrepreneur and financier in their own right, in practice the great majority of Islamic banks, including those in Iran, have opted for the former role. The reason is that banks as traditional money managers have always sought to assume only credit risks, and not business or transaction risks. Direct involvement in business activities usually entails retraining the bank employees in the direction of real business, agriculture, housing and manufacturing activities, which is extremely complicated, time-consuming and of uncertain outcome. Islamic banks' reluctance to enter into *mushārakah* and *muḍārabah* contracts, which would involve the banks in a greater degree of business risks, is a case in point. According to the Iranian Civil Code (Article 576), management of the partnership's common pool of assets is subject to agreement among the partners. But banks delegate this responsibility to the other party because they do not have the expertise and know-how to manage a business venture. Section 3.2 will expand on this point.

Supervision of the activities of the banks' partners, or of the activities of the agents in *muḍārabah* contracts, is essential and is usually stipulated in all contracts. This will be discussed in more detail in the section on *mushārakah*. In the case of instalment sales contracts, it is stipulated that the banks should make sure that the asset purchased on credit by the client is used for the intended purpose, as specified in the contract. The banks, based on this stipulation, reserve the right to check the premises of the client, and the client is obliged to facilitate such visits.

Another insertion in the contract relates to collateral. Collateral can take many forms, such as real estate, machinery and equipment, bank accounts, promissory notes, and so on. Collateral accepted by banks under instalment sales contracts can be movable or immovable, which, in the latter case, must be registered at the notary public's offices. The taking of collateral is considered as added insurance by Iranian banks, in addition to the self-enforcing character of the contract.

However, in order to further safeguard the depositors' investment resources placed with the banks, and in recognition of the banks' intermediary role, the wording of the instalment sales contract is such as to require the credit applicant to pay the instalments promptly. The contract stipulates that delay in payment of each instalment, or the client's default and failure to abide by the other contract conditions, will make the total financial commitment of the client under the contract, including all the unpaid instalments, become due and payable at once. On top of this, there are also penalties for late payment, which the defaulting client has to shoulder, the amount of which is determined by the law.

3.2 *Mushārakah* (Partnership)

There are two forms of *mushārakah* (partnership) in Iranian banking contracts: civil partnership and equity partnership contracts. As seen in Table 8.2, civil partnership financing dominates as a mode of financing. Equity partnership, as the name implies, is based on the banks' participation in a productive project through purchasing stocks and shares in a company. In this chapter, only civil partnership contracts are examined.

The Iranian Civil Code defines civil partnership as a 'mixture of the ownership rights of several owners concentrated on a single item, with the share of each partner remaining indistinguishable or indistinct'. The predetermined share of each partner in the common ownership fund will be the basis for the distribution of profits and losses, unless the partners themselves make other arrangements. Such other arrangements may give one or more partners a larger share, in accordance with their greater efforts. Management of the joint assets (property) will be in accordance with the conditions laid down by the partners.[4]

The Usury (Interest)-Free Banking Law of 1983 (Article 7) authorizes banks to enter into partnership contracts with clients, while the banks' standard operating procedure on *mushārakah* (civil) defines these as 'the mixing of cash and/or non-cash partnership shares of several real or juridical persons, in a profit-seeking partnership venture based on an agreement, such that the pre-determined share of each partner in the common asset remains indistinguishable'.

The civil partnership contract, unlike the equity partnership, does not require formation of a company to manage the affairs of the partnership business; nor does the partnership acquire juridical identity separate from the partners. All partners are fully responsible for any related liabilities. Accordingly, each partner in civil partnerships is responsible up to the amount of the partnership assets. Therefore in the civil partnership contracts concluded by banks, it is usually stipulated that non-bank partners responsible for managing the joint partnership are not authorized financially to commit the joint venture beyond the common partnership capital, thereby making the bank, as one of the partners, liable beyond its share in the partnership capital.

In civil partnerships, each partner has the right to transfer his intermingled (mixed) share to any other person without the consent of the other partner(s). However, he must offer it to the other partners[5] before offering it to anyone else. Accordingly, in civil partnership contracts, banks make sure that this legal transfer of rights of the other partners, as well as their legal right to annul the 'revocable' contract of *mushārakah* unilaterally, are voluntarily abrogated.

As mentioned before, the intermingled and hence indistinguishable share of each partner in the common partnership fund means that each partner has an ownership stake in each infinitesimal unit of the common partnership assets, up to his or her partnership share. Therefore no single partner can, without the consent of the other partner(s), unilaterally interfere in the management of the partnership business. As banks do not regard themselves competent to manage the partnership business, they delegate this right to the other partner(s).

In civil partnership contracts, banks insist upon and require their partner(s) to accept and shoulder any potential capital loss that may arise during the joint-venture operation. In addition, they require the partner(s) to provide the bank with sufficient collateral security to protect the banks' partnership share from any potential mismanagement or abuse of the common partnership fund by the partners. The collateral security and loss-recovery commitments demanded from non-bank partners have been justified on the ground that the partner who also manages the partnership business may well misuse the common partnership funds.

Banks are obliged, according to the *mushārakah* standard operating procedure as reflected in the *mushārakah* contracts, to exercise proper supervision and control over satisfactory implementation of civil partnership ventures until termination of the partnership contract and settlement of all claims. In practice, supervision has proved extremely arduous for the banks' personnel, as the banks' partners charged with running the joint ventures on their own take advantage of the banks' lack of familiarity with the business operations and dictate their own priorities and preferences, not to mention cases where true profits are deliberately disguised or misreported.

The termination of the *mushārakah* contracts occurs either when the partnership has run its course and the assets are divided up among the partners, or when one of the partners decides unilaterally to annul the contract, when a partner dies, or when the partnership assets are squandered or destroyed. Banks, therefore, protect themselves by incorporating proper provisions in the *mushārakah* contracts.

4. IMPLICATIONS OF ISLAMIC CONTRACTS FOR THE IRANIAN BANKING SYSTEM

(a) From the very beginning, the drafters of the Usury (Interest)-Free Banking Law were fully aware of the fact that the structure and organization of the Iranian banking system were suited to, and would support, only an intermediary role for the banks. The personnel of the typical commercial bank, as well as the bank's structure and organization, were trained and designed to operate as a financial intermediary only, and not as an investment company or trading and manufacturing concern. Division of labour and the principle of specialization required that commercial banking as a short-term, trade-oriented activity be kept separate from long-term investment and infrastructural financing, which are usually in the domain of investment banks and capital markets, notwithstanding the fact that some overlapping naturally occurs during such operations. As mentioned earlier, several references in the Law and in the contracts refer to bank financing being based only upon the request of the client and the borrowers. Banks are not allowed to engage in trade and manufacturing activities on their own volition. In Islamic banking, however, banks can act as an intermediary of funds, as well as engage in real business activities on their own and on behalf of their depositors. In practice, this pooling of diverse activities has posed problems for the Islamic banks, which do not regard themselves as having enough business expertise to venture into real business transactions, thereby taking business risks, in addition to the usual conventional banking practice of accepting credit risks. Mostly for this reason, Islamic banks in Iran, as well as elsewhere, prefer *murābaḥah* and instalment sales contracts to the full-risk contracts of *mushārakah* and *muḍārabah*, in which the banks as partners must be thoroughly familiar with the real economy and real-sector transactions. Supervision of the clients' operations in joint ventures has also proved complicated and demanding for the banks' personnel.

(b) It is important for Islamic banking contracts to operate in a legally solid environment, free from ambiguous interpretations and fully supported by binding legal measures. An accommodating judicial setting goes a long way to creating an appropriate condition for the prompt enforcement of Islamic banking contracts. In Iran, this objective has been achieved by enacting a separate, tailor-made law that makes all such contracts legally binding and enforceable without resort to an executive order or decision by a court of law, in case of any violation by either party to the contract.

(c) The contracts unambiguously stipulate that in the case of instalment sales, the commodity has been received and collected by the client in a good form and condition at a specified price. All such contracts are worded in such a way as to prevent the defaulting client from claiming ignorance of the law and/or ignorance of the contract conditions.

(d) The taking of collateral by banks, especially in *mushārakah* contracts, may seem unjustified, but because of the banks' unfamiliarity with the joint-venture operations and problems in supervision, they are practically obliged to demand collateral in order to safeguard their depositors' interest. In addition, the *mushārakah* contracts contain several other provisions that treat the banks' partners not as a party to the joint-venture operations, but as a borrower of funds who must repay their debts, no matter what happens to the joint-venture profitability.

In this regard, even if the joint venture should suffer a normal business loss, the bank's partner must shoulder full responsibility and must unilaterally make up for the loss. Or if the subject of the *mushārakah* is trade-related, and the commodity cannot be sold by the end of the contract period, the partner undertakes to buy that commodity out of his personal funds.

(e) One problem that Iranian banks, unlike other Islamic banks operating outside Iran, seldom face is the likelihood that the partnership project or instalment sale commodity might be of a nature contrary to the *Sharīʿah*.

This problem may exist in countries in which interest-free banks operate alongside the interest-based banks, thus prompting the interest-free banks to seek advice and rulings from their *Sharīʿah* boards. In the Islamic Republic of Iran, however, un-Islamic activities such as gambling, purchase and sale of alcohol, hoarding and the like are strictly forbidden and are never carried out in the open. Accordingly, no reference is made thereto in the contracts.

(f) The minimum expected rate of profit (MERP) is a cut-off rate announced annually by the government, so that banks may accept all the submitted projects with an equal or higher expected prospective rate of return, and reject those with a prospective rate below the minimum level. The MERP is a monetary-policy instrument used by the Iranian Central Bank to adopt a restrictive (higher MERP) or expansionary (lower MERP) monetary policy. However, some Iranian commercial bankers, in conformity with their traditional reluctance to commit their depositors' funds to the *mushārakah*-type contracts with uncertain outcomes, use the MERP as a fixed and final rate, charged and collected at the beginning of both *mushārakah* and *muḍārabah* contracts, thus treating both contracts as *murābaḥah*-type contracts. The Iranian Central Bank, of course, tries to rectify such malpractice, but the growing number of these cases is another sign that bankers as money managers are inherently reluctant to venture into uncharted business territories beyond their area of competence. A proposed solution to this problem is a comprehensive change in the organization of Islamic banks and in the training of bank personnel towards greater acceptance of business risks and more familiarity with real-sector business operations.[6]

(g) The state-owned banking system charges the users of bank resources different profit rates, thus giving priority to selected sectors of the economy such as agriculture, and charging higher rates for trade transactions, to which the government accords lower priority. In practice, however, some bank borrowers try to circumvent this policy by declaring their business to be in the priority sector with a lower rate, and switching later to their intended field of operation. The contracts have a provision to penalize such practices.

(h) The state ownership of the entire banking system has led to a lack of effective competition in both sources and uses of bank funds. Since bank charges are usually lower than the prevailing rate of inflation, there is a greater demand for bank loans and facilities than supply. The banks can therefore dictate their own terms, usually without challenge, reflecting a lack of alternative sources.

NOTES

1. Article 3 of the Law.
2. Debt purchase is a mode of Islamic transaction that has proved controversial for the Islamic jurists. In Iran and Malaysia, it is conditionally allowed. In Iran, some jurists approve of this practice on condition that the debt instrument is sold at less than face value. (See Daily *Kayhan*, 1999). However, in Iran in the past few years, it has been gradually phased out as a mode of transaction because of problems arising out of establishing the authenticity of the debt instruments used in banking transactions. In Malaysia, however, this mode is still operative.
3. Articles 185 and 186 of the Civil Code of Iran.
4. See Yasseri (1999).
5. This right is enjoyed by all partners under the Law.
6. See Yasseri (1997).

REFERENCES

Daily Kayhan (29 November 1999), Tehran, Iran.

Yasseri, Ali (1997), 'Risk Exposure in Islamic Banking: Balancing the Outcomes', *Islamic Banker*, February.

Yasseri, Ali (1999), 'The Experience of the Islamic Republic of Iran in *Mushārakah* Financing', *The Arab Law Quarterly*, **14** (3).

COMMENTS

Mohamed Ali Elgari

We all know that Muslims everywhere aspire to see a banking system that is free of *ribā*. We also know that Islamic banking is everywhere and that three Muslim countries did adopt a global approach towards Islamization of the financial system. These are Pakistan, Iran and Sudan. And that is about all that most of us know. This chapter is, therefore, a welcome contribution into a rather improvised literature on the experience of countries in Islamization. The subject matter of this chapter is clearly very important, because it affords both researchers and policy-makers an opportunity to benefit from a rich experience in Islamization of banking.

I would like to make the following comments.

First, the writer mentioned that banking law considers the instalment sale contract as a self-enforcing legal document, which makes it unnecessary for banks to obtain a court order to force a defaulting debtor. Those of us who are involved in the practical side of Islamic banking appreciate the importance of this rather bold step. In a financial system where creditors are not permitted to compensate themselves for delayed payment of debt, this is actually an essential requirement for the survival of the system. This is one aspect of Islamic banking law we can all benefit from. More studies will be needed to explore the possibilities and implications in other environments.

Second, there is no hope that we can conclude the long debate on whether an Islamic bank is a merchant (trader) or purely a financial intermediary. However, in the case of Iran, we have an example where legislators realize that a bank, Islamic or otherwise, will not be of much use unless it confines itself to financial intermediation. The writer tells us that the Usury (Interest)-Free Banking Law in Iran adopted this route from the very beginning. However, such an approach must have its own limitation, that is, not allowing the banks to cross the line of *Sharīʿah* permissibility. The writer mentions that banks treat partners in a *mushārakah* as simple debtors who are not only obliged to pay back their partners' capital and profit, but will have to furnish the bank with collateral to support such an obligation. This is clearly not acceptable. With the policy of setting by decree a minimum expected rate of profit, *mushārakah* and *muḍārabah* clearly lose their participatory aspect and are abrogated from the *Sharīʿah* point of view.

Third, the rationale for prohibition of *ribā* is the fact that it is unjust. It goes without saying that other contractual arrangements, which include injustice, should also be prohibited. The form of civil partnership is clearly biased in favour of the bank, in such an excessive way that the spirit of partnership completely disappears. This comment is addressed to the writer as a suggestion that he should bring it to the attention of the authorities in Iran.

9. Islamic financial institutions of India: their nature, problems and prospects*

M.I. Bagsiraj

1. INTRODUCTION

There are over 300 Islamic financial institutions (IFIs) operating in India.[1] They are not banks, but are bank substitutes, because the Indian Banking Act does not provide for interest-free banking operations. Thus it is against great handicaps and constraints that various IFIs are operating and gradually expanding their sphere of economic influence in India. Without any statutory provisions or backing from the secular government, they are struggling admirably to promote the Islamic financial system to generate economic welfare through an alternative financial model. At a time of economic liberalization, privatization and globalization, they are creating new avenues and hopes for the betterment of the socio-economically beleaguered Muslim minority of India.

The IFIs of India are neither uniform in composition nor homogeneous in their operations. They may be classified into four broad categories:

1. Financial Associations of Persons, small *baitulmāls*[2] or funds which are not registered under any provision and which are part of the unorganized Islamic financial sector.
2. Muslim Funds or Islamic Welfare Societies registered either under the Societies Act or the Trust Act.
3. Islamic Cooperative Credit Societies registered with the registrar of co-operative societies.
4. Islamic investment companies registered under the Companies Act.

The growing environment of economic liberalization and privatization has opened new opportunities for IFIs and Indian Muslims. However, the enactment of the Non-Banking Financial Companies (NBFC) Act in 1998 is posing a great

* This chapter is based on data collected for a research project sponsored by King Abdulaziz University of Jeddah, Saudi Arabia, entitled 'Islamic Financial Institutions of India: Progress, Problems and Prospects'.

many operational difficulties for IFIs in India. For the first time, they have come under greater scrutiny of the Reserve Bank of India's prudential norms. This study highlights these and other problems encountered by IFIs in India, and assesses their nature, performance, potential and prospects.

2. METHODOLOGY

This is the first-ever empirical study of the functioning IFIs in India. It is based on primary as well as secondary data of some selected organizations. Four prominent IFIs in India, one from each category mentioned earlier, have been selected from different parts of the country. Performance data have been collected from annual reports of the selected institutions and a questionnaire. The questionnaire was divided into five parts. Part I called for general information. Parts II and III were concerned with collection of economic information about fund mobilization and fund utilization functions respectively. Part IV dealt with social information and the last part was devoted to the collection of managerial information. All questionnaires were filled in through personal interviews. All the tables in this chapter are based on the data collected from institutions surveyed through these questionnaires. Simple statistical and economic tools and techniques have been applied for analysis and interpretation. Another survey was also conducted in 24 cities and towns of India to assess the awareness and acceptability by Indian Muslims of the functioning of IFIs. The study can be helpful in determining the future scope of IFIs in India and the course of action to be taken to make them effective vehicles of the community's and country's march towards economic independence.

3. ASSOCIATIONS OF PERSONS

Associations of Persons are unregistered, privately operated, small functional groups operating in mosques, educational institutions or markets, throughout the country. In mosques or *anjumans*[3] they have taken the form of small *baitulmāls* wherein *zakāh* funds are mobilized along with membership fees and donations. Needy persons are helped on a charitable basis. Interest-free loans (*qarḍ al-ḥasan*) are also extended. In the educational institutions they have taken the form of interest-free chit funds.[4] Groups of 25 to 30 members contribute a fixed sum each month and one or two persons share the monthly collections at no cost. In the market, associations or groups of Muslim businessmen coming together for mutual financial assistance are slightly bigger.

Denied finance by bankers and exploited by *mahājan*[5] money-lenders who charge over 36 per cent interest, groups of 50 to 100 Muslim businessmen come together to form an association for mobilizing their own savings and providing interest-free, low-cost loans.

The majority of these Associations of Persons are actually self-help groups mobilizing and providing low-cost interest-free capital. These loans are used both for consumption as well as production purposes, so far more for the former. But recently more and more Muslim businessmen are adopting this pattern to augment their business capital. There are hundreds of Associations of Persons operating throughout India. It is very difficult to quantify them. The amount of interest-free loans extended by them may be running into a few hundred crores[6] of rupees. It is difficult accurately to calculate the amount or its impact. However, an attempt can always be made to understand their functioning. The Barkat Association of Belgaum has been selected for detailed study because it represents the emerging Associations of Persons, which have an impact that is more economic than social.

3.1 Barkat Association, Belgaum

Belgaum is a city of about 7 lakh[7] people with 20 per cent Muslim population situated in Northern Karnataka bordering Maharashtra. The city is known for its good climate, culture, education and trade. The Muslims of Belgaum are mostly engaged in road transport, both passenger and goods, spare parts for vehicles and their repairs, vegetable and fruit business, beef and mutton shops and footwear trade. During the 1990s, Belgaum's Muslim businessmen made reasonable progress and diversified their business, thanks mainly to the establishment of various self-help groups based on Islamic finance. Like Indian Muslims in general, Belgaum Muslims are also unable to get the necessary assistance from commercial banks. To avoid the 3 per cent monthly interest burden charged by *mahājan* money-lenders on short-term business loans, some Muslim entrepreneurs, following the example of small chit funds, started an Association of Persons called Federation in 1986. It was closed down in 1997 because of a misunderstanding among its organizers, but it led to the birth of seven similar groups between 1995 and 1999. The experiences gained by managers of these groups led them to register a Cooperative Society in 1997 called Barkat Society, which they intend to run on interest-free Islamic principles.

For detailed study we will take up only one of the seven groups, the Barkat Association. It started in 1994, with a membership of 75 Muslim businessmen of Belgaum. Table 9.1 gives the economic details of its performance.

Table 9.1 Economic performance of the Barkat Association, Belgaum, 1994–98 (figures in rupees lakh)

Years (1)	No. of members (2)	Fixed deposits per member (Rs) (3)	Total deposits (4)	No. of loans disbursed (5)	Total loans (6)	No. of outstanding loans (7)	Outstanding loans (8)	Bad debts (9)	Total operational costs (10)	Surplus funds (11)	Reserve funds (12)
1994–95	75	0.22	16.50	129	90.00	4	2.0	NIL	0.56	0.25	0.45
1995–96	100	0.22	22.00	152	105.00	4	2.0	NIL	0.60	0.40	1.00
(%)	33.33	0.0	33.33	17.83	16.67	0.0	0.0	NA	0.57	60.0	122.2
1996–97	120	0.22	26.40	177	130.00	12	6.0	NIL	1.30	0.60	1.60
(%)	20.00	0.0	20.00	16.45	23.81	300.0	300.0	NA	1.00	50.0	60.0
1997–98	140	0.22	30.40	114	142.00	18	9.0	NIL	0.50	0.95	2.00
(%)	16.67	0.0	15.15	–35.59	9.23	50.0	50.0	NA	0.35	58.0	25.0

Note: Percentages in column (10) represent percentages of column (6). All other percentages represent annual growth rates.

3.1.1 Economic performance

Fixed deposit per member, which includes membership fees, has remained fixed at Rs 22,000. But total deposits have increased from Rs 16.5 lakh in 1994–95 to Rs .30.4 lakh in 1997–98 because of the increase in membership from 75 to 140. The total number of interest-free annual disbursal of loans during the same period increased from 129 to 177 in 1996–97 but declined to 114 in 1997–98, the average loan amount increasing from about Rs 70000 up to 1996–97 to about Rs 1.25 lakh in 1997–98. The operational cost of loan disbursals was very low in 1994–95 (0.56 per cent). It increased to 1.00 per cent in 1996–97 because a computer was purchased in that year. The cost in the following year declined to 0.35 per cent, whereas larger and registered IFIs of India are struggling to keep their operational costs below 10 per cent. The Barkat Association is also maintaining a reserve fund for acquiring its own office premises.

The *modus operandi* is that membership is only open to permanent Muslim businessmen of Belgaum. Each member has to pay membership fees of Rs 10 000 and a deposit of Rs 5000 on each loan of Rs1 lakh. A further amount of Rs 650 is to be paid per loan towards meeting the operational costs of the Association and Rs 350 as building fund. A loan of Rs 50 000 to one lakh is given to the members for a period of not more than six months. Every borrower has to immediately start paying a daily instalment of Rs 350 on a loan of Rs 50 000, Rs 450 on a loan of Rs 75 000 and Rs 600 on a loan of Rs 100 000. A member who delays the repayment for more than ten days gets only 75 per cent of the next loan. For a delay of more than 15 days, the next loan amount is cut to only 50 per cent and for more than one month's delay no loan is sanctioned for the next six months. Any shortfalls in repayment of the loan amount are recovered from the two guarantors. Thus there are some outstanding loans but no bad debts at all. Operational costs are minimized by voluntary work by all the office holders of the managing committee, which is selected unanimously by the members each year.

All the other six associations of businessmen of Belgaum follow more or less the same model. In different towns there are different types of financial Associations of Persons. The majority of them are philanthropic in nature. In a secular country like India, where the financial rules and regulations are not conducive to establishment and operation of interest-free Islamic banking, these financial non-profit Associations of Persons are providing significant economic services to the minority businessmen. Their role is, however, limited, as they cannot have more than 150 members. Nor can they finance large businesses for longer periods. Nevertheless, in the absence of helpful legal provisions, where Islamic interest-free banking cannot be established, this model of financial Associations of Persons can serve the Muslim businessmen well at the grass-roots level and sustain their business in an era of increasing privatization and market competition.

4. INTEREST-FREE FUNDS AND WELFARE SOCIETIES

The Muslim clergy of India was mainly responsible for the establishment of Muslim Funds and Islamic Welfare Societies. Both of these are either registered under the Societies Act or the Trust Act. These are non-profit institutions and are generally small in size. They mobilize interest-free local savings and extend interest-free loans usually against the security of gold ornaments. Muslim Funds operate widely in North India, mainly in Uttar Pradesh (UP), and Islamic Welfare Societies in South India, mainly in Kerala. More than 200 Islamic Welfare Societies are functioning in Kerala alone.[8] Overall, there may be more than 300 Muslim Funds and Islamic Welfare Societies functioning in India. Their total working capital is estimated to be around one crore rupees.

The meeting of operational costs is a big hurdle in the way of growth of interest-free, non-profit IFIs of India. Generally, part of the operational cost is met from donations, and a part from service charges, which are fixed arbitrarily. The service charge is collected in various forms. Some institutions collect it in the form of monthly fees, some on a quarterly basis, some collect it by selling loan application forms, while others collect a fixed sum based on the amount and period of loan.

The regulatory framework for Non-Bank Financial Companies (NBFCs) issued by the Reserve Bank of India (RBI) in 1998 has clouded the future of these institutions. However, since these institutions are welfare-oriented and non-commercial and non-profit, they are expected to survive. More recently they have been exempted from seeking RBI registration.

Muslim Fund Najibabad has been selected for intensive study because it is the largest fund and represents the characteristics of most of the other funds which dominate the Islamic financial sector in North India.

4.1 Muslim Fund Najibabad

After the partition of India and the abolition of the *zamindārī* system,[9] the Muslim masses of North India became increasingly poor. Their poverty and indebtedness drove them into the vicious clutches of money-lenders who exploited them to the hilt. The Islamic model of interest-free economic funds was developed to encourage poor farmers and workers to save small amounts on a daily or weekly basis and to get interest-free loans. Dozens of such Funds, led by the Muslim Fund Deoband, started in northern India, especially in UP between 1960 and 1980. The Muslim Fund Najibabad (MFN), which started in 1971, is the biggest one, with 29 branches throughout the country.

4.1.1 Deposits

The economic performance of MFN is given in Table 9.2. Spot deposits are the only deposits collected from people, who are mostly poor. They are like

Table 9.2 Economic performance of Muslim Fund Najibabad, 1971–98 (figures in rupees)

Year (1)	Spot deposits (2)	Gold loans (3)	Surety loans (4)	Educational loans (5)	Total loans (6)	Total operational costs (7)	Operational costs received from borrowers (8)	Bank interest earnings (9)	Dividend & misc. income (10)	Total income (11)	Excess of income over costs (12)	Total reserve funds (13)	Total assets and reserves (14)
1971–72	91 328	64 772	8 230	0	73 002	3 294	3 813	0	0	3 814	519	0	0
(%)	NA	NA	11.27	NA	79.93	4.51	115.76	NA	NA	NA	13.61	NA	NA
1975–76	1 079 265	872 792	0	0	872 792	28 889	39 056	3 884	0	42 941	14 051	42 483	0
(%)	1081.75	88.73	NA	NA	80.87	3.31	135.19	9.05	NA	1025.84	32.72	NA	NA
1980–81	6 044 357	3 538 870	0	0	3 538 870	165 413	181 495	26 529	0	208 025	42 611	267 537	0
(%)	460.04	100.00	NA	NA	58.55	4.67	109.72	12.75	NA	384.44	20.48	529.75	NA
1985–86	18 425 007	11 837 460	238 912	16 200	12 092 572	907 191	785 531	218 300	22 400	1 026 231	119 040	440 091	1 925 824
(%)	204.83	100.00	1.98	0.13	65.63	7.50	86.59	21.27	2.18	393.32	11.60	64.50	NA
1990–91	44 064 995	34 408 744	1 079 410	30 400	35 518 554	3 714 492	1 977 089	1 718 278	25 291	3 720 658	6 166	449 172	6 445 870
(%)	139.16	97.89	3.04	0.09	80.60	10.46	53.23	46.18	0.68	262.56	0.17	2.06	234.71
1995–96	89 409 442	27 908 492	3 441 717	58 650	31 408 859	3 888 116	1 181 595	2 086 441	71 763	3 339 799	–548 317	3 745 697	15 403 973
(%)	102.90	96.88	10.96	0.19	35.13	12.38	30.39	62.47	2.15	–10.24	–16.42	733.91	138.97
1996–97	101 471 642	33 166 426	2 639 134	56 400	35 861 960	5 963 665	3 119 049	2 915 409	71 041	6 105 499	141 834	3 603 863	20 428 070
(%)	13.49	88.86	7.36	0.16	35.34	16.63	52.30	47.75	1.16	82.81	2.32	–3.79	32.62
1997–98	125 922 828	38 312 917	4 481 743	71 000	42 865 660	8 231 521	3 542 407	4 651 746	954 017	9 148 170	916 649	3 545 823	23 662 487
(%)	24.10	92.48	10.46	0.17	34.04	19.20	43.03	50.85	10.43	49.83	10.02	–1.61	15.83

Notes:

1. Column (6) percentages represent percentage of spot deposits.
2. Column (7) percentages represent percentage of total loans.
3. Column (8) percentages represent percentage of total operational cost.
4. Columns (9), (10) and (12) percentages represent percentage of total income.
5. Rest of the percentages represent annual growth rates.

pigmy deposits collected by agents going from door to door on a daily or weekly basis. Over a period of 27 years, spot deposits have increased from Rs 91 328 in 1971–72 to Rs 12.59 crore in 1997–98. These deposits are withdrawable any time. In fact, frequent withdrawals are a big problem. Many depositors (especially non-Muslim traders) have been using the facility for overnight safe keeping of their daily collections and getting rid of small change and soiled currency notes. Exchange, disposal and utilization of soiled, unwanted currency notes are big problems for the management.

4.1.2 Loans

MFN mainly provides three types of loans: loans against the security of gold ornaments; loans against personal security of two signatories, which are actually unsecured loans; and educational loans. Both gold and surety loans are given for only three months. But most of the loans are renewed until they are refunded. Hence no data on outstanding or bad debts are available. Although some of the loans are a decade old, no serious effort has been made to recover them. Neither has the deposited jewellery ever been sold to recover bad debts by any of the dozens of Muslim Funds. In fact, the managements of Muslim Funds have built the credibility of their institutions and operations on the basis of their policy of never selling deposited ornaments to recover loans. They are apprehensive about changing this policy. It is only when the borrower himself so desires, or if he dies and his inheritors decide to sell these ornaments to settle the dues, that the jewellery is auctioned or sold. Keeping the unsecured loans in check is the only measure these funds seem to be taking to reinstate a float. For instance, they stopped providing unsecured loans between 1975 and 1984. Subsequently they could only contain them at a comparatively low level of around 10 per cent. The total of gold-secured loans increased from Rs 64 772 in 1972 to Rs 3.83 crores in 1998. The unsecured loans during the same period increased from Rs 8230 to Rs 44.82 lakh. Educational loans, which started in 1981–82 with nominal loans of Rs 16 200, are more of a community welfare service.

4.1.3 Costs

No service charges are imposed on educational loans, but service charges are imposed on other loans. Initially Rs 10 were collected as service charges on loans of Rs 1000, that is, 1 per cent. This was increased to 5 per cent in 1980, 7 per cent in 1985 and 10 per cent in 1990. The total operational costs have increased gradually from 4.51 per cent in 1971–72 to 7.5 per cent in 1985–86, 10.46 per cent in 1990–91, 16.63 per cent in 1996–97 and 19.20 per cent in 1997–98. But since 1985 operational costs also include the expenditure on charitable education and health projects. Neither separate nor systematic accounting of interest-free lending costs is maintained, which is always a tough proposition for the low-paid, non-qualified, untrained and ill-equipped managerial staff of almost all the Muslim Funds in India. The current monthly salary of a junior branch manager is Rs 3575 and of a senior manager Rs 4500 per month, which works out at just about $82 and $104 respectively.

MFN, and dozens of similar Funds, cannot afford to employ professional staff because they seek to keep their operational costs down. Their average operational costs are comparatively high because their scale of operations is very small, in turn, because, in secular India, they have neither independent statutory status nor any appropriate regulatory body. As charitable financial societies, they cannot accept more than 250 deposits. Hence MFN, which is the biggest, and one of the comparatively better-managed Funds, started a company called Al-Najib Milli Mutual Benefits Ltd in 1990 under the Indian Companies Act. Since 1990 both institutions have been operating from the same offices with common staff and almost the same office-holders.[10]

4.1.4 Recovery of costs

The recovery of operational costs is a big issue for the interest-free, non-profit financial institutions of India. Until 1980–81, when the number of offices and the loan disbursals were comparatively low, the operational costs recovered from borrowers was more than 100 per cent but from 1985–86 cost recovery continued to fall, from 86.59 per cent in 1985–86 to 43.03 per cent in 1997–98. The Muslim Fund management was forced to meet part of the costs from other sources of income, including bank interest from fixed deposits, dividend from investments in the Unit Trust of India (UTI), and other miscellaneous income.

4.1.5 Income

The MFN, like all other IFIs of India, has no alternative but to keep its excess cash in commercial banks. Initially they were keeping such cash in current accounts, which earn no interest, but subsequently many of them have started placing it in fixed accounts, and the interest accruals are being used to meet some of the welfare and building expenses when absolutely necessary. Bank interest earnings of the MFN have gradually increased from around 9.05 per cent of total income in 1975–76 to 50.85 per cent in 1997–98, after touching 62.47 per cent in 1995–96. Dividends earned from investments in UTI (Unit Trust of India) and miscellaneous income have increased from around 2.18 per cent in 1985–86 to over 10.43 per cent in 1997–98. Except in 1995–96, when the MFN made a net loss of Rs 54 8317, the total earnings have always been more than operational costs. The losses in 1995–96 were mainly due to failure and liquidation of a computer education centre run by the Fund.

4.1.6 Problems

The main economic problem of the MFN is that, while its deposit mobilization efforts are very good, the spot deposits have grown to over Rs 12.59 crores at the end of 1997–98; total loans outstanding in the same period are only about Rs 4.29 crores, that is, 34.04 per cent of the deposits. In fact, in 1971–72, 1975–76 and 1990–91 over 80 per cent of deposits were loaned but between 1995 and 1998 the loans have fallen to only around 35 per cent. In other words, the MFN has substantial liquid funds without any avenues of use. In addition to the substantial liquid funds, they also have gold jewellery worth more than Rs 4.00 crores. However, we cannot apply yardsticks of a commercial bank to judge the operational efficiency of Muslim Funds. Loans are not the assets of Muslim Funds; neither is credit creation their objective. Besides, the spot deposits of Muslim Funds are current deposits liable to be withdrawn more frequently. In fact, the withdrawals during some months of the year, and in some of the branches, are very heavy. Public confidence also swings wildly whenever an NBFC closes a shop or when relations between India and Pakistan worsen, leading to substantial withdrawals, especially from branches where the proportion of non-Muslim depositors is high. In general, non-Muslim depositors are about 10 per cent, but in some of the branches, they are over 35 per cent. Out of 90 per cent of Muslim depositors, Muslim women form only about 20 per cent.

The management feels that the lower productivity of employees, the higher cost of deposit mobilization, the government's changing financial policies, the failure of other NBFCs, and corruption of the government officials are the main problems facing their Fund, in that order. Little do they realize that their limited objectives, lack of professional management, and compromise with interest-free financial principles are also significant problems.

The stated objective of the management is 'to save lowest classes of people especially Muslims from the clutches of 60 per cent interest charged by money lenders, and also to provide them some education and health care facilities'. According to I.M. Zaki, General Manager of the MFN, 75 per cent of UP Muslims belong to lower and backward classes; 15 per cent belong to the middle class. Only about 10 per cent of Muslims are rich enough to have savings in banks from which they may be earning 5 per cent to 10 per cent interest. Unless 75 per cent of lower-class Muslims, mainly small farmers and workers, who are living in perpetual debt, are saved from the clutches of *mahājans* and money-lenders, they will end up paying 60 per cent interest and also lose their jewellery. Their economic condition will go on worsening. Thus, what MFN and other Muslim Funds and Islamic Welfare Societies are doing is saving some of the backward Muslims from exploitative interest payments and safeguarding their jewellery. Other economic benefits (if any) and welfare activities are only incidental.

5. INTEREST-FREE COOPERATIVE CREDIT SOCIETIES

Given the constraints of Indian banking and financial regulations, the cooperative model has been the most amenable to interest-free Islamic finance.

Unfortunately, because of widespread ignorance, ethnic and linguistic differences, and a lack of industriousness, Indian Muslims did not adopt the interest-free cooperative model so successfully developed by The Patni Cooperative Credit Society Ltd of Surat as far back as in 1938. It took 37 years for Indian Muslims to successfully establish another interest-free cooperative society in Bombay in 1976, that is, Bait-un-Nasr Cooperative Credit Society Ltd. It has been followed by just one more successful cooperative society, again in Bombay, namely *Baitulmāl* Cooperative Credit Society Ltd.

Generally, ten or more persons can come together to contribute their own share capital and start a cooperative credit (consumers' or producers') society. The only problem is that every state in India has its own Cooperative Society Act under which a cooperative society can be established only within that state. Though multi-state cooperative societies can be started under the Multi-State Cooperative Societies Act of the Central Government, it is rather cumbersome and time-consuming. So far, Indian Muslims have not been able to start any multi-state cooperative society, even though Bait-un-Nasr has been contemplating it for a long time.

The Patni Cooperative Credit Society Ltd of Surat, Gujarat, has been selected for detailed study because it is the earliest effort to establish an Islamic financial institution.

5.1 The Patni Cooperative Credit Society Limited, Surat

As the first IFI in India, the Society was established in Surat in Gujarat before Independence (1947). The Muslim businessmen from Patan, who settled in Surat, had started the Patni Cooperative Credit Society Ltd as early as in 1938.[11] The British authorities of the state registered it in 1942. The Society is functioning successfully even today. Table 9.3 provides data on its economic performance.

5.1.1 Deposits

The Patni Cooperative Credit Society started in 1938–39 with an authorized capital of Rs 15 000 which was increased to Rs 9.00 lakhs in 1994–95. The society initially accepted deposits but they were gradually converted into shares to avoid payment of compulsory interest. The share capital was increased from Rs 36 354 in 1949–50 to Rs 7.71 lakhs in 1997–98. Membership fees of Rs 3 are collected from each member but by the following year they are converted into shares. An entry fee of Rs 1 is also collected from new members. The Society was also running a consumer's cooperative called Hilal Store until 1983. The value of the store's stock in 1959–60 was worth Rs 188 777. The idea was to use the profits earned by the store to meet the operational costs of extending interest-free loans by the Society. But when the store made a loss of Rs 49 in 1982–83, it was closed.

Table 9.3 Economic performance of the Patni Cooperative Credit Society Ltd, Surat, 1939/40–1997/98 (figures in rupees)

Year (1)	Authorized capital (2)	Deposits (3)	Shares (4)	No. of loans (5)	Total loans (6)	Investment in equities (7)	Investment in handlooms (8)	Total dividend after tax (9)	Total operational costs (10)	Out-standing loans (11)	Bad debts (12)	Total reserves (13)
1939–40	15 000	3 254	NA	18	1 374	2 324	NIL	62	40	0	NIL	610
1949–50	115 000	83 869	36 354	NA	27 200	54 258	NIL	2 198	15 080	18 940	NIL	42 143
(%)	666.67	2477.41	NA	NA	1879.62	2234.68	NA	3445.16	NA	NA	NA	6808.69
1959–60	115 000	102 643	76 749	NA	45 615	162 375	NIL	9 103	6 545*	32 260	NIL	92 489
(%)	0.00	22.38	111.12	NA	67.70	199.26	NA	314.15	–56.60	70.33	NA	119.46
1969–70	300 000	11 000	138 501	236	94 900	191 825	NIL	12 971	20 246*	56 296	NIL	154 600
(%)	160.87	–89.28	80.46	NA	108.05	18.14	NA	42.49	209.34	74.51	NA	67.16
1979–80	300 000	1961	271 602	483	197 200	200 448	NIL	29 373	36 560*	156 950	NIL	399 900
(%)	0.00	–82.17	96.10	104.66	107.80	4.50	NA	126.45	80.58	178.79	NA	158.67
1989–90	715 000	NIL	461 601	361	215 800	944 978	390 000	113 440	52 625**	213 895	NIL	1 315 486
(%)	138.33	NA	69.95	–25.26	9.43	371.43	NA	286.21	43.94	36.28	NA	228.95
1994–95	900 000	NIL	764 841	448	381 800	1 456 542	NIL	135 307	73 126**	322 360	NIL	1 546 551
(%)	25.87	NA	65.69	24.10	76.92	54.14	NA	19.28	38.96	50.71	NA	17.56
1997–98	900 000	NIL	771 465	586	711 500	2 675 772	15 000	387 981	537 656***	682 410	NIL	3 761 800
(%)	0.00	NA	0.87	30.80	86.35	83.71	NA	186.74	635.25	111.69	NA	143.24

Notes:
* Running costs of store are also included.
** Provision of Rs 25 000, for tax on dividend.
*** Income tax Rs 1.5 lakhs + Rs 1.85 lakhs spent on souvenir printing are also included.

5.1.2 Loans

Only 18 persons were given interest-free loans of Rs 1374 during the entire year of 1939–40. The average loan was just Rs 77.33. It must be noted, however, that in 1940 the daily wage of an unskilled worker was only about Rs 0.25 and the salary of a new primary school teacher was Rs 15 per month. In 1988, 586 persons were given an average loan of Rs 1214, totalling Rs 711 500.

5.1.3 Investments

The Society (which extends not only interest-free but totally cost-free loans) is the only Islamic Society to have invested part of its share capital in equities and handlooms. The income from this is used to meet operational costs and to maintain scores of reserve funds. The after-tax dividend of the Society increased from just Rs 62 in 1939–40 to Rs 387 981 in 1997–98. The investment in equities has registered an impressive growth. It grew from just Rs 2324 in 1939–40 to Rs 26.76 lakh in 1997–98. The operational costs of the Society until 1979–80 also include the costs of running the cooperative store. Subsequently, they include income tax payments. Hence the cost of advancing loans alone cannot be effectively determined.

5.1.4 Problems

The Society is an illustrious example of the small Muslim community of Surat, Gujarat finding their own way to eschew *ḥarām* interest in an economy and polity which is alien to the concept and unhelpful to the practice of interest-free transactions. Its first limitation is the scope of its operations. It caters only to the members of the Patni Society rather than Muslims in general. Its second limitation is that the Society is not a commercial endeavour. Its functions are more of a philanthropic nature. However, the Society has been proving its worth since 1938 for other Muslims in India to follow suit and emulate the example. Perhaps if other Muslims throughout the country had also established such cooperative societies earlier, their economic condition would have been much better today.

6. ISLAMIC FINANCIAL COMPANIES

Non-Bank Financial Companies are an important part of the Indian financial system bordering its banking sector. Indian commercial banks can only accept deposits and lend on an interest basis. They cannot accept equity finance or invest on a profit/loss-sharing basis. It is left to NBFCs to perform these functions. It was in 1980 that the first Islamic Financial Company (IFC), called Al-Mizan, was established at Madras. It was promoted by leading Muslim leather merchants of Tamil Nadu. It consisted of a mother company and a group of 19 partnership firms, each with 19 members. The share capital of each partner was in multiples of Rs 25 000. Thus, share capital of more than Rs 350 crores was raised. Each partnership firm was responsible for the purchase of raw leather from its area and for supplying it to the mother company at a reasonable profit. The managing partner of every partnership firm was the representative of the mother company. Unfortunately, the experiment failed miserably in 1984–85 when the company incurred heavy losses due mainly to dishonesty and lack of professional and efficient management.

Bait-un-Nasr of Bombay has promoted a number of investment companies. Two public limited investment companies (Falah Investments Ltd and Ittefaq Investments Ltd) were established in 1983. In 1988 Barkat Investments Ltd was established. Barkat Leasing and Financial Services Ltd (BLFSL) was established in 1991. The deposit base of the Barkat Group of companies had shown remarkable progress until 1997, increasing from a few lakh rupees in 1984 to Rs 32 crore in 1997. However, since 1997–98 it has been incurring heavy losses due to huge unprofitable investments in real estate.

The Al-Ameen educational group of Bangalore had established an interest-based urban cooperative bank called Amanat Bank, which is running successfully and has recently secured scheduled bank status. The group also started Al-Ameen Islamic Financial and Investment Corporation (AIFIC) in 1986, which is functioning mainly as a leasing company. It has 25 branches all over the country. Its share capital increased to Rs 1.32 crores and deposits to about Rs 11 crores in 1996–97. AIFIC was making steady profits until 1995–96, but since 1996–97 it has been incurring losses.

The story of many other Islamic financial companies is not much different. Except for Albaraka Finance House Ltd of Bombay and Assalam Financial and Investment Co. Pvt. Ltd of Calicut, Kerala, none of the IFCs of India was able to secure RBI registration until April 1999. This is because they did not fulfil the prudential norms set by the RBI. Whereas the applications of Al-Falah Finance Ltd and Fateh Leasing and Finance (P) Ltd of Delhi have been rejected by the RBI, the applications of other IFCs are still pending.

Sayad Shariat Finance Ltd of Tamil Nadu is another leasing company which is doing well in spite of the limitations set by the RBI's norms for NBFCs. It was established in 1987–88. Its share capital has increased to Rs 2.37 crores and deposits to Rs 13.93 crores. It has earned net profit of Rs 26.67 lakh and declared a 16 per cent dividend in 1997–98 even after refunding public deposits worth Rs 4.76 crores in the year as per the RBI norms.

Some of the economically unsound and mismanaged IFCs of India such as Al-Falah Investments of Lucknow and Baitul Islam Finance and Investment (P) Ltd of Calicut, Kerala, have been wound up. Many others are struggling to survive not only due to strict RBI norms but also because of lack of professional management and public support, especially of the Muslim community, mainly because they are not transparent in their dealings.

Barkat Leasing and Financial Services Ltd of Bombay has been selected for detailed study because it has a national character and fairly represents the endeavour of IFCs of India.

6.1 Barkat Leasing and Financial Services Limited, Mumbai

Barkat Leasing and Financial Services Ltd (BLFSL) of Mumbai is a flagship of the Barkat group of companies which are the offshoots of Bait-un-Nasr Cooperative Credit Society Ltd. The Barkat Group of Companies includes Falah Investments Ltd and Ittefaq Investments Ltd, established in 1983, the Barkat Investment Corporation, established in 1988, and Muhafiz Credit and Investment India Pvt. Ltd, established in 1994. The Barkat group also includes four partnership firms, namely Barkat Finance and Investments, Barkat Savings, Barkat Securities and Finance and Barkat Stocks and Investment. BLFSL was established in 1991 as a non-deposit accepting leasing company to accept variable-rate fully convertible debentures (FCD) and equity.[12] It had the advantage of operating from as many as 15 branches mainly in the southern and western states of the country. In addition, since 1994 it has entered into an understanding with Muslim Fund Najibabad to promote each other's business from their offices.

6.1.1 Working capital

IFCs of India are mobilizing their funds largely through *muḍārabah* term deposits from both resident and non-resident Indians. The depositors are generally entitled to bonuses distributed usually at half-yearly intervals on the basis of profits earned by the company on *murābaḥah* investments. Scheme deposits, such as advance linked deposits, *taufīr* (savings) deposits and housing deposits, are also employed by some of the IFCs. Share capital is the other source of working capital raised by IFCs in India. The Albaraka Finance House Ltd is the only IFC which is also raising its working capital either through interest-free loans from its principal, Dalalh Albaraka, or through interest-based loans from Bank of Baroda, which it calls Islamically permissible back-to-back lease finance. BLFSL is, however, raising its working capital either through FCDs with a variable rate of return or share capital (Table 9.4). The contribution of FCDs has gradually increased to 90.25 per cent in 1997–98.

6.1.2 Investment pattern

Generally, most of the income of IFCs of India is earned from *ijārah* (leasing) investments. Hire purchase and mark-up pricing (which involves a contract in which a client wishing to purchase equipment or goods requests the company

Table 9.4 Fund mobilization and deployment by Barkat Leasing and Financial Services Ltd, Mumbai, 1991–98

Year (1)	Authorized capital Rs lakhs (2)	Share capital Rs lakhs (3)	Convertible debentures Rs lakhs (4)	Profits C/F Rs (5)	Total funds Rs (6)	Investment in equity Rs (7)	*Ijārah* investments Rs (8)	Inv. in call money Rs (9)	Fixed deposits Rs (10)	Inv. in real estate Rs (11)	Total investments Rs (12)	Bank balances Rs (13)
1991–92	10	5.00	0	2 604	593 191	0	322 100	0	0	0	32 210	479 420
(%)	NA	84.29		0.44			1000.00	NA	NA	NA	NA	NA
1992–93	100	25.00	0	15 589	2 515 589	196 750	1 479 042	424 000	0	0	2 099 792	609 022
(%)	NA	99.38		0.62	324.08	9.37	70.44	20.19	NA	NA	6419.07	27.0
1993–94	100	25.00	32.75	127 908	5 902 908	1 071 910	4 086 581	213 400	0	0	7 292 491	750 455
(%)	NA	42.35	55.48	2.17	134.65	14.70	56.04	2.93	NA	NA	247.30	23.2
1994–95	100	28.07	147.65	246 485	17 818 485	5 469 936	11 398 535	2 194 000	0	0	19 062 471	1 679 142
(%)	NA	15.75	82.86	1.38	201.86	28.69	59.80	11.51	NA	NA	161.40	21.3
1995–96	100	62.63	616.60	652 511	68 575 511	2 680 330	22 080 741	47 722 254	5 000	0	72 488 325	2 037 594
(%)	NA	9.13	89.92	0.95	284.86	3.70	30.46	65.83	NA	NA	280.27	
1996–97	200	91.26	902.85	764 218	100 175 218	2 623 898	36 805 098	78 879 528	5 000	0	118 313 624	1 205 548
(%)	NA	9.11	90.13	0.76	46.08	2.22	31.11	66.67	NA	NA	63.22	40.8
1997–98	200	143.6	1340.18	0	148 378 000	2 496 130	33 383 820	77 022 504	5 000	40 527 016	153 434 470	4 489 630
(%)	NA	9.68	90.32	NA	48.12	1.63	21.76	50.20	NA	26.41	29.68	–2.7

Notes:
1. Columns (6), (12) and (13) percentages represent annual growth rates.
2. Columns (3), (4) and (5) percentages represent percentage of total funds.
3. Columns (7), (8), (9) and (11) percentages represent percentage of total investments.

to purchase these items and resell them to him at cost plus a reasonable profit payable on the terms agreed to between the parties) is another important source of earnings of IFCs. *Mushārakah*, *muḍārabah* or joint-venture financing on a profit/loss-sharing basis are also employed as tools of investments and earnings in a small number of cases. Investments in equity shares of the blue-chip companies, and in real estate or housing finance, are other income earning avenues of IFCs of India.

BLFSL is investing most of its funds in the leasing business, followed by investments in call money and in equity shares of leading companies listed on the stock exchange. In 1997–98, BLFSL invested Rs 4.05 crores, in real estate and lost heavily. The investment pattern of BLFSL shows that investments in call money with Barkat Savings and Barkat Investment Corporation are its unique feature. This is an avenue which none of the other IFCs of India have access to. Thus, unlike other IFCs of India, BLFSL is the only one that has been utilizing its idle cash for short-term investments and income-earning opportunities. In fact, BLFSL is in a better position to do this because the Barkat group has several companies (including partnership firms) that can effectively utilize idle cash. BLFSL is also investing in their variable-return deposits. In fact, the investments in call money have gradually increased to over 50 per cent, whereas in leasing they have declined to 22 per cent, and in equities to 2 per cent in 1997–98.

6.1.3 Earnings

The RBI has classified most of the IFCs in India as leasing companies because they have been earning more than 50 per cent of their earnings in this way. BLFSL is also earning a substantial portion of its income from leasing office equipment and vehicles. Together with lease management fees, lease rentals account for over 60 per cent of its total earnings except for two years, 1995–96 and 1996–97, when income from other sources, which mainly include earnings from short-term investments in call money, were higher (Table 9.5). Whereas earnings from leasing activities are steadily growing, the returns from investments in equity are fluctuating, which may be why the majority of IFCs of India do not invest in stocks. The general impurity of stocks listed on stock exchanges may be the other reason. The lack of innovative entrepreneurship of Muslim businessmen may be why IFCs of India usually do not invest or earn much from joint-venture and project financing on a profit/loss-sharing basis.

6.1.4 Problems

Economic recession has severely affected the performance of BLFSL, especially in 1997–98. The sudden and substantial investment in the crashing real estate market is not the only cause of huge losses. Returns from investments in stocks, as well as in call money (other income from investments in deposits with

Table 9.5 Income of Barkat Leasing and Financial Services Ltd, Mumbai, 1991–98 (figures in rupees)

Yearwise distribution of income						
Year (1)	Lease rentals (2)	Lease mgt fees (3)	Other income (4)	Profit from sale of equities (5)	Profit from sale of assets (6)	Total (7)
1991–92	0	16 105	0	0	0	16 105
(%)	NA	100.00	NA	NA	NA	NA
1992–93	246 562	1 250	44 906	0	0	292 718
(%)	84.23	0.43	15.34	0.00	0.0	1717.56
1993–94	523 029	15 071	62 434	35 460	0	635 994
(%)	82.24	2.37	9.82	5.58	0.0	117.27
1994–95	1 790 971	67 208	431 181	913 199	0	3 202 559
(%)	55.92	2.10	13.46	28.51	0.0	403.55
1995–96	3 540 013	134 941	4 523 661	1 663 133	0	9 861 748
(%)	35.90	1.37	45.87	16.86	0.0	207.93
1996–97	6 557 929	230 870	8 901 104	26 025	139 584	15 855 512
(%)	41.36	1.46	56.14	0.16	0.88	60.78
1997–98	7 623 420	80 674	92 454	12 343	65 253	7 874 144
(%)	96.82	1.02	1.17	0.16	0.83	–50.34

Note:
Column (7) percentages represent annual growth rates. Rest of the percentages represent percentage of total income.

variable returns), have also declined sharply. For example, a marginal decline of investments in call money in 1997–98 has led to a staggering 55 per cent decline in income from short-term investments. Thus effective investments of BLFSL in real estate in 1997–98 were more than Rs 11.75 crores, that is, over 75 per cent of total investment. In retrospect, it may be said that the inability of the management to foresee the crash in the real-estate market and the lack of wisdom in its investment strategy led to the downfall of BLFSL. The Barkat group, in their eagerness to earn quick income, invested even short-term funds in long-term investments without paying due attention to the on-setting recession and their own liquidity position. Nor did they maintain enough reserves to meet any contingency. The result was that, with a working capital of about Rs 15 crores, BLFSL could not withstand losses of Rs 1.07 crores in 1997–98, due to the liquidity crunch. As a result, their operations came to an almost standstill. The so-called call money investments could not be called back because they were blocked in the sliding real-estate market. Even the entire Barkat group, which claimed a total fund resource of Rs 32 crores in 1997–98, could not save the situation. Almost similar was the fate of many other leading IFCs except Albarka of Bombay and Sayed Shariat Finance of Tamil Nadu, which did not invest in real estate and the Assalam Financial and Investment Company (P) Ltd of Calicut to a lesser extent, which had maintained enough liquidity to refund public deposits as per the new NBFC norms imposed by the RBI since 1997. All other IFCs had either to close shop or drastically reduce their operations.

7. FUTURE PROSPECTS OF IFIs IN INDIA

The future prospects of IFIs of India are in the hands of the people of India and especially the Muslims. If Indian Muslims adopt Islamic financial principles and practices, its institutionalization cannot be far away. Unless they themselves firmly adhere to the values of interest-free finance and IFIs, they cannot convince non-Muslims, or create a lobby so essential to influence decision-makers in a democracy, to get the necessary statutory support to establish and manage IFIs in India. Al-Ameen Islamic Financial and Investment Corporation Ltd (AIFIC), Barkat Leasing and Financial Services Ltd (BLFSL), and Muslim Fund Najibabad (MFN) together have about 100 branches in different parts of the country. But their membership is only in thousands in a country where there are more than 120 million Muslims. The doors of these institutions are open to non-Muslims only in name, as their membership is less than 3 per cent of the total. The total working capital of IFIs of India is only about Rs 300 crores, whereas the total income share of Indian Muslims is at least Rs 1200 billion, 10 per cent of the Indian net national product. With the national saving rate being around 24 per cent, even if Muslims save just 15 per cent of their incomes, their annual savings should be around Rs 180 billion. It means that the present IFIs of India have mobilized only 0.37 per cent of the savings of Indian Muslims. Is this because IFIs of India do not enjoy the confidence of Indian Muslims? Or is it because Indian Muslims are ignorant of the principles of interest-free finance? Or perhaps it is because IFIs of India cannot perform banking functions. It may be all of these and other factors.

To find out the answers to the above and related questions, a survey on awareness about IFIs of India and Islamic financial principles was conducted in 24 Indian cities and towns. The survey is based on towns, where people are supposed to be more knowledgeable. All the cities, except six, do not have a prominent IFI. All the states, which have a substantial Muslim population except Assam, Andhra and West Bengal, have been covered (See Table 9.6). Thirty persons from each city, two from each of the 15 different professions, were interviewed. In all, 720 persons were interviewed, 90 of them women.

Table 9.6 Awareness survey sample universe

Panel A: Geographical Distribution				Panel B: Professional Distribution	
Serial no.	City	State	Sample size	Professional status of sample	Sample size
1	Agra	Uttar Pradesh	24	Religious scholars	48
2	Aligarh	Uttar Pradesh	24	Bank employees	48
3	Deoband	Uttar Pradesh	24	Farmers	48
4	Najibabad	Uttar Pradesh	24	Fishermen	48
5	Delhi	Delhi	24	Govt officials	48
6	Gurgaon	Haryana	24	Labourers	48
7	Chandigarh	Punjab	24	Large businessmen	48
8	Bhopal	Madhya Pradesh	24	Large industrialists	48
9	Patna	Bihar	24	Mechanics	48
10	Ajmer	Rajastan	24	Petty traders	48
11	Badoda	Gujarat	24	Private officials	48
12	Surat	Gujarat	24	Small industrialists	48
13	Mumbai	Maharashtra	24	Teachers	48
14	Pune	Maharashtra	24	University students	48
15	Sangli	Maharashtra	24	Vendors	48
16	Bangalore	Karnataka	24		
17	Belgaum	Karnataka	24		
18	Bhatkal	Karnataka	24		
19	Dharwad	Karnataka	24		
20	Mysore	Karnataka	24		
21	Kudchi	Karnataka	24		
22	Chennai	Tamil Nadu	24		
23	Calicut	Kerala	24		
24	Kasarkod	Kerala	24		
				Total:	720

7.1 Main Findings

About 56 per cent of urban Indian men and 69 per cent of women (overall 57.5 per cent) are totally unaware of the existence of IFIs in their own city or nearby. Only 31 per cent know that IFIs mobilize interest-free or profit/loss-

Table 9.7 Results of awareness survey about IFIs of India and Islamic financial principles

Subject	Yes			No			Yes (%)			No (%)		
	M	F	T	M	F	T	M	F	T	M	F	T
1 Are you aware of operation of IFIs in India?	278	28	306	353	61	414	44.05	31.46	42.5	55.95	68.53	57.5
2 Are you aware that IFIs mobilize interest-free/PLS deposits?	194	30	224	438	58	496	30.7	34.09	31.11	69.3	65.91	68.89
3 Are you aware that IFIs give interest-free loans?	200	30	230	431	59	490	31.7	33.71	31.94	68.3	66.89	68.05
4 Are you aware that IFIs provide funds for investment on PLS basis?	91	7	98	540	82	622	14.42	7.87	13.61	85.58	92.13	86.39
5 Are you aware that IFIs provide hire-purchase facilities?	112	17	129	519	72	591	17.75	19.1	17.92	82.25	80.9	82.08
6 Are you aware that IFIs work on the basis that interest is not permissible?	520	48	568	111	41	152	82.41	53.93	78.89	17.59	46.07	21.11
7 Are you familiar with alternative Islamic financial instruments?	119	13	132	512	71	583	18.86	15.48	18.46	81.14	84.52	81.54
8 Do you think that IFIs are for Muslims only?	375	54	429	255	36	291	59.43	60	59.58	40.57	40	40.42
9 Does Islamic finance lead to development and welfare?	573	71	644	59	17	76	90.66	80.68	89.44	9.34	19.32	10.56
10 Do you invest in shares?	193	19	212	434	71	505	30.78	21.11	29.57	69.22	78.89	70.43
11 Do you invest in shares for speculation?	76	17	93	554	73	627	12.06	18.89	12.92	87.94	81.11	87.08
12 Do you invest in shares for earning dividends?	171	19	190	462	68	530	27.01	21.83	26.39	72.99	78.17	73.61
13 Will you deposit with an IFI?	526	49	575	105	40	145	83.36	55.06	79.86	16.64	44.94	20.14
14 Will you borrow from IFI?	427	58	485	204	31	235	67.67	65.17	67.36	32.33	34.83	32.64
15 Do you have an account with any IFI?	76	16	92	558	70	628	11.99	18.6	12.78	88.01	81.4	87.22

Note: M = Male. F = Female. T = Total.

sharing (PLS) deposits. Only 32 per cent know that IFIs provide interest-free loans. Only 14 per cent know that IFIs provide funds on PLS basis. Only 18 per cent know that IFIs also provide leasing or hire-purchase facilities. In other words, between 69 per cent and 86 per cent do not know about the functions performed by the IFIs in India. Although 79 per cent of urban Muslims know that interest is not permissible, 82 per cent, including some religious scholars, do not know about alternative Islamic financial instruments. This, perhaps, is the main problem, that is, the lack of involvement of Muslim masses with the IFIs of India.

The majority (60 per cent) of urban Indian Muslims believe that IFIs are for Muslims only. A large percentage (89 per cent) of Muslims believe that interest-free PLS Islamic finance can lead to economic development and welfare. Only 30 per cent of Muslims invest in shares, many of them in the shares of small cooperative societies or partnership firms. Only 13 per cent of the investors in stocks do it for speculative purposes, while 26 per cent do it for dividends. This means that 61 per cent purchase the shares of cooperative credit societies, perhaps because it is compulsory for getting loans, rather than for dividend earnings.

Given an opportunity, 80 per cent of urban Indian Muslims are willing to deposit or invest in IFIs on a PLS basis. Some of the respondents would like to invest only if the IFIs are genuine. However, fewer Muslims (67 per cent) are willing to borrow from IFIs on a PLS basis. This may be because of a comparative lack of entrepreneurship among Indian Muslims. In fact, the experience of IFCs in India is that the demand for, and returns from, PLS capital investments are much lower. Finally, only 13 per cent of urban Muslims have an account in IFIs. It is interesting to note that, proportionately, more women than men have accounts in IFIs. This is because in Muslim Funds and Islamic Welfare Societies, where interest-free loans of Rs 5000 to Rs 10 000 are given, these loans are given against the security of gold ornaments. Therefore, women clients outnumber men.

8. CONCLUSIONS

There are over 300 IFIs operating in India. Most of them (95 per cent) are small, welfare-oriented and philanthropic in nature. They mobilize return-free savings and extend interest-free loans generally against the security of gold ornaments. They recover service charges to meet their operational costs. Financial Associations of Persons formed by Muslim businessmen are fairly successful in providing short-term business loans. Interest-free cooperative credit societies are also doing well. However, the cooperative format is not utilized extensively by Indian Muslims, perhaps due to lack of education. The majority of the non-profit IFIs of India cannot afford to employ qualified staff. Hence, they are not managed professionally. Nevertheless, smaller non-profit IFIs can continue to flourish as interest-free micro credit financial institutions and satisfy the credit needs of economically backward Muslims.

The financial laws in India do not favour IFIs. As a result, Islamic banks cannot be established in India. Nor can they totally eliminate interest earnings on account of compulsory investments in government securities to comply with a statutory liquidity ratio and other norms. However, Islamic financial companies are being established as Non-Banking Financial Companies that are mobilizing *muḍārabah* deposits and investing mainly in *ijārah*, *murābaḥah* and *mushārakah* business avenues. They are yet to gather financial expertise and strength to make a favourable impact on the economic conditions of Indian Muslims. They are also struggling to fulfil new prudential norms of capital adequacy and credit rating set by the RBI. The lack of transparency and professionalism, together with the absence of a regulatory authority to standardize and monitor the operations of IFIs, have led to failure of some of the IFCs. However, with increasing economic liberalization and globalization of the Indian economy, IFIs of India (especially IFCs) have better prospects provided they come up to the RBI norms, professionalize their operations and enter into national as well as international collaboration.

The awareness survey about IFIs of India reveals that a vast majority of Indian Muslims are unaware of the existence and functioning of IFIs in their own towns and cities. The sooner they learn, adopt and practise the principles of Islamic finance and patronize the existing IFIs, the better will be the prospects of IFIs in India. The IFIs for their part will have to improve their transparency, credibility and proficiency, and reach out not only to the Muslim masses but also to non-Muslims if they desire to improve their prospects and generate significant impact on the economic conditions of Indian Muslims in particular and others in general.

NOTES

1. Rahmatullah (1992), pp. 11–12.
2. Some of the mosques in India have small and medium-size charitable societies called *baitulmāls*.
3. An *anjuman* is a social organization of Muslims in most of the cities and towns of South India.
4. Chit funds are contributions by groups of people on a monthly basis. One member wins the draw every month.
5. *Mahājan* is a Hindu community of money-lenders.
6. One crore is equal to 10 million.
7. One lakh is equal to 0.1 million.
8. Rahman (1998), pp. 53–8.

9. The *zamindārī* system refers to ownership of land by absentee landlords and cultivation by tenants.
10. Nasir (1997), pp. 20–21.
11. Nuroddin (1968), pp. 3–4.
12. Khatkhate (1997), p. 18.

REFERENCES

Khatkhate, M.H. (1997), 'Islamic Investment Activities in India', paper presented at the Second Conference on Islamic Banking and Finance, Toronto, Canada.

Nasir, M.H. (1997), *Twenty-Five Years of Travelogue of Muslim Fund Najibabad* (in Urdu), Rampura, Najibabad, India.

Nuroddin, A.H. (1968), *Silver Jubilee Souvenir, The Patni Cooperative Credit Society Ltd*, Surat, Gujarat, India.

Rahman, K.T. Abdul (1998), *Interest Free Banking Institutions in Kerala: An Economic Analysis*, M.Phil. Dissertation, Pondicherry Central University, Kerala, India.

Rahmatullah (1992), *Directory: Islamic Banks in India*, Mumbai, India: AICMEU.

COMMENTS

Fazlur Rahman Faridi

This survey of Islamic financial institutions in India is a pioneering study. It represents the first attempt to critically examine and evaluate the establishment and working of such institutions. Before this study our only source of information comprised substandard and infrequent reports of these institutions themselves that intended only to score some propaganda points and concealed more than they revealed.

The study is significant in many respects. It begins with a brief statement of the legal and institutional constraints in which Islamic finance has to operate in India. The banking legislation in India is based on interest-based financial transactions and, as a consequence, creates hurdles for any alternative system of financial intermediation. Although Indian banking law does not directly prohibit interest-free financial intermediation, it does prohibit banks from practising direct equity financing and ownership. In addition to this basic constraint, the rules and regulations frequently imposed by the Reserve Bank of India (RBI) to control the liquidity and viability of banks work against the establishment of medium and large-scale financial cooperatives. In view of this built-in constraint, interest-free banking institutions fall out of the purview of the RBI and are denied whatever benefits are provided to conventional banks by this authority.

Two important considerations weigh heavily with the controlling authorities in India, similar to the perception of such authorities elsewhere. First is the apprehension that direct investment in production ventures by financial intermediaries promotes undue monopolization of industry and trade. Second is the belief that interest-free banks' activities cannot be controlled by traditional tools of credit control, which rely mostly on the variation of market rates of interest. Hence the RBI does not favour the establishment of Islamic banks in India.

Bagsiraj has carefully examined the tortuous journey of Islamic financial institutions. He has correctly classified these institutions into (a) charitable, (b) financial cooperatives, and (c) finance leasing and investment companies. He has selected some model institutions and tried to examine critically their proximity to Islamic values. His examination of these institutions is hampered by the lack of data and also lack of transparency in their working. But despite these handicaps he has been able to point to the fundamental strengths and weaknesses of these institutions.

He points to a lack of coordination and absence of any countrywide or region-wise network to provide infrastructure services that leads to several problems. Foremost among these is the non-existence or inadequacy of any liquidity funds. In times of crises each institution has to depend on its own resources. Second is the absence of any consultation or coordination in investment policies or avenues. For this purpose also, each institution has to depend on its own sources. Being small in size, their task is difficult and costly. The inadequacy of liquidity provision has landed some of these institutions in a curious situation. Some of them, like Najibabad Muslim Fund (NMF), maintain credit balances with conventional banks and meet their expenses from interest accruing on their deposits.

A second weakness of these institutions is their failure to find profitable investment opportunities that are Islamically valid. The author is right when he says that smallness of size and lack of innovative endeavour on the part of the institutions are factors responsible for this.

However, the author has not examined the reasons why the financial authorities in India view Islamic finance with suspicion. It could be a worthwhile endeavour. Many sincere activists attribute it to religious bias only. While this may be partially valid, the truth is that financial authorities, being conversant only with the traditional armoury of credit control, are at a loss to understand how they could be able to oversee and regulate financial institutions that are interest-free. It is therefore necessary to work out an alternative set of devices and convince the regulatory authorities of the willingness of interest-free institutions to submit to their control provided it is exercised through these devices. Effective control of financial intermediation is possible even without resort to interest-based techniques.

In our view the concluding part of the chapter (where the author reviews the prospects of Islamic financial institutions in India) is very encouraging and needs to be considered seriously.

COMMENTS

Sule Ahmed Gusau

The chapter is full of factual evidence on an area that is highly important but grossly neglected. However, I would like to draw the attention of the author to the following points.

1. The section on 'methodology' talks of appropriate statistical and economic tools and techniques being applied without specifying which ones they were. It would have been better if these tools had been specified so that those who wish to cross-check the work could do so.
2. The finding that 80 per cent of urban Indian Muslims are willing to deposit or invest in IFIs on PLS basis is interesting, but it should be interpreted with extreme caution. This is because in a piece of research in Nigeria covering major cities, the present discussant found similar results, but when Habib Nigeria Ltd opened Islamic windows in those same cities, the finding was not confirmed. Only very few Muslims have opened accounts with the window and nobody so far has closed his account with the commercial banks in order to patronize the Islamic window. Many are just waiting to see what happens before they venture into it.
3. One wonders why some of the institutions discussed by the author are called Islamic financial institutions when in fact they earn interest, and charge variable and arbitrary service charges. To the present discussant, unless these institutions stop these Islamically objectionable activities, they do not deserve to be called Islamic.
4. The discussion on bad debts (which the chapter argues do not occur) leaves one wondering what happens in the event of the death of a borrower and in the light of the policy of the IFIs not to sell the ornaments given as security for the loans.
5. Also, the evaluation of the performance of the IFIs, which concentrates on the deposits, investments and loans, leaves one wondering about the deeper implications of the activities of the IFIs for their members and the economy as a whole. This aspect has not been touched by the chapter. To that extent the chapter neglects an area worthy of investigation.
6. It is generally agreed that one of the most important distinguishing characteristics of IFIs is the provision of interest-free loans (*qarḍ al-ḥasan*). It would, therefore, be interesting to know what part of the loans that the Indian IFIs give goes to *qarḍ al-ḥasan* and what part goes to other kinds of loans. The chapter is silent on that. To that extent, it fails to show how IFIs help the poor to obtain cheaper loans even for consumption purposes.

10. The interface between Islamic and conventional banking

Rodney Wilson

1. INTRODUCTION

The chapter will focus on the following issues:

1. Can conventional banks legitimately offer Islamic financing facilities given their involvement, at least in part, with *ribā*-based finance?
2. Are Islamic and conventional banking practices converging or becoming increasingly distinct?
3. What lessons can Islamic banks learn from the experiences of conventional banks, and what can conventional banks learn from Islamic banks?
4. Where Islamic banks are involved in inter-bank transactions with conventional banks, what pitfalls should be avoided to ensure *Sharīʿah* compliance?
5. To what extent do national bank regulations designed for conventional banks pose problems for Islamic banks?

2. COMMERCIAL BANKS OFFERING ISLAMIC FACILITIES

Since the late 1980s one significant development has been for commercial banks, both within and outside the Muslim world, to offer Islamic financing facilities to their clients as an alternative to *ribā* dealings. In Egypt the National Bank and the Banque du Caire, leading state-owned banks, now offer Islamic services.[1] In Saudi Arabia the National Commercial and Riyadh Banks provide similar facilities, as does the Saudi British Bank.[2]

The National Commercial Bank (NCB) is particularly committed to Islamic finance, with a specialist network of over 35 dedicated branches throughout Saudi Arabia by 1999 offering a range of the *Sharīʿah*-compatible products. This includes the NCB International Trade Fund, a low-risk, non-interest-bearing investment fund, with clients' money earmarked for the purchase of goods and their resale at a mark-up on the *murābaḥah* principle. This is the largest fund of its kind in the world, with assets worth over $3 billion. Only major companies are financed, and all transactions are short term, with an average portfolio life of three months and no individual transaction allowed to exceed one year.

For National Commercial Bank clients wanting to invest in local currency rather than dollars the NCB Saudi Riyal Trade Fund is proving popular. The fund functions in a similar manner to the International Trade Fund, but its investments include purely domestic trade. For clients of high net worth the National Commercial Bank offers a Personal Investment Portfolio (PIP) management service, with the Islamic Banking Division acting as *muḍārib* for funds placed in a range of merchandise and commodities, including oil and gas, but excluding gold, silver, currencies and commodities prohibited under *Sharīʿah* law.

The NCB Global Trading Equity Fund represents a medium- to longer-term investment vehicle, with this open-ended fund designed to provide high returns over a minimum period of at least three years. Investors can fully or partially redeem their funds at any time on a weekly basis. Hence the client has a high level of flexibility. As the name implies, funds are invested in international equity markets, with the investments dollar-denominated.

In Bahrain, Citibank opened an Islamic Investment Bank in 1996, while the Dutch bank, ABN AMRO, added a dedicated Islamic banking division to its offshore operations.[3] The Bahrain-based Arab Banking Corporation has provided Islamic fund management services since 1987. It has its own *Sharīʿah* committee comprising three scholars who are members of the *Fiqh* Academy in Jeddah. Much of its financing has involved trade through *murābaḥah* and *bayʿ al-salam*.

Citibank had been offering Islamic financing services since 1983, 15 years before the opening of its Islamic Investment branch in Bahrain. Over this period it managed assets worth over $1 billion for Islamic investors. With the opening of the Bahrain Islamic Investment Bank, it is planning to extend the range and depth of its Islamic financing services. It has already developed new trade financing instruments combining features of *muḍārabah* and *mushārakah* financing. It aims to provide both liquidity and private portfolio management, private banking and professional asset management services, as well as asset-based finance and investment and financial advisory services. It also intends to play a major role in the development of an Islamic capital market, including encouraging the trading of secondary instruments.

In London, Islamic financing services are offered by Saudi International Bank, United Bank of Kuwait, Kleinwort Benson and ANZ, the Australia and New Zealand Bank Group, which has significant interests in Pakistan and Malaysia. The United Bank of Kuwait has been particularly active through its specialist Islamic financing division.[4] This provides Islamic fixed repayment mortgages for home buyers and investors in private property, and has built up a significant leasing portfolio worth over $300 million. In a further development, the United Bank of Kuwait opened an office in Dubai in 1997 to provide Islamic financial services to clients in the lower Gulf.

These developments are likely to have profound significance for Islamic banking development, even though some clients will always prefer to bank with exclusively Islamic banks rather than Islamic affiliates of multinational institutions. The advantage of these institutions is their substantial size and perceived solidity, the possibility of cross-selling Islamic services to existing Muslim clients, the wealth of in-house expertise available and the efficiency with which they provide their services. The much smaller exclusively Islamic banks cannot hope to compete in these areas, but they can still claim purity and much greater distance from any *ribā*-based transactions.

3. CONVERGENCE OR DIVERGENCE OF CONVENTIONAL AND ISLAMIC BANKS

As with any private financial institution the activities of Islamic banks reflect the needs of their clients. Much of the demand is for basic retail and commercial business services rather than for the more specialist services which investment banks offer.

3.1 Retail Deposits

Retail deposit services include the provision of current accounts, as well as low-risk investment accounts usually on a *muḍārabah* basis with clients sharing in any bank profits. Conventional banks provide similar deposit services at the retail level, but there are some notable differences. First, conventional banks allow overdrafts on current accounts, which often incur both fixed-rate charges and interest, with the former varying according to whether the overdraft is below or exceeds pre-arranged credit limits. Islamic banks cannot offer overdraft facilities on current accounts, which have to be maintained in surplus. However, depositors who get into temporary financial difficulties due to events beyond their control such as illness may receive interest-free loans (*qarḍ al-ḥasan*).

Conventional banks offer savings rather than investment accounts, the major attraction of such accounts being the interest paid to depositors. This often increases as the minimum notice period for withdrawals lengthens, with accounts which for example require three months' notice for withdrawals paying more interest than those requiring one months' notice. Some Islamic banks apply similar stepped returns with their investment accounts, with a higher proportionate profit share as the period of notice for withdrawals increases.

Increasingly, conventional banks are promoting themselves as financial supermarkets at the retail level offering a wide range of financial services, including investment products and fund management. In Saudi Arabia these include Islamically designated investment funds, which aim to invest in *ḥalāl* enterprises, both locally and in Western countries. Some Islamic banks, notably the Jordan Islamic Bank, have offered a type of equity exposure through specified investment accounts, where the bank identifies the possible investment opportunities from existing or new business clients and invites existing account-holders to subscribe. Instead of sharing in the bank's profit the investors gain a share of the profits of the enterprise in which the funds are placed, with the bank taking a management fee for its work.

3.2 Housing Finance

Conventional retail banks are increasingly concentrating on personal lending rather than loans for business, but in most Muslim countries and communities there is much less demand for consumer credit, partly because there is much less of a culture of materialistic consumerism than in the West. A large proportion of conventional bank consumer lending is through mortgages on house purchases, usually secured on the value of the property. Clients make monthly interest and instalment repayments, usually by direct debit from their current accounts into which their salaries and other income is paid. Such payments often extend over periods as long as 25 years, with the interest charges either fixed for the duration of the loan, or variable at a premium over inter-bank rates. Some housing loans are only repaid at the end of the mortgage period rather than on a monthly basis, the client instead paying into an endowment insurance policy, the proceeds from which should be sufficient to meet the debt obligations. If the borrower dies before the termination of the mortgage, the insurance cover will meet the repayments in full. Most conventional mortgage lenders require the borrower to take out insurance, both on himself and on the property.

There have been several attempts by Islamic banks to make available similar housing finance facilities, notably the Islamic mortgages provided through the London offices of Al Baraka in the early 1990s, where repayments were based on the implicit rental value of the property rather than on the basis of interest. The most ambitious Islamic mortgage scheme in the UK was that provided by the Islamic Investment Banking Unit of the United Bank of Kuwait. It has sought to attract business from the local Muslim community, from both United Kingdom residents and citizens through its Manzil scheme, which was launched in 1996.[5]

Unlike conventional mortgages, which operate on the basis of a loan or mortgage account on which interest is charged, the Manzil scheme is based on a purchase and sale with the payment deferred over an agreed term. It is the client who agrees the purchase price with the vendor, but the bank that buys the property on the client's behalf, and then immediately resells it to the client at a mark-up. The client has to pay at least 25 per cent of the purchase price in cash, but the remaining 75 per cent can be deferred over 5, 7.5, 10, 12.5 or 15 years, with repayments made monthly by direct debit. Those who get into financial difficulties and have payments arrears will be treated sympathetically, in line with the voluntary code of conduct of the UK Council of Mortgage Lenders.[6] The mortgage scheme was discussed with the Bank of England, which was satisfied with the plans.

Manzil mortgages are being distributed through independent financial advisers (IFAs) and solicitors who have significant dealings with the British Muslim community, and often have employees who speak Urdu or Arabic. It can be extended for the purchase of any suitable property in England or Wales, and, following legal advice about the position of the scheme under Scottish law, the scheme will be extended there. As most Muslims in the UK, as in the rest of the population, are keen to own their homes, the demand for mortgages is very large, most of which at present is covered by conventional interest-based loans.

3.3 Consumer Finance

Conventional banks increasingly provide finance to their clients for the purchase of 'big ticket' consumer durables such as cars or other vehicles, home improvements such as kitchen and bathroom refurbishment, or the purchase of major 'white' goods such as washing machines, freezers, dishwashers and other similar items of household equipment. As with mortgages, such finance can be provided on a fixed or variable interest basis, usually the former, with the loan running over a two- or three-year period with constant monthly repayments.

A number of Islamic banks provide similar types of financing, but usually on a leasing (*ijārah*) or hire-purchase basis with the bank owning the asset for the duration of the financing contract, and therefore taking on ownership obligations that justify its return in accordance with the *Sharīʿah* law. The Kuwait Finance House has run a car purchase scheme for its clients since the 1980s, with referrals both from car retailers and as a result of direct demand from its own customers. Other institutions, such as the Jordan Islamic Bank, have financed the purchase of equipment by professionals such as dentists, but have not been involved in consumer credit for household purchases. There would seem much scope for Islamic banks to become involved in consumer finance, although this may be more a matter of facilitating purchases rather than encouraging consumerism and materialist aspirations.

3.4 Small Business Finance

Retail conventional banks often extend their remit to cover small business finance that is conducted on similar terms to personal lending. In the case of very small loans to high-risk ventures, the loan is often covered by personal assets such as housing serving as collateral. For more established ventures with a regular cash flow and a good business plan, unsecured finance may be granted, although not usually on very generous terms. Conventional banks may refer borrowers seeking equity finance to a venture capital company, but they will not provide this type of finance themselves because of the risks involved and the problems of disinvestment.

Islamic finance would seem at first sight to be ideally suited to the needs of small business, as *muḍārabah* (profit-sharing) provides the Islamic bank the opportunity to share in the success of any enterprise, without penalizing businesses unduly for any failure. The partial transfer of risk from the entrepreneur to the bank inevitably makes the bank reluctant to engage in such financing unless a higher return is anticipated. Having such a return in the form of a substantial share of anticipated profits may deter the entrepreneur from seeking the finance in the first place. There is in addition a principal–agent problem of asymmetric information. Where the bank is the principal and the entrepreneur the agent, there will always be the temptation to report a lower profit. This is why financial reporting by the entrepreneur for successful *muḍārabah* is very important as it avoids the moral hazard problem.

Mushārakah is the other route to avoid this problem, as it involves a partnership between the Islamic bank and the entrepreneur with both having more equal access to information. Islamic banks are often deterred from taking this route because of the set-up and administrative costs, but it could provide a viable option if these can be reduced.

In practice most Islamic bank financing is through *murābaḥah* trade financing, a reflection partly of the low-risk nature of such finance, which involves the bank purchasing a good on behalf of a client and reselling the good to the same client at a predetermined mark-up. Such financing in many countries throughout the Muslim world simply reflects business demands and the trading character of much economic activity. In these countries the types of financing do not differ significantly between conventional and Islamic banks; rather it is the financing methods that differ.

Leasing or *ijārah* is the second most popular method of financing for many Islamic banks, but this has also become more significant for conventional banks. The latter often provide leasing facilities through specialized subsidiaries, but Islamic banks tend to view leasing as a mainstream activity and part of their core business. Again unlike *mushārakah*, there is little risk involved, as the goods or equipment being leased serve as collateral for the financing.

4. LESSONS ISLAMIC AND CONVENTIONAL BANKS CAN LEARN FROM EACH OTHER

There are lessons in the field of technology which Islamic banks can learn from conventional banks in the most advanced industrialized countries that may facilitate their entry to these markets. Conventional banks can, however, learn from Islamic banks concerning staff and client motivation, as well as about staff–client relationships, which are at the heart of Islamic banking. In other words there can be a technology transfer one way, but a human value transfer in the opposite direction.

4.1 Technology Transfer

Banking practices largely reflect the business environment in which they operate. There can be much debate about how far they can lead their customers in promoting change and modernization and to what extent this is brought about as a result of customers' demands and expectations. In other words, is change, including technological change in the provision of banking services, supply or demand led? How labour-intensive or capital-intensive banking services are, tends to mirror relative factor costs. In this respect, the banking industry is no different from other industries, with more paper-based labour-intensive services provided in low-wage countries and more electronic and automated services in high-wage countries. As most Islamic banks operate in relatively low-wage countries, they are often less advanced technologically than leading multinational banks, although in higher-wage countries such as those of the Gulf, more use is made of information technology and automated systems such as cash dispensers for current account-holders.

There is probably relatively little that Islamic banks can learn from conventional banks in a similar low-wage environment, but arguably more that Islamic banks can learn from conventional banks in high-wage technologically advanced countries.[7] Traditionally banking services have been delivered through a branch network, which places Islamic banks at a disadvantage, as they do not have a significant presence in any Western market. This makes it very difficult to serve scattered Muslim communities. Conventional banks have developed telephone banking, on-line services using proprietary software and Internet banking, probably the innovation of greatest long-term significance.

Although the start-up costs of these remote delivery services are substantial, they are much less than those of branch network expansion. Provided Muslim clients have the necessary equipment, they can easily undertake most of their banking business without actually visiting a branch. As virtually the entire population has access to fixed-line telephones in the advanced industrialized countries, including the Muslim population, and increasing numbers also have mobile telephones, account balances can be checked, payments made and transfers between accounts conducted from home, office or car 24 hours a day. Client service staff are not required, as communication can be made by voicemail or key-number entry on the telephone pad to a computer. The same services can be made available via the Internet, with clients themselves also able to print off account statements and records of their transactions. As the Internet becomes accessible through television and personal organizers as well as through personal computers, a large segment of the population will be able to become involved in home and office banking.

4.2 Islamic Financial Values

There are many reasons why customers choose to place their financial business with particular banks rather than others, the most usual being that the institution is where family and friends bank. Reputation is also important, as banks have to be seen as safe and reliable places to deposit funds without risk of default. There is much customer inertia in banking, and if institutions are seen as having served families well over long periods of time, there is often little desire to change banks, even when competitors offer better returns. Transferring to another bank can involve transactions costs, not only in terms of money but also of time, as standing orders and direct debits are changed, and personal identification numbers are entered on credit and debit cards.

Despite these impediments to account movement, bank clients in the advanced industrialized countries are becoming less loyal to their financial institutions. There is greater customer mobility as depositors and borrowers shop around for competitive deposit and borrowing rates. Branding and image are of some significance, but the greatest incentives appear to be financial. However, much of the customer account migration is to remote-access banks which offer telephone or Web-based banking, as these often offer higher savings deposit rates and cheaper lending due to their lower cost bases.

Being relatively new, Islamic banks have fewer long-standing customers, although some of the earliest established Islamic banks have customers who have been banking with them for over 20 years. A majority of Islamic bank customers have already banked with conventional institutions before the Islamic banks' opening, and many retain these accounts. There are some parallels with the ethical investment industry, where most investors with ethical investments also have conventional asset holdings.

What distinguishes Islamic banks from their conventional counterparts is not only the unique products they have on offer but also the commonality of their client base. All have been attracted to Islamic banks because they provide products compatible with the *Sharīʿah*, which the clients themselves respect and believe in. In conventional finance what is sometimes described as relationship banking is confined to the provision of private banking services for clients of high net worth, but with Islamic banking there is the possibility of a close relationship between the bank and the client, even though this does not have to be developed through a highly personalized level of service. Rather, because the clients themselves share similar characteristics, notably a common faith that affects their economic and financial behaviour, the bank can provide a standardized service which nevertheless the client feels is designed for their particular circumstances.[8] Islamic banks can 'connect' with their clients through appropriate marketing and sponsorship activity.[9]

Furthermore, because there is a higher level of trust between Islamic banks and their clients than is the case with conventional banking, the risks of moral hazard are less. Clients are more likely to disclose the true levels of their business profits if they view the relationship with the bank as a partnership rather than being adversarial. Higher levels of trust reduce risk and uncertainty, and result in lower monitoring costs for Islamic banks. Commercial risks of course remain, but the risks associated with actual or potential dishonesty or disclosure failures are reduced considerably when both the bank and the client are on the same moral plane.

5. ISLAMIC BANKS' TRANSACTIONS WITH CONVENTIONAL BANKS

Many Islamic banks use the facilities of conventional banks for treasury management, foreign exchange, portfolio services and investment banking. Major multinational conventional banks have the critical mass to provide specialist services while Islamic banks are usually too small in size to take on such services themselves. Outsourcing makes sense for organizations when the benefits of internalization are outweighed by the administrative costs of trying to extend their functions into new areas where demand is limited. As most Islamic banks are located in the Muslim world, where most of the demand is for core banking services rather than for highly specialized finance, it is a potential management distraction to widen the facilities on offer excessively. This could actually result in deterioration in the quality of the basic level of deposit and funding services.

5.1 Treasury Management

Many Islamic banks cannot manage their cash balances profitably, as they cannot redeposit temporary excess funds with other institutions and earn interest returns. Multinational conventional banks can accept such deposits on a *muḍārabah* basis, and use *murābaḥah* financing to generate profits that can be passed on in part to the Islamic banks. Islamic banks can and do of course undertake *murābaḥah* financing, but they have a more restricted client base than major international banks. The latter can have trade financing facilities maturing on each working day. At the same time international banks, because of the scale of their business, can work on finer margins than smaller national banks. International banks may also have locational advantages, such as the Islamic Investment Banking Unit of the United Bank of Kuwait, which can identify a large number of *murābaḥah* financing opportunities through their London and New York offices that banks based in the Islamic world cannot easily match.

When conventional banks accept deposits from Islamic banks, the latter will need assurance of *Sharīʿah* compliance, and in particular that the funds are separated from other conventional deposits, and that the financing is maintained on a segregated basis given that the conventional bank will be involved with *ribā*. Accountability by the conventional bank to a recognized *Sharīʿah* adviser or committee can provide assurance for the Islamic bank, as will initial and final reports on how the funds have been used for the period of redepositing when the conventional bank is custodian of the funds. Where the conventional bank only operates as an adviser to the Islamic bank or provides introductions to potential fund users, the cash deposits may not appear as liabilities on the balance sheet of the conventional bank and the trade financing receivables may not appear as assets. Such off-balance-sheet activities can be helpful for many conventional banks in certain jurisdictions given requirements such as reserve ratios or capital-to-asset ratios.

5.2 Foreign Exchange Facilities

Islamic banks provide foreign exchange facilities for their clients in major currencies such as the US dollar, and many offer dollar deposit and financing facilities. In any bank there is inevitably a mismatch between clients' demand for foreign exchange and the supply of foreign exchange, which is usually covered through inter-bank transactions. Islamic banks buying and selling foreign exchange through the inter-bank market will inevitably be dealing with conventional banks.

It is the largest international banks such as Citibank or Hong Kong Shanghai Banking Corporation (HSBC) that can offer the widest range of foreign exchange services and the most competitive margins between buying and selling rates. They can offer spot rates on minor as well as major currencies as well as forward contracts, although many *Sharīʿah* scholars believe the latter are not permissible as they involve a future commitment with respect to uncertain funds rather than an immediate tangible transaction. A contrary view is that forward transactions increase certainty as the parties agree the rate in advance, whereas relying on uncertain future spot rates is inevitably a gamble. It can be argued that to some extent both sides are debating at cross purposes, as there are two different uncertainties, one relating to future spot rates and the other to completion risk, as the foreign exchange which it is assumed will be supplied or demanded in the future may not actually materialize due to changed commercial circumstances.

5.3 Portfolio Management Services

Islamic banks, which offer mutual funds to their clients, may use the services of international banking or fund management groups who have expertise and research specialists, which smaller institutions cannot match. Islamic banks using the services of international banks and fund management groups will need assurance that the companies included in any portfolio have been screened so that they are acceptable to Muslim investors, with companies such as breweries and distilleries excluded as well as those involved in pork production or distribution. Companies with excessive reliance on debt financing will also be excluded, and hence gearing ratios will need to be monitored.

The Swiss Banking Corporation and groups such as Wellington Asset Management provide portfolio services for Islamic funds, the former serving the International Investor of Kuwait while the latter is involved with the Islamic mutual funds offered by the National Commercial Bank of Saudi Arabia. Islamic banks such as Al Rajhi of Saudi Arabia offer a number of mutual fund products for their clients, but most Islamic banks do not offer equity-based alternatives to their standard *muḍārabah* deposit facilities, even though this can increase client choice and result in greater asset diversification.

5.4 Investment Banking Functions

In the United States, investment banking functions were historically separated from retail banking, partly to protect retail depositors as investment banking, which can involve derivatives trading, is more risky. Investment banks make much of their profit from advising clients on acquisitions and merger activity, and through arranging corporate financing through instruments such as bonds and floating-rate notes. The banks often act as underwriters for such financing instruments, which can again bring considerable risks if the pricing of the instruments is misjudged and the banks have to take up the unsold stock.

Some investment banking activities such as derivatives trading or the issue of conventional interest-bearing bonds is not legitimate under the *Sharīʿah*, but other types of corporate financing activity are permissible, including advice on and the financing of mergers and acquisitions. In practice, in most Muslim countries there has until recently been little merger and acquisition activity, as most companies in these countries are national rather than international in focus and operations, and many are state owned rather than being public liability companies in the private sector.

With globalization and the growth of multinational companies, many of the national companies in the Islamic world look increasingly weak, as they can only survive through tariffs, quotas, subsidies and discriminatory purchasing arrangements which in those Muslim countries that are members of the World Trade Organization are expected to be phased out. Furthermore, nationally oriented companies, especially in the smaller Muslim countries, lack critical mass, and cannot easily fund research and development activity. Their clients often get poor value for money, and products that are outdated. One solution is to embark on joint ventures with Western multinationals, which Islamic banks can be involved in financing, but often they may need the specialist advice of investment banks.

A case can be argued for Islamic banks encouraging cross-border merger and acquisition activity involving companies in two or more Muslim countries. For this to work, those governments that maintain restrictions on capital movements would have to move towards full currency convertibility. There is much that Islamic banks can learn from investment banks with respect to mergers and acquisitions. As a number of Islamic banks, notably the Faisal Banks, Al Rajhi and the Al Baraka group, have branches in several Muslim and Western countries, they are in a position to encourage cross-border mergers and acquisitions, not least because their local knowledge can complement the technical expertise of the international investment banks.

Investment banks can also help with the development of the *Sharīʿah*-compliant financial instruments in cooperation with Islamic banks. Conventional bonds are not permissible, but it is possible to have Islamic synthetic bonds, with a fixed redemption value like their conventional counterparts, but with returns based on profit shares rather than interest. The government of Pakistan issued this type of bond, and Citi Islamic Bank in Bahrain has tried to develop similar facilities.

6. ISLAMIC FINANCIAL INSTRUMENTS AND WESTERN SECULAR LAW

Apart from issues of conformity with the *Sharīʿah* law and the *fatāwā*[10] (rulings) of the *Fiqh* Academy, there is also the issue of how Islamic financial institutions should structure their instruments to comply with the secular law of the countries in which they operate, including Western countries. Where co-financing between Islamic and conventional financing institutions is involved, the latter are solely governed by secular law, even though through their cooperation with Islamic institutions they become indirectly liable under the *Sharīʿah* law for the limited joint funding operations.

The different structure of Islamic from conventional financial instruments means consideration must be given to legal issues such as owner liability, the consequences of default and what happens in the event of loss or destruction of the assets. There are also legal issues with respect to export credit cover when Islamic trade financing instruments are used and inter-creditor issues involving ownership of assets, amortization of investment and voting rights.

6.1 Ownership Liability

In Islamic finance, the provider of the funding usually assumes an ownership liability, which may be of brief duration in the case of *murābaḥah*[11] trade financing or medium to long term as in the cases of leasing, *muḍārabah* or *mushārakah*. In all these instances the financier is exposed to a greater liability under national or international laws than a conventional lender, who does not assume ownership responsibilities. These include not only the risk of loss or damage to the asset being funded but also any liabilities arising out of the use of the asset. For example, if the asset is an item of equipment that causes death or injury during its use, then the Islamic financier could be held legally responsible. If the asset being financed is an oil tanker that is involved in an accident, causing oil spillage that results in serious pollution, then the Islamic financier may also be liable for claims relating to the environmental damage. This liability will arise even if the Islamic bank or financial institution has little control over the use of the asset.

Islamic banks will always expect to obtain title to the goods or equipment being financed as proof of its ownership. However, sale structures are quite different from lease structures under Islamic financing provisions, and are treated differently under Western secular law. It is obviously convenient if the user of the asset can acquire it directly, as the user will have greater knowledge of the asset and the supplier than the financier. Under an Islamic lease structure, this is not a problem as the leasee is permitted under the *Sharīʿah* to acquire the asset from a supplier and immediately sell the asset to the lessor at the same price. The lessor will then have a leasing contract with the lessee who is actually using the asset.

With a sale contract, the Islamic financier must acquire the asset directly from the supplier, rather than the user taking ownership through acquiring the asset. This presents several problems for both the Islamic financier and the supplier, which may be a Western company with no knowledge of Islamic finance or experience of dealing with Islamic banks. First, the financier may wish to undertake a full risk analysis of what can be complex sale contracts given the level of exposure. Second, the user may be concerned about getting the benefit of any supplier warranties, when it is the financier rather than the user who is the buyer. Third, the supplier may wish to maintain title to the goods or equipment until it can confirm that the payment has been made, but this may be unacceptable to the Islamic financier, who will want the ownership deeds on assuming legal liability.

6.2 Project Delays and Payments Defaults

As the Islamic bank or financial institution will always expect to receive an ownership title relating to its financing, as already indicated, this can cause problems when there are project delays. In such cases the Islamic financier may fail to acquire a title to the unfinished equipment or goods, or may receive a title to some items but not others. For a conventional bank this is not a problem, as it has only lent money to the end user, and delays are therefore the concern of the latter and not the bank to which the end user will still be liable. The Islamic financier will not have carried out their obligations, however, until they obtain the title deed, which means the problem is between them and the supplier or contractor rather than the end user and the contractor.

Similar difficulties arise in the case of adverse developments before project completion, which may affect the viability of the project being funded. Conventional banks may call in their loan, although how easily this can be done will depend on the terms of the loan. In the case of an Islamic financier the position is more complex. If a damaged or destroyed asset is leased from an Islamic bank, the lessee may refuse to make further rental payments on the grounds that the asset has become of minimal or no further value. The Islamic bank as lessor with responsibility for the asset under the *Sharīʿah* will have difficulty in overcoming such objections and obtaining further payment.[12] In the case of *murābaḥah* or *istiṣnāʿ* deferred payment sales, the position is even worse, given the responsibilities of the Islamic financier. If the good being financed is damaged or destroyed, the purchaser may refuse to proceed to completion and the bank may be left with a valueless asset that cannot be sold.

6.3 Co-financing Rights and Responsibilities

Where Islamic financial institutions are involved in co-financing projects with conventional banks, it is important to ensure that none of the parties will have greater rights or responsibilities than the other. This can be far from straightforward given that each institution functions differently. A conventional bank will be owed principal and interest, and mechanisms can be put in place to ensure all principal is amortized at the same rate for conventional co-financiers. There will be no interest payments accruing to the Islamic bank or repayment of principal, its return being based on profit or a leasing or instalment arrangement.

The best way forward is to establish how much the Islamic and conventional banks have invested in the project, either through the initial purchase of the asset in the case of the former or the loan in the case of the latter. Each party can then agree what the order of precedence should be with respect to rights over repayments. For example, sums received may be charged first against fees, next against profits, next against amortization of investment and finally against payment of indemnity sums, the objective being to ensure that investments are amortized uniformly. In the event of default, the Islamic bank will want to assure itself that any claims by the conventional banks for principal and accrued interest do not take precedence over their claims as investors in the failed business.

There are also the issues of decision-taking and voting rights by Islamic and conventional co-financiers. Normally there should be unanimous agreement, but if this is impossible, then the parties should vote according to their funding contributions.

6.4 Security and Guarantees under Islamic Financing

Islamic banks can accept securities for leasing and *murābaḥah* contracts, and may resort to national secular courts to ensure their rights over securities are enforced in the event of payments failure or default. Securities can be accepted in the form of a personal guarantee, real estate or property, and the assignment of funds relating to supply contracts. Goods are also acceptable as security, provided they are not subject to a sale contract. A reserve can also be placed on an amount of money from the current or investment account of the client. Guarantees from other banks can also be accepted as security.

Islamic banks can also use pledges, which are concluded through the offer and acceptance of a contract. Pledges give the pledgee the right to possession of the goods being pledged until the debt is repaid. They are irrevocable once made, but the pledgee can annul the contract. Pledges can be exchanged or used to secure financing. Only physical goods can be pledged, not intangibles because of concern over valuation and repossession. One pledge may be offered to two different financiers, but each of the parties must be informed about what is envisaged. A pledge is not a substitute for the repayment of a debt, and the bank's right to repayment is not diminished by the pledge. If a pledgor dies, then the pledge will have to be honoured from the estate of the deceased. If a pledgor refuses to repay a debt subject to a pledge, then the pledgee has the right to secure the good pledged through the courts.

Islamic banks are commercial institutions, not charities, but they may, at their discretion, act leniently with a client who has offered security for financing, but who then finds that he cannot repay due to unforeseen developments which have adversely affected the business. Nevertheless, Islamic banks must always balance the interests of those being funded with those of their depositors and shareholders. A distinction is made between not being able to repay and unwillingness to repay. In the former case, if a client has difficulty with payments he should consult the bank, which may not call in the pledged security. In the latter case the security will be sought, and the bank may claim compensation for 'harm or injury' through the courts in lieu of interest.

In summary, Islamic banks and financial institutions can act within secular commercial and contract law, and it is possible to use national laws to serve their legitimate interests.

7. CONCLUSION

Islamic banks and conventional banks should not regard each other as a threat. They of course compete with each other, but not usually by the pricing of their services. Instead Islamic banks compete by offering differentiated products that they believe will appeal to Muslim clients given their *Sharīʿah* compliance. Islamic banking, despite being in existence in its modern form for over three decades, is still in many respects an infant industry. The banks themselves lack the critical mass to be major international players. Hence they need to cooperate with conventional banks to identify attractive financing opportunities, and for international client appraisal. Islamic banks can draw on expertise in the *Sharīʿah*, but they are often lacking in knowledge of sophisticated financing techniques and instruments, and have little experience of financial engineering. In this field cooperation with major international banks can also prove fruitful.

Islamic banks can learn from the experiences of conventional banks in information technology, but conventional banks can learn from Islamic banks new facets of relationship banking and how to achieve client loyalty by the convergence of bank and customer values. Islamic banks dealing with conventional banks need to ensure that any cash or portfolio management is conducted in accordance with the *Sharīʿah*. Nevertheless, the experience of the last two decades demonstrates that conventional banks can legitimately offer Islamic financing facilities. There would seem to be many promising areas for cooperation between Islamic and conventional banks, but that does not mean that both types of institutions will not continue to compete with each other.

NOTES

1. Galloux (1997), pp. 167–92.
2. Wilson (1997), pp. 44–5.

3. Measures (1999), p. 4.
4. Smith (1997), pp. 8–11.
5. Leach (1997), pp. 3–4.
6. Ibid.
7. Maad (1999), pp. 10–12.
8. Hume (1999), pp. 10–12.
9. Sheikh (1999), pp. 6–7.
10. DeLorenzo (1997). This volume, which provides details of the *fatāwā* issued by the religious supervisory boards of leading Islamic banks, has become a standard reference work for conventional bankers managing operations where there is a need for *Sharīʿah* compliance.
11. Vogel and Hayes (1998), pp. 241–4 provide details of 'ownership in transit' under *murābaḥah.*
12. Although optional clauses can be built into the contract to cover such situations through *khiyār ash-sharṭ*. See Comair-Obeid (1996), pp. 67–8.

REFERENCES

Comair-Obeid, Nayla (1996), *The Law of Business Contracts in the Arab Middle East*, London: Kluwer Law International.

DeLorenzo, Yusuf Talal (1997), *A Compendium of Legal Opinions on the Operations of Islamic Banks*, London: Institute of Islamic Banking and Insurance.

Galloux, Michel (1997), *Finance Islamique et Pouvoir Politique: le Cas de l'Egypte Moderne*, Paris: Presses Universitaires de France.

Hume, James (1999), 'The development, marketing and selling of Islamic Financial Products', *New Horizon* (93), November, 10–12.

Leach, Keith (1997), 'Britain's first Islamic mortgage', *New Horizon* (63), May, 3–4.

Maad, Soha (1999), 'Technology to support Islamic banks in facing global competition in the new Millennium', *New Horizon* (94), December, 10–12.

Measures, Peter (1999), *Islamic Banking and Finance*, London: Clyde and Co.

Sheikh, Shahzad (1999), 'The customer knows best', *New Horizon* (90), August, 6–7.

Smith, Duncan (1997), 'Islamic banks, Conventional banks and combinations of the two', *New Horizon* (64), June, 8–11.

Vogel, Frank and Samuel Hayes (1998), *Islamic Law and Finance*, London: Kluwer Law International.

Wilson, Rodney (1997), *Islamic Finance*, London: Financial Times Publishing.

COMMENTS

Muhammad Abdul Mannan

I would like to divide my observations on this chapter into two parts:

Part One covers our perceptions of Islamic finance and its motivational properties of the 'interface' between Islamic and conventional banking and finance, which tends to be significantly different from either the market or the command economy. It would link all the issues involved to the key thrust of Islamic finance.

Part Two will deal with some specific aspects of this chapter.

Part One: General Observations

A careful study of the 'interface' between Islamic and conventional banking as reflected in the chapter reveals that Islamic banking and finance, without built-in provisioning for social, ethical and moral ingredients, will most likely be submerged in the mainstream of the Western conventional banking system and consequently in the wave of the market economy operating through Western materialistic and secular values. This is perhaps what is happening either consciously or unconsciously in the case of the operation of Islamic banking in the corporate sector. The comparative advantage of conventional banks over Islamic banks in terms of their systems, management experience and techniques of product innovation is expected to bring competition, resulting in a sharpening of the techniques and procedures of Islamic banking modes. In the process, profitability is becoming more dominant in Islamic banks' operations. Conventional banks having Islamic windows lack knowledge and know-how of social, ethical and moral foundations of Islamic finance.

It appears that the Islamic banks in the corporate sector are running the risk of getting submerged in the wave of market economy and marginalizing social and ethical elements of Islamic finance. While the resultant convergence may bring efficiency in the operations of Islamic banks, it is feared that it will also bring at least five dilemmas for Islamic banks in the corporate sector:

1. Increasing concentration of ownership and beneficiaries of Islamic banking and finance having a link to a global elite and its network of reciprocal obligations.
2. Crucial neglect of the vast masses of people in Muslim countries incapable of entering into the financial market.
3. An increasing trend towards secularization of Islamic economics, banking and finance.

4. Marginalizing social, ethical and moral ingredients of Islamic modes of financing.
5. Developing barriers to the growth of perpetual social capital, which expresses the shared values of a society, reinforces them and stimulates a caring society.

To me, in the study of Islamic economics, banking and finance, it is to be recognized that the best business may not be the one that always makes the most profit; and that the technically most efficient may not necessarily be the socially most efficient. Its distinctiveness arises from its integrated study of social, ethical and moral issues involved in economic problems and financial transactions and their solution in conformity with the *Sharīʿah.* It follows that the overall limits of Islamic banking and finance are to be found in its economic, social, ethical and moral imperatives. On the conceptual level, Islamic banking decisions are intended to bring real material benefits, and visible social advantages and moral fulfilment – all three in one package – in varying proportions ranging from credit to constructions, trading to transport, farming to fishing, manufacturing to mining and so on. As such, the operations of Islamic banking must be seen within the framework of total societal values and culture. The mere transaction without interest does not necessarily make the operation Islamic. Even in Western market societies, many economic enterprises run on a profit-sharing basis. Are these operations to be called Islamic? Contrary to the popular view, I am inclined to label such activities as secular economic transactions. In their form they may be called Islamic, but not in their content and spirit. The fact is that the mere mechanical replacement of interest by profit-sharing may not necessarily capture the true spirit of Islam if it does not bring about the required change in the attitude of the participants – an attitude that generates the forces of group participation, sharing and altruism among savers, investors, producers and consumers as well. Thus, this emphasis on totality having a number of facets brings out the true nature of Islamic banking operations.

This human approach to comprehensive, socio-economic banking offers a contrast to the prevailing narrow view of Islamic banking, which usually treats banks as mere financial intermediaries, working on the principles of interest-free transactions. The operations of such Islamic banking should go much beyond the mere replacement of the interest rate by the profit-sharing ratio. It is expected to generate forces of interdependency and mutual concern in life-style, affecting the behaviour of savers, depositing investors, consumers, producers, labourers, farmers, and both poor and rich members of the society. The uniqueness of such banking should lie not only in integrating economic, social and moral dimensions in every transaction but also in controlling their results and directing their consequences to achieve the desired economic and social welfare within the framework of the totality of the human situation at an earthly macro level and the dual notion of accountability (life on earth and life Hereafter) on the spiritual level. Seen in this light the classic mechanics of operations (*murābaḥah, mushārakah* and *muḍārabah*) and other tools need to be designed or redesigned in a manner so as to manifest economic, social and moral dimensions for giving them the distinctive Islamic character of banking and finance. Thus the common tools of economic analysis, such as scarcity, choice, opportunity cost, marginal efficiency of capital, discount rate, profit, rent, wages, and a host of other concepts, will have different meanings in Islamic economics, banking and finance. The interface between Islamic and conventional banking needs to be understood from this perspective. It appears that the chapter has not been able to articulate different meanings of interface in this context.

Part Two: Specific Observations

The main strength of the chapter is that it is informative and educative. It provides a fairly good survey of a number of commercial banks offering Islamic banking facilities and vice versa. The chapter has indicated a number of areas of cooperation between commercial and Islamic banks in terms of technology transfer, sophisticated financial engineering, technologies and instruments. Similarly, it is good in terms of explaining the mechanics and forms of operations of different Islamic modes of financing rather than articulating social and ethical imperatives of Islamic finance as indicated earlier. It is clearly written on the assumptions of the neoclassical orthodox paradigm based on the market. It lacks depth in its understanding of some philosophical underpinnings of Islamic economic ideas and values. Besides, what is missing in the author's analysis is the key thrust of Islamic banking beyond the frontiers of the market. In this respect, Wilson's survey of Islamic banking operations in different Muslim countries remains inadequate and incomplete.

I agree with the author's basic conclusion that 'Islamic and conventional banks should not regard each other as a threat.' Both Islamic banks and financial institutions can co-exist and act within secular commercial and contract law, and it is possible to use national laws to serve their legitimate interests. Islamic banks can of course compete by offering differentiated products and services and can learn from the experiences of conventional banks in technology transfer and financial engineering. Conventional banks can learn from Islamic banks' new facets of participatory finance as well as banking beyond the frontiers of the market. The legacy of banking may be viewed as a part of the common heritage of mankind. We find the evolution of banking services in Baghdad for the first time in the middle of the eighth century, allowing a merchant to write a cheque in one part of an Islamic state and having it encashed in a distant place. Taken all in all, the author deserves our appreciation for this valuable piece of work on Islamic finance.

COMMENTS

Abdurrahman Lahlou

The first three sections of the chapter are mainly descriptive. They give an overview of the Islamic branches and Islamic facilities offered by conventional banks in the Western as well as the Muslim world. Many innovative and relevant banking products have been developed and marketed here and there. It is important to mention that the main justification for this marketing success in many Western countries is that the products cater for the needs of the Muslim populations there, and thus conform to their religious beliefs, and not because of their technical relevance or efficiency. This part does not call for any fundamental remark.

In section 4, the author imagines a two-way transfer between conventional and Islamic banks; with banking technology one way and human value the other way. I find this plan a bit idealistic. If banking technology is transferable, because of its merchant nature, we cannot say the same for values. First, and to be realistic, the relationship between Islamic banks and their clients is not that pure and selfless. On the contrary, the trend in many Islamic societies is to consider that feelings have no place in financial deals. Bankers have to stick to the professional character of the relationship.

The author mentions that a high level of trust is supposed to exist between the Islamic banker and his client, which reduces risk, and therefore reduces monitoring costs. The only remark I would like to add is that the Islamic banker in our Muslim countries acts unfortunately in a secular environment. All of his clients are not necessarily good Muslims or unconditional supporters of Islamic banking. A study conducted by the National Commercial Bank in Saudi Arabia shows that this category represents only 19 per cent of the market.[1] Integrity is unfortunately not an economic feature, but a social and educational one, and it is hard to integrate it into a model. Therefore, the Islamic banker has to be very selective when dealing with clients.

Second, human values that the banker shares with his client, such as mutual respect, honesty and self-discipline, are a part of Islam, and probably spread through preaching as well as acquaintance. But it is not easy to imagine that values are transferable between parties linked by business agreements. On the other hand, the motivation that differentiates the staff of Islamic banks from the staff of conventional banks dealing with Islamic products is really transferable in my view. As long as Islamic bankers consider their activity as a challenge and its success as an achievement, which does not exclude the search for profit, they are definitely highly motivated. This kind of motivation is also necessarily higher than that of a conventional banker dealing with Islamic modes of financing for the sake of expansion and maximization of profit.

As far as technology transfer is concerned, I do not agree with the author when he says that Islamic banks can learn more from Western banks than they can learn from conventional local banks in their countries, because of the technological advance of the former, due to capital-intensive choice and high wages. While this description may apply to the industrial sector and many other services, I think it does not apply to the banking sector in many underdeveloped countries. The banking sector in Muslim countries is highly profitable. The lack of growth and prosperity that is the lot of the commodity sector does not afflict the banking sector. Therefore, you can easily find in this prosperous business the same features you find in developed countries: high wages, modern processes, professional management, which all bring high technology. These features are probably shared by many Islamic banks. If they are not, Islamic banks must learn from their fellow compatriots as much as they learn from Western banks, especially as most of our conventional banks are in joint ventures with Western prestigious banks and necessarily develop a permanent technology transfer flow. It is a kind of triangular technology transfer that we can design, where Islamic banks get technology directly from fellow conventional banks, rather than from Western banks because of the similarity of their environment.

The fifth section of the chapter deals with the transactions between Islamic banks and conventional banks or financial institutions, including fund managers, for whom the author spares a whole section. His analysis shows that the most *Sharīʿah*-compliant way of cooperation between the two categories of banks is the support in fund management given by Western institutions to Islamic banks in search of excess funds investment. Furthermore, this way of cooperation gives Islamic banks a profitable means of managing cash balances, without prejudice to their autonomy.

But are Islamic funds in Western countries the right place to invest the excess funds of Islamic banks? In my opinion, the Muslim countries' markets should have priority, although the traditional Western mature markets remain the best places to pursue a profit maximization strategy.

In the case of leasing, the author thinks it is a problem that Islamic banks, in order to obtain title to the equipment being financed, need to lead the purchase operation themselves, which deprives the client of mastering the operation and getting the greatest advantages from the supplier. Then the solution for the author is the lease-back, which enables the client to make the purchase himself. I do not see any need for that, as long as the client could deal with the whole operation, and at the end of the process, provide the lessor with a pro-forma invoice on the basis of which the leasing contract with the supplier can be made.

My final remark relates to the interface between Islamic and conventional banking. The Islamic banking system, though dominated by sales-based business, remains a relevant alternative in Muslim countries to the funding needs of Muslim investors. However, it is well known that equity funding is more developmental than debt, but the constraints that sharing-based banking faces in our countries seem to be insurmountable, due to the uncertain environment. It is no secret that the general trend in Islamic banking activity is the domination of leasing and sale financing modes over sharing-based contracts.

In terms of cooperation and technology transfer, the question is how conventional banks in the Western arena can contribute to promote these ungovernable modes of financing. If they succeed in that, Islamic banks could then learn much from them. At least, this success could constitute a laboratory experiment for the 'infant industry' that is Islamic banking.

NOTE

1. Said Al Martan, 'Islamic branches in Conventional banks', paper presented to the conference on Contemporary Implementations of Islamic Economics, ASMECI-IRTI, Casablanca, 1998.

11. Alternative visions of international monetary reform

M. Umer Chapra*

1. INTRODUCTION

The international financial system has experienced a number of crises over the last two decades.[1] Not a single geographical area or major country has been spared the effect of these crises. In general, the early-warning indicators such as interest rate spreads and credit ratings have proved to be ineffective in predicting the crises (BIS, 1999b, p. 56). Even the IMF was unable to foresee the crises in spite of its access to a great deal of information not available to others. Moreover, the policies it adopted after the crises came under severe criticism, in particular its rescue operations which, according to some of its critics, have only created a moral hazard that would tend to weaken market discipline in the future (Schultz et al., 1998; Meltzer, 1998). Hence there is an uneasy feeling that there is something basically wrong somewhere. This has led to a call for comprehensive reform of the international financial system to help prevent the outbreak and spread of financial crises or, at least, minimize their frequency and severity. The needed reform has come to be labelled 'the new architecture'.

There is perhaps no one who would challenge this call for a new architecture for the international financial system. However, as Andrew Crockett, General Manager of the Bank for International Settlements and Chairman of the newly created Financial Stability Forum, has rightly pointed out: 'More than two years after the outbreak of the Asian financial crisis, and after innumerable conferences and papers on the subject, a grand new design for the international financial system has still to be devised' (Crockett, 2000, p. 13). What could be the reason for the inability to prepare a convincing reform

* This chapter is a substantially expanded version of a section of the author's paper (2000), 'Why Has Islam Prohibited Interest?' The author is indebted to Habib Ahmed, Tariqullah Khan and Munawar Iqbal for their valuable comments on an earlier version of the chapter. The views and opinions expressed herein are personal and do not represent those of the Islamic Research and Training Institute.

programme in spite of so much investment in terms of time and effort? Could it be the failure to determine the ultimate cause of the crises?

2. CAUSES OF THE CRISES

A number of economists have tried to determine the causes of the crises. Some consider financial liberalisation to be the cause in an environment where financial systems of many countries are not sound as a result of improper regulation and supervision (Glick, 1998; Bisignano, 1998). Others feel that the ultimate cause is the bursting of the speculative bubble in asset prices driven initially by the excesses of financial intermediaries (Krugman, 1998). It has also been argued that the root cause of the crises was the maturity mismatch: short-term international liabilities were far greater than short-term assets (Chang and Velasco, 1998; Radelet and Sachs, 1998). The available literature indicates a number of other causes as well. However, even though all these factors may have had some role to play in the crises, no consensus seems to have developed so far in pinpointing the ultimate cause or the cause of all causes. In the absence of a proper understanding of the ultimate cause, conflicting remedies have been proposed. This makes it difficult to lay down an effective reform programme. Hence the proposals for the new architecture have been unable to step beyond the basic principles of conventional wisdom that emphasizes sound macroeconomic policies along with healthy financial systems that incorporate sustainable exchange rates, proper regulation and supervision, and greater transparency. (For these principles, see Camdessus, 2000, pp. 1 and 7–10.)

These principles are undoubtedly indispensable because in the last analysis all crises have their roots in unhealthy fiscal, monetary and exchange rate policies. Hence, no one has ever denied the need for their honest implementation. They have, nevertheless, been violated. This brings to mind a number of questions. The first is about what it is that enables the continuation of macroeconomic imbalances, unsustainable exchange rates and unhealthy financial systems over a prolonged period. One would expect that market discipline itself would normally ensure the honest and effective implementation of these principles. However, the persistence of the crises suggests that either market discipline does not exist or it is ineffective in preventing the continued rise in macroeconomic imbalances in the public sector and living beyond means in the private sector, such that it becomes possible to have excessive leverage and to blow the speculative bubble to the point of bursting. A second related question is why some of the countries that have followed sound fiscal and monetary policies have also faced crises. The European Exchange Rate Mechanism (ERM) crisis of the early 1990s challenges the view that foreign exchange market crises stem from undisciplined fiscal and monetary policies. Many of the countries caught up in the crisis did not have overly expansionary policies (IMF, 1999, p. 67). Even the East Asian countries do not convincingly fit into the mould of inconsistent exchange rates and macroeconomic policies. A third but equally important question is why some of the apparently well-regulated financial systems have also faced crises and whether greater regulation, supervision and transparency will by themselves help minimize the volatility of the international financial system.

3. WHY THE INADEQUATE MARKET DISCIPLINE?

The available literature has been unable to answer these questions satisfactorily. It may not be able to do so without looking at the underlying reason for the failure to implement the basic principles of the new architecture in spite of their being a part of conventional wisdom. The primary cause, in our view, is inadequate market discipline in the conventional financial system. Instead of making the depositors and the bankers share in the risks of business, it assures them of the repayment of their deposits or loans with interest. This makes the depositors take little interest in the soundness of the financial institution. It also makes the banks rely on the crutches of the collateral to extend financing for practically any purpose, including speculation. The collateral cannot, however, be a substitute for a more careful evaluation of the project financed. This is because the value of the collateral can itself be impaired by the same factors that diminish the ability of the borrower to repay the loan. The ability of the market to impose the required discipline is thus impaired, which leads to an unhealthy expansion in the overall volume of credit, to excessive leverage, and to living beyond means. This tendency of the system is further reinforced by the bias of the tax system in favour of debt financing – dividends are subject to taxation while interest payments are allowed to be treated as a tax-deductible expense.

The system's inadequate market discipline is, however, not something new. It has existed all along with the development and spread of the conventional financial system. Then, why, one may ask, has there been greater volatility in the last two decades compared with what prevailed before? What has created the difference is the rise in the volume of funds as a result of rapid economic development after the Second World War, the revolution in information and communications technology, and liberalization of foreign exchange markets. These developments are, however, a manifestation of human progress and cannot be blamed for the crises. When the volume of funds was small and there were also controls on their free movement, inadequate market discipline was not able to create havoc. However, the position is different now.

Therefore, instead of blaming the new developments, it would be more appropriate to examine carefully the fault line in the international financial system resulting from the lack of adequate market discipline because of the absence of explicit risk-sharing. It is this fault line that makes it possible for the financier to lend excessively and also to move funds rapidly from place to place at the slightest change in the economic environment. A high degree of volatility is thus injected into interest rates and asset prices. This generates uncertainty in the investment market, which in turn discourages capital formation and leads to misallocation of resources (BIS, 1982, p. 3). It also drives the borrowers and lenders alike from the long end of the debt market to the shorter end. Consequently, there is a steep rise in highly leveraged short-term debt, which has accentuated economic and financial instability. The IMF has acknowledged this fact in its May 1998 *World Economic Outlook* by stating that countries with high levels of short-term debt are 'likely to be particularly vulnerable to internal and external shocks and thus susceptible to financial crises' (p. 83).

One may wish to pause here to ask why a rise in debt, and particularly short-term debt, should accentuate instability. One of the major reasons is the close link between easy availability of credit, macroeconomic imbalances, and financial instability. The easy availability of credit makes it possible for the public sector to have a high debt profile and for the private sector to live beyond its means and to have a high leverage. If the debt is not used productively, the ability to service the debt does not rise in proportion to the debt and leads to financial fragility and debt crises. The greater the reliance on short-term debt and the higher the leverage, the more severe the crises may be. This is because short-term debt is easily reversible as far as the lender is concerned, but repayment is difficult for the borrower if the amount is locked up in loss-making speculative assets or medium- and long-term investments with a long gestation period. While there may be nothing basically wrong in a reasonable amount of short-term debt that is used for financing the purchase and sale of real goods and services, an excess of it tends to get diverted to speculation in the foreign exchange, stock and property markets.

3.1 The East Asia Crisis

The 1997 East Asia crisis has clearly demonstrated this. The Eastern tigers had been considered to be among the global economy's shining success stories. They had high domestic saving and investment rates coupled with low inflation. They also pursued healthy fiscal policies, which could be the envy of a number of developing countries. Since one of the major causes of financial instability is the financing of government deficit by bonds or fixed-interest-bearing assets (see Christ, 1979 and Searth, 1979), the fiscal discipline of these countries should have helped save them from such instability. However, it did not. The rapid growth in bank credit in local currency to the private sector by domestic banks on the basis of easily available short-term inflows in foreign currency loans from abroad created speculative heat in the stock and property markets and generated a mood of 'irrational exuberance' which pushed up asset prices far beyond what was dictated by fundamentals.

The large foreign exchange inflows from abroad also enabled the central banks to peg exchange rates. This helped provide the assurance needed by foreign banks for lending and, along with high domestic interest rates, attracted further inflows of funds from abroad in foreign currencies to finance direct investment as well as the ongoing boom in the assets markets. Since about 64 per cent of the inflows in the five seriously affected countries (South Korea, Indonesia, Thailand, Malaysia and the Philippines) were short term (BIS, 1999b, p. 10), there was a serious maturity and currency mismatch. This joined hands with political corruption and ineffective banking regulation to lend heavily to favoured companies, which became highly over-leveraged.

The fast growth of these companies was thus made possible by the availability of easy money from conventional banks which do not generally scrutinize the projects minutely because of, as indicated earlier, the absence of risk-sharing. It was the old mistake of lending on collateral without adequately evaluating the underlying risks. Had there been risk-sharing, the banks would have been under a constraint to scrutinize the projects more carefully, and would not have yielded even to political pressures if they considered the projects to be too risky. Therefore, there is a strong rationale in drawing the conclusion that one of the most important underlying causes of excessive short-term lending was the inadequate market discipline resulting from the absence of risk-sharing on the part of banks as well as depositors. It is very difficult for regulators to impose such a discipline unless the operators in the market are themselves rightly motivated. The assurances of receiving the deposits or the principal amount of the loan with the predetermined rate of return stand in the way.

There was a reverse flow of funds as soon as there was a negative shock. Shocks can result from a number of factors, including natural calamities and unanticipated declines in the economies of borrowing countries due to changes in interest rates or relative export and import prices. Such shocks lead to a decline in confidence in the borrowing country's ability to honour its liabilities in foreign exchange. The rapid outflow of foreign exchange, which would not have been possible in the case of equity financing or even medium- and long-term debt, led to a sharp fall in exchange rates and asset prices along with a steep rise in the local currency value of the debt. Private sector borrowers who were expected to repay their debts in the local currency were unable to do so on schedule. There was a domestic banking crisis, which had its repercussions on foreign banks because of the inability of domestic banks to meet their external obligations.

Governments have only two options in such circumstances. The first is to bail out the domestic banks at a great cost to the taxpayer, and the second is to allow the problem banks to fail. The second alternative is not generally considered to be politically feasible in spite of the recent calls to the contrary (Schwartz, 1998; Meltzer, 1998; Calomiris, 1998). In a financial system that assures, in principle, the repayment of deposits with interest and does not, therefore, permit the establishment of Islamic banks because they do not provide such an assurance, it would be a breach of trust on the part of the governments to allow the violation of this principle. Moreover, there is also a presumption, right or wrong, that if the big problem banks are allowed to fail, the financial system will break down and the economy will suffer a severe setback as a result of spillover and contagion effects. Hence the 'too big to fail' doctrine. The governments, therefore, generally feel politically safer in choosing the first alternative.

Since the domestic banks' external liabilities were in foreign exchange and the central banks' foreign exchange reserves had declined steeply, a bailout of external banks was not possible without external assistance, which the IMF came in handy to provide. This has, as indicated earlier, raised a storm of criticism and a call for the reform of the IMF itself by reducing its role (Schwartz, 1998; Meltzer, 1998). The IMF did not perhaps have a choice. Not having any way of assuring its influential members that its refusal to provide resources would not destabilize the entire international financial system, it chose the safer way out. The IMF bailout, however, got the debt unintentionally transferred from the private foreign banks to the central banks and the governments of the affected countries. Professor James Tobin, the Nobel Laureate, has hence rightly observed that 'when private banks and businesses can borrow in whatever amounts, maturities and currencies they choose, they create future claims on their country's reserves' (World Bank, 1998, p. 3).

Discussion of the role of excessive reliance on short-term credit or inflow of funds in the Asian crisis need not lead to the false impression that this is not possible in industrial countries with properly regulated and supervised banking systems. The IMF has clearly warned of the existence of such a possibility by stating that 'whatever their causes the market dynamics of surges and reversals are not peculiar to emerging markets and it is unrealistic to think that they will ever be completely eliminated' (IMF, 1998b, p. 98). The boom in the US stock market has been fed to a great extent by short-term flows of funds from abroad just as it had been in East Asia. If these inflows dry up or are reversed for some unpredictable reason, there may be a serious crisis. This happened in the late 1960s when confidence in the US dollar declined as a result of the persistent US budgetary and current account deficits. Consequently, there was a substantial outflow of funds from the US, leading to a steep decline in the US gold and foreign exchange reserves, a significant depreciation in the dollar's external value, and the demonetization of gold. This flight away from the dollar also fuelled inflation through a rise in international commodity prices.

3.2 The Collapse of Long-Term Capital Management

The collapse of the US hedge fund, Long-Term Capital Management (LTCM), in 1998 was also due to highly leveraged short-term lending. Even though the name 'hedge fund' brings to mind the idea of risk reduction, 'hedge funds typically do just the opposite of what their name implies: they speculate' (Edwards, 1999, p. 189). They are, according to *The Economist*, 'nothing more than rapacious speculators, borrowing heavily to beef up their bets' (*The Economist*, 1998, p. 21). These hedge funds are left mostly unregulated and are not encumbered by restrictions on leverage or short sales and are free to take concentrated positions in a single firm, industry, or sector – positions that might be considered 'imprudent' if taken by other institutional fund managers (Edwards, 1999, p. 190). They are, therefore, able to pursue the investment or trading strategies they choose in their own interest without due regard to the impact that this may have on others.

There is a strong suspicion that these hedge funds do not operate in isolation. If they did, they would probably not be able to make large gains, and the risks to which they are exposed would also be much greater. They therefore normally tend to operate in unison. This becomes possible because their chief executives often go to the same clubs, dine together, and know each other intimately (Plender, 1998). On the strength of their own wealth and the enormous amounts that they can borrow, they are able to destabilize the financial market of any country around the world whenever they find it to their advantage. Hence they are generally blamed for manipulating markets from Hong Kong to London and New York (*The Economist*, 1998). Mahathir Muhammad, Malaysia's Prime Minister, charged that short-term currency speculators, and particularly large hedge funds, were the primary cause of the collapse of the Malaysian ringgit in summer 1997, resulting in the collapse of the Malaysian economy (Muhammad, 1997, p. C1). It is difficult to know whether this charge is right or wrong because of the skill and secrecy with which these funds collude and operate. However, if the charge is right, then it is not unlikely that these funds may also have been instrumental in the collapse of the Thai baht and some other South Asian currencies.

The LTCM had a leverage of 25:1 in mid-1998 (BIS, 1999a, p. 100), but the losses that it suffered reduced its equity (net asset value) from the initial $4.8 billion to $2.3 billion in August 1998. Its leverage, therefore, rose to 50:1 on its balance-sheet positions alone. However, its equity continued to be eroded further by losses, reaching just $600 million, or one-eighth of its original value, on 23 September 1998. Since its balance-sheet positions were in excess of $100 billion on that date, its leverage rose to 167 times capital (IMF, 1998c, p. 55). The Federal Reserve *had* to come to its rescue because its default would have posed risks of systemic proportions. Many of the top commercial banks, which are supervised by the Federal Reserve and considered to be healthy and sound, had lent huge amounts to these funds. If the Federal Reserve had not come to their rescue, there might have been a serious crisis in the US financial system with spillover and contagion effects around the world.[2] If the misadventure of a single hedge fund with an initial equity of only $4.8 billion could take the US and the world economy to the precipice of a financial disaster, then it would be perfectly legitimate to raise the question of what would happen if a number of hedge funds got into trouble.

A hedge fund is able to pursue its operations in secrecy because, as explained by Chairman of the Board of Governors of the Federal Reserve System, Alan Greenspan, it is 'structured to avoid regulation by limiting its clientele to a small number of highly sophisticated, very wealthy individuals' (Greenspan, 1998b, p. 1046). He did not, however, explain how the banks found it possible in a supposedly very well-regulated and supervised banking system to provide excessively leveraged lending to such 'highly sophisticated, very wealthy individuals' for risky speculation when it is well known that the higher the leverage, the greater the risk of default. The unwinding of leveraged positions can cause major disruption in financial markets by exaggerating market movements and generating knock-on effects (IMF, 1998c, pp. 51–3).

This shows that a crisis can come not merely because of improper regulation of banks, as it did in East Asia, but also in a properly regulated and supervised system, as it did in the US. Even though the hedge funds were not regulated, the banks were. Then why did the banks lend huge amounts to the LTCM and other funds? What were the supervisors doing and why were they unable to detect and correct this problem before the crisis? Is there any assurance that the regulation of hedge funds would, without any risk-sharing by banks, stop excessive flow of funds to other speculators?

3.3 Foreign Exchange Market Instability

The heavy reliance on short-term borrowing has also injected a substantial degree of instability into the international foreign exchange markets. According to a survey conducted by the Bank for International Settlements, the daily turnover in traditional foreign exchange markets, adjusted for double-counting, had escalated to $1490 billion in April 1998, compared with $590 billion in April 1989, $820 billion in April 1992 and $1190 billion in April 1995 (BIS, 1998).[3] The daily foreign exchange turnover in April 1998 was more than 49 times the daily volume of world merchandise trade (exports plus imports).[4] Even if an allowance is made for services, unilateral transfers, and non-speculative capital flows, the turnover is far more than warranted. Only 39.6 per cent of the 1998 turnover was related to spot transactions, which have risen at the compounded annual rate of about 6.0 per cent per annum over the nine years since April 1989, very close to the growth of 6.8 per cent per annum in world trade. The balance of the turnover (60.4 per cent) was related largely to outright forwards and foreign exchange swaps, which have registered a compounded growth of 15.8 per cent per annum over this period. If the assertion normally made by bankers that they give due consideration to the end use of funds had been correct, such a high degree of leveraged credit extension for speculative transactions might not have taken place.

The dramatic growth in speculative transactions over the past two decades, of which derivatives are only the latest manifestation, has resulted in an enormous expansion in the payments system. Greenspan himself, sitting at the nerve centre of international finance, finds this expansion in cross-border finance relative to the trade it finances startling (Greenspan, 1998a, p. 3). Such a large expansion implies that if problems were to arise, they could quickly spread throughout the financial system, exerting a domino effect on financial institutions. Accordingly, Crockett has been led to acknowledge that 'our economies have thus become increasingly vulnerable to a possible breakdown in the payments system' (Crockett, 1994, p. 3).

The large volume has also had other adverse effects. It has been one of the major factors contributing to the continued high real rates of interest that have tended to discourage productive investment. Foreign exchange markets, being driven by short-run speculation rather than long-run fundamentals, have become highly volatile. This impedes the efficient operation of these markets, injects excessive instability into them, and creates pressures in favour of exchange controls, particularly on capital transfers. The effort by central banks to overcome this instability through small changes in interest rates or the intervention of a few hundred million dollars a day has generally not proved to be particularly effective.

The Tobin tax on foreign exchange transactions has, therefore, been suggested to reduce the instability. This proposal needs to be reviewed against the ineffectiveness of the securities transaction tax which is levied on the sale of stocks, bonds, options and futures by a number of major industrial countries, including the US, the UK, France, Germany and Japan. This tax proved to be ineffective in preventing or even diluting the October 1998 stock market crash (Hakkio, 1994). Is there any guarantee that the foreign exchange transactions tax would fare any better? Critics of the Tobin tax have accordingly argued that even this tax would be ineffective. One of the reasons given for this is that the imposition of such a tax would be impractical. Unless all countries adopted it and implemented it faithfully, trading would shift to tax-free havens. However, even if all countries complied, experienced speculators might be able to devise ways of evading or avoiding the tax because all countries do not have an effective tax administration.[5]

4. THE REMEDY

If heavy reliance on short-term debt is desired to be curbed, then the question is about the best way to achieve this goal. One of the ways suggested, as already indicated, is greater regulation (Edwards, 1999; Calomiris, 1999; Stiglitz, 1998). Regulations, even though unavoidable to a certain extent, cannot be relied upon totally, due to a number of reasons. First, it is difficult to reach an agreement on what and how to regulate. There are serious disagreements even on fundamental issues. For example, the Basle Committee has found it difficult to decide how to calculate how much capital banks need and whether hedge funds should be regulated (*The Economist*, 2000, p. 93). Without a proper consensus, regulations may not be uniformly applied in all countries and to all institutional money managers. In such a situation, there will be a flight of funds to offshore havens where almost half of all hedge funds are already located (Edwards, 1999, p. 191). Second, even if there is agreement, regulations may be difficult to enforce because of the off-balance-sheet accounts, bank secrecy standards, and the difficulty faced by bank examiners in accurately evaluating the quality of banks' assets. Emerging market banking crises provide a number of examples of how apparently well-capitalized banks were found to be insolvent as a result of the failure to recognize the poor quality of their loan portfolio. Even the LTCM crisis shows how banks in an apparently well-regulated system can become entangled in a speculative spree. Third, bringing banks under a water-tight regulatory umbrella may not only raise the costs of enforcement but also mislead depositors into thinking that their deposits enjoy a regulatory stamp of security.

This does not mean that regulation is not necessary. However, regulation and supervision would be more effective if they were complemented by a paradigm shift in favour of greater discipline in the financial system by making investment depositors as well as the banks share in the risks of business. Just the bailing-in of banks, as is being suggested by some analysts (Meltzer, 1998; Calomiris, 1998; Yeager, 1998), may not be able to take us far enough. What is necessary is not just to make the shareholders suffer when a bank fails, but also to strongly motivate the depositors to be cautious in choosing their bank and the bank management to be more careful in making their loans and investments. Without such risk-sharing, the depositors may keep on receiving competitive rates of interest because the banks receive a predetermined higher rate. However, the quality of the assets may not be good from the very beginning and may even be declining. Suddenly, one day, there may be a revelation to the bank examiners about the poor quality of the banks' assets. It would be unjust to dump these losses on deposit insurance or the taxpayers through a bail-in process if the banks' capital is not adequate to cover them. However, if the banks share in the risks, and the depositors get a share only of what the users of bank funds *actually* earn, then the quality of the banks' assets will remain transparent all along by the return that the banks and the depositors are actually able to get every quarter/year. Bank managers are better placed to evaluate the quality of their assets than regulators and depositors, and risk-sharing would motivate them to take the decisions that they feel are in the best interest of banks and depositors.

Therefore, reinforcing regulation and supervision of banks by profit/loss-sharing by both the banks and the investment depositors would help ensure the soundness of banks. It would help introduce a dimension of self-discipline into the financial system. The depositors would not then be led into a state of complacency by the regulatory framework but would rather be motivated to exercise greater care in choosing their banks. Bank management would also be obliged in their own self-interest to scrutinize more carefully the projects they finance. A good deal of the credit available for unhealthy speculation and unsound projects would thus be eliminated and the possibility of speculative bubbles would thereby be reduced substantially. Governments would also be unable to obtain financing for everything and would thus be under a constraint to rely less on debt by streamlining their tax systems and reducing their unproductive and wasteful spending.

4.1 Speculation?

If credit for speculative purposes is to be curbed, speculation would need to be defined precisely because of the different forms in which it is expressed (see Tirole, 1994, pp. 513–14). We are not concerned here with all kinds of speculation but only with that which is related to short sales and long purchases in the stock, commodity, and foreign exchange markets. The speculator either sells short or buys long. A 'short' sale is a sale of something that the seller does not own at the time of sale and does not intend to deliver from his own portfolio. The short seller, popularly called a bear, expects the price of the security sold short to decline and hopes to be able to 'cover' his short sale through an 'offsetting' purchase at a lower price before maturity date so as to be able to secure a profit. The long buyer, known as a bull, buys stock which he does not want in the hope of making an 'offsetting' sale at a higher price before the date of maturity. Only about 2 per cent of all futures contracts are settled by actual delivery and the rest, about 98 per cent, are liquidated before the delivery date by offsetting transactions (Madura, 1992, p. 246). In fact it is generally felt that trading in futures contracts is for purposes other than the exchange of titles (Altman, 1981, pp. 21 and 15; Hieronymus, 1971, p. 28).

The ability to make margin purchases provides the speculator with a high degree of leverage and enables him to make a larger purchase with a smaller amount. In a margin purchase, the customer is required to deposit with the broker a fraction of the purchase price, either in cash or in acceptable securities, to protect the broker against loss in the event of default. The balance is loaned to the customer by the brokerage house that obtains the funds, usually by pledging the purchased asset with a bank for a collateral loan. The long buyer is required to keep the margin good by depositing additional cash or acceptable securities in the event of a decline in prices by more than the minimum margin requirement. Conversely the customer may withdraw cash or securities from his account if a rise in price should increase his margin substantially above the requirement.

Speculative sales combined with margin purchases bring about an unnecessary expansion or contraction in the volume of transactions and, hence, contribute to excessive fluctuations in stock prices without any real change in the fundamentals. A strong evidence of this is the stock market crash of October 1987. Hardly any fundamental change can be identified to justify the precipitous plunge of 22 per cent in stock prices. A study by Shiller (1981) also reinforces this conclusion. It found that stock prices have been more volatile than is justified by variations in dividends.

Variations in margin requirements and interest rates tend only to add a further dimension of uncertainty and instability to the stock markets. The lowering of margin requirements and/or interest rates generates unnecessary heat in the market. Raising them afterwards with the objective of restoring 'sanity' to the market only forces speculators to liquidate their positions. This brings down prices and ruins some of the speculators at the altar of others who are usually 'insiders' and know what is coming. In a study of 23 industrial countries, Roll (1989) failed to find any relationship between stock price volatility and stock market regulatory devices like market price limits, margin requirements and transactions taxes. Hence speculation has attracted widespread criticism for the role it has played in stock price volatility, and particularly in the stock market crashes of 1929 and 1987 (see Karpoff, 1994, p. 446).

The claim that speculation helps stabilize prices would be true only if the speculators operated in different random directions and their separate actions were mutually corrective. The claimed stabilizing effect would require that there be no marked disparity in the speculators' purchases and sales. But speculation involves judgement, or anticipation of a rise or fall in prices, and is accentuated when something happens or some information is available on which judgement can be based. The same events or rumours give rise to the same judgements. In the real world, rumours, sometimes purposely spread by insiders and vested interests, lead to a wave of speculative buying or selling concentrated in the same direction and brings about an abnormal and unhealthy fluctuation in prices. It is generally acknowledged that prices in the stock markets are susceptible to manipulation and rigging. There are, in the words of a stock market insider, 'intrigues, lethal competitions, tense lunch-time deals, high-stake gambles, the subterfuges, cover-ups, and huge payoffs that make Wall Street the greatest playground in the world' (Sage, 1980, p. I). There are 'safeguards against such rigging but they don't work' because 'Wall Street plays its games seriously, sometimes so well that neither you nor I – nor, seemingly, the Securities Exchange Commission – knows who is in there playing' (Lechner, 1980, pp. 108 and 94).

Continued sanity in the stock market could only be attained through a number of reforms. The most important of these may have to be the abolition of short sales and the imposition of 100 per cent margin, which implies that buyers can make only cash purchases. Speculators will not then be able to take a large position with a small amount at risk. Largay has concluded, on the basis of his analysis of 71 New York Stock Exchange and 38 American Stock Exchange stocks placed under special margin requirements during 1968–69, that, 'the empirical results support the a priori hypothesis that banning the use of credit for transactions in individual issues is associated with a "cooling off" of speculative activity in these stocks'.[6] Bach has also observed that:

> if rising stock prices have been financed by borrowed money, a downturn in the market may precipitate a major collapse in stock prices, as lenders call for cash, and may place serious financial pressure on banks and other lenders. A high market based on credit is thus far more vulnerable than a cash market and is more likely to be a cyclically destabilizing force. (Bach, 1977, p. 182)

The only adverse effect of such moves would be a decline in the short-term trading volume in the stock market. As Gordon has aptly remarked, 'the market machinery encourages turnover and consequently price fluctuations' because 'the greater the volume of sales, the more money made by the brokers' (Gordon, 1980, p. 223). The near-elimination of gyratic movements in prices would exert a healthy effect on the long-run trend. If the purpose of financial markets is to channel household savings into productive investments for boosting employment and output, then speculation in the stock market does the reverse. It rather diverts resources away from productive activity. Accordingly, the Nobel Laureate, Professor James Tobin, stated that:

> Very little of the work of the securities industry, as gauged by the volume of market activity, has to do with the financing of real investment in any very direct way. Likewise those markets have very little to do, in aggregate, with the translation of the saving of households into corporate investment. (Tobin, 1984, p. 11)

The elimination of speculative short sales and long purchases need not necessarily close the door for hedging future payments and receivables arising out of trade in real goods and services.

4.2 Greater Reliance on Equity Finance

The reduction in reliance on short-term borrowing and confining such borrowing to the financing of real goods and services would result in greater dependence on medium- and long-term borrowing and equity financing. Of these two, equity financing would be preferable because, by making the financiers participate in the risks of business, it would induce them to assess the risks more carefully and to monitor the borrowers. The double assessment of investment proposals by both the borrower and the lender would help raise market discipline and introduce greater health into the financial sector. The IMF has also thrown its weight in favour of equity financing by arguing that:

> Foreign direct investment, in contrast to debt-creating inflows, is often regarded as providing a safer and more stable way to finance development because it refers to ownership and control of plant, equipment, and infrastructure and therefore funds the growth-creating capacity of an economy, whereas short-term foreign borrowing is more likely to be used to finance consumption. Furthermore, in the event of a crisis, while investors can divest themselves of domestic securities and banks can refuse to roll over loans, owners of physical capital cannot find buyers so easily. (IMF, 1998a, p. 82)

Moreover, as Hicks (1982) has argued, interest has to be paid in good or bad times alike, but dividends can be reduced in bad times and, in extreme situations, even passed. So the burden of finance by shares is less. There is no doubt that in good times an increased dividend would be expected, but it is precisely in such times that the burden of higher dividend can be borne. 'The firm would be insuring itself to some extent', to use his precise words, 'against a strain which in difficult conditions can be serious, at the cost of an increased payment in conditions when it would be easy to meet it. It is in this sense that the riskiness of its position would be diminished' ibid., p. 14). This factor should tend to have the effect of substantially reducing business failures, and in turn dampening, rather than accentuating, economic instability.

Greater reliance on equity financing has supporters even in mainstream economics. Rogoff, a Harvard Professor of Economics, states that 'In an ideal world equity lending and direct investment would play a much bigger role.' He further asserts that: 'With a better balance between debt and equity, risk-sharing would be greatly enhanced and financial crises sharply muted' (Rogoff, 1999, p. 40). However, the linking of credit to the purchase of real goods and services would take us a step further in reducing instability in the financial markets by curbing excessive credit expansion for speculative transactions. Thus it is not necessary to be pessimistic and to join Stiglitz in declaring that 'volatile markets are an inescapable reality' (Stiglitz, 1999, p. 6). With the introduction of the above-mentioned basic reforms in the financial system, it should be possible to reduce volatility substantially.[7]

4.3 Raising Savings

This leads to the question of why developing countries are so heavily dependent on external loans for financing their development. The answer lies in their low saving rate, which forces them to import savings. The greater their dependence on an inflow of capital, the less capable they are to liberalize capital outflows. This makes it more difficult for them to attract equity capital and thereby increases their reliance on debt with government guarantees.

Raising domestic savings should hence receive high priority in the national reconstruction plans of developing countries. How can this be achieved? By raising interest rates and tax incentives? The evidence generally shows that interest rates and tax incentives have little or no effect on saving (Schmidt-Hebbel et al., 1996, p. 101). Hence cutting of consumption, particularly that of luxury goods and services, may prove to be more productive. This would make it necessary to restrain the spread of Western consumer culture in developing countries. The insistence of the industrial countries that developing countries reduce their tariffs on all goods and services may, therefore, be uncalled for. Moreover, while the resort to higher taxation of luxury goods would undoubtedly be helpful, greater success may be attained if an effort is also made to bring about a change in life-styles so that consumption of status symbols becomes a social taboo. This may not be possible without the injection of a moral dimension into the life-styles. This may perhaps be one of the reasons why all religions, and in particular Islam, have encouraged humble life-styles and discouraged ostentatious consumption. One of the important elements of this moral dimension in all major religions is the abolition of interest because of the living beyond means that an interest-based financial system promotes and the adverse effect that this tends to exert on saving, investment and employment.

However, in spite of a rise in savings, developing countries may need to attract a larger volume of medium- and long-term capital. For success in this goal, there can be no escape from providing all the needed incentives and facilities and also liberalizing repatriation of capital with dividends. This they would be more willing to undertake when the speculative part of the foreign exchange markets has been substantially reduced and the fear of exchange rate volatility is minimized. Howard Davies, Director of Britain's Financial Services Authority and Chairman of the Committee on highly leveraged institutions set up by the Financial Stability Forum, has rightly remarked that: 'If you cannot give open economies some kind of assurance that they will not be subject to speculative attack, then they will close up' (*The Economist*, April 2000, p. 94).

5. THE ISLAMIC REFORM PROGRAMME

Implementation of the above-mentioned reform programme for the financial system may be difficult in the Western world because, as Mills and Presley have put it, 'Western societies have been stripped of the ethical presuppositions conducive to the proscription of interest' (Mills and Presley, 1999, p. 113). Even the proscription of short sales may not be possible in spite of a great deal of support for it because it is difficult to reverse a system once it has become significantly advanced in a certain direction. Moreover, there is the vested interest of stockbrokers who are able to gain from the large volume of transactions. These limitations need not, however, create a great difficulty in the Muslim world because all elements of the suggested reform programme are an integral part of the Islamic paradigm. The prohibition of interest in Islam should help increase reliance on equity and profit/loss-sharing (*muḍārabah* and *mushārakah*) and reduce the proportion of credit in total financing. However, while the *Sharīʿah* has banned interest, it has not prohibited credit. It has allowed credit but through the sales-based modes of financing which are intended not only to remove interest but also to restrain excessive credit expansion by confining the availability of credit to only real goods and services. Some of these modes are: *murābaḥah*, *ijārah*, *salam* and *istiṣnāʿ*. All these are essentially sales transactions related to real goods and services. The return on capital in all these transactions becomes a part of the price.

Since the additional purchasing power created by the credit available under these Islamic modes is backed by real goods and services, there is no possibility of creating unnecessary heat in the market. Credit available for speculative purposes would at least be minimized, if not eliminated, thereby creating a balance between the expansion of credit and the expansion of output of real goods and services. Hardly anyone should have qualms about this because lending against the collateral of stocks to purchase stocks does not create wealth. It only breeds speculation and instability. The purpose of credit should be to finance productive investments and not to encourage speculative buying or hoarding. Paul Volcker, Ex-Chairman of the Federal Reserve System, had, in a letter to the chief executives of all member banks, warned against speculative loans, loans made to retire stocks, loans to finance takeovers, and loans involving any extraordinary finance, 'except as they may clearly involve the improvement in the nation's productive capabilities' (Volcker, 1979, p. 110). This warning of Volcker has remained more or less unheeded in the conventional system because the system is not tuned to its acceptance. In the Islamic system, however, the participation of banks in the risks of business should help minimize the use of scarce credit resources for all unproductive purposes.

The *Sharīʿah* has also put a stricture on speculative short sales by prohibiting the sale of something that the seller does not own and possess.[8] The *Sharīʿah* has not, however, prohibited all forward transactions. It has allowed the forward purchase or sale of agricultural commodities (*salam*) or manufactured goods (*istiṣnāʿ*). Forward transactions in real goods and services with the intention of taking and giving delivery perform an important economic function. They make an allowance for the time period it takes to produce the goods and thus provide producers as well as users with the assurance that they can sell or receive the goods when ready or needed. In contrast with this, short speculative sales do not perform such a function. In such sales, the 'forward' seller has no role to play. He sells 'something he cannot consume or use in his business, upon which he performs no work, and to which he adds no value' (Rix, 1965, p. 204). Spot purchases against cash payment and the reciprocal receipt constitute a real investment and cannot be equated with speculation irrespective of when the purchaser decides to resell what he has purchased. This is because the spot seller already owns the sold items which he purchased against cash, and his decision to resell them will be determined by changes in his economic circumstances or his perception of the market, both of which may not necessarily change immediately. The prohibition of interest and the sharing of the depositor and the lender in the risks of business, along with the removal of speculative sales, should help inject greater discipline into the financial market.

6. CONCLUSION

The establishment of Islamic banks in the Muslim world, even though in an embryonic stage, has created a hope that the programme may ultimately be implemented in the future and thus set the stage for its acceptance by the rest of the world. However, due to a number of problems. Islamic banks have so far not been playing a significant role in promoting greater reliance on profit-sharing modes. They are primarily involved in extending credit. Nevertheless, since this credit is on the basis of Islamic modes, it remains confined to the purchase and sale of real goods and services and does not become available for speculative purposes. Moreover, the proportion of total banking assets of the Muslim world that the Islamic banks have so far been able to bring under their financial net is relatively small. There are also a number of *fiqhī* issues that still need to be resolved. The shared institutions that are necessary for the proper functioning of Islamic banks have yet to be established. A proper regulatory and supervisory framework for Islamic banks has also not yet been formulated. This may not even be possible until the central banks start taking a keen interest in Islamic banking and all the *fiqhī* issues related to banking and finance are satisfactorily resolved. Hence it may be quite a while before the implementation of the Islamic programme makes real headway in the Muslim world in spite of a great deal of support for it among the masses.

NOTES

1. The more important of these are the US stock market crash in October 1987, the bursting of the Japanese stock and property market bubble in the 1990s, the breakdown of the European Exchange Rate Mechanism (ERM) in 1992–93, the bond market crash in 1994, the Mexican crisis in 1995, the East Asian crisis in 1997, the Russian crisis in August 1998, the breakdown of the US hedge funds in 1998, and the Brazilian exchange rate crisis in 1999.
2. This was clearly acknowledged by Alan Greenspan in the following words: 'Had the failure of the LTCM triggered the seizing up of markets, substantial damage could have been inflicted on many market participants, including some not directly involved with the firm, and could have potentially impaired the economies of many nations, including our own' (Greenspan, 1998b, p. 1046).
3. The Bank for International Settlements (BIS) conducts a survey of foreign exchange markets every three years in the month of April.
4. World trade (exports plus imports) rose from $499.0 billion in April 1989 to $908.7 billion in April 1998 (IMF, *International Financial Statistics*, CD-ROM and November 1998). The average value of daily world trade in April 1998 comes to $30.3 billion.
5. See the arguments in favour of and against the feasibility of the Tobin tax by various writers in Haq et al. (1996).
6. Reported by Irwin Friend in his paper 'Economic Foundations of Stock Markets' in Bicksler (1979), p. 156.
7. A number of Islamic economists have argued this point. See, for example, Chapra (1985), pp. 117–22; Chishti (1985); Khan (1987); Mirakhor and Zaidi (1987), Siddiqui and Fardmanesh (1994).
8. For a valuable discussion on stock and commodity market speculation from the point of view of the *Sharīʿah*, see the *Fiqhī* decision entitled '*Sūq al-Awrāq al-Māliyyah wa al-Baḍā'iʿ* (*al-Brusah*)' issued by the Majlis al-Majmaʿ al-Fiqh al-Islāmī of the Rābitah al-'Ālam al-Islāmī in *Qarārāt Majlis al-Majmaʿ al-Fiqh al-Islāmī* (Makkah, al-Amānah al-ʿĀmmah, Rābiṭah al-ʿĀlam al-Islāmī, 1985), pp. 120–25; and the article of Ahmad Yusuf Sulayman in Al-Ittiḥād al-Dawlī lī al-Bunūk al-Islāmiyyah, *Al-Mawsūʿah al-ʿAmaliyyah*, vol. 5, pp. 389–431, particularly the summary on pp. 429–31. See also, Bayt al-Tamwīl al-Kuwaitī, *Al-Fatāwā al-Sharʿiyyah* (Kuwait, 1980, pp. 45–9).

REFERENCES

Altman, Edward I. (ed.) (1981), *Financial Handbook*, 5th edn, New York: John Wiley.

Bach, G.L. (1977), *Economics: An Introduction to Analysis and Policy*, 9th edn, Englewood Cliffs, NJ: Prentice Hall.

Bank for International Settlements (1982), *Annual Report*, June.

Bank for International Settlements (1998), *Press Release*, 19 October, giving preliminary results of the foreign exchange currency survey for April 1998.

Bank for International Settlements (1999a), *Annual Report*.

Bank for International Settlements (1999b), Basel Committee on Banking Supervision, *Supervisory Lessons to be Drawn from the Asian Crisis*, Working Paper No. 2.

Bicksler, James L. (1979), *Handbook of Financial Economics*, Amsterdam, The Netherlands: North Holland Publishing Co.

Bisignano, Joseph (1998), 'Precarious Credit Equilibria: Reflections on the Asian Financial Crisis', paper presented at the Conference, Asia: An Analysis of Financial Crises, 8–10 October. Proceedings to be published by the Federal Reserve Bank of Chicago.

Calomiris, Charles (1998), 'The IMF's Imprudent Role as Lender of Last Resort', *The Cato Journal*, **17** (3).

Calomiris, Charles (1999), 'How to Invent a New IMF', *The International Economy*, January/February.

Camdessus, Michael (2000), 'Main Principles for the Future of International Monetary, Financial System', *IMF Survey*, 10 January.

Chang, Roberto and Andres Velasco (1998), *The Asian Liquidity Crisis*, Working Paper No. 6796, Cambridge, MA: The National Bureau of Economic Research.

Chapra, M. Umer (2000), 'Why Has Islam Prohibited Interest? Rationale Behind the Prohibition of Interest in Islam', *Review of Islamic Economics* (9), 5–20.

Chishti, Salim U. (1985), 'Relative Stability of an Interest-Free Economy', *Journal of Research in Islamic Economics*, Summer, 3–11.

Christ, Carl (1979), 'On Fiscal and Monetary Policies and the Government Budget Restraint', *American Economic Review*, 526–38.

Crockett, Andrew (1994), Address at the 24th International Management Symposium in St. Galen on 1 June, *BIS Review*, 22 June.

Crockett, Andrew (2000); 'A Pillar to Bolster Global Finance', *Financial Times*, 22 March.

Economist, The (1998), 'The Risk Business', 17 October .

Economist, The (2000), 'Financial Regulation: Basle Bust', 15 April, 93–4.

Edwards, Franklin R. (1999), 'Hedge Funds and the Collapse of Long-Term Capital Management', *Journal of Economic Perspectives*, Spring, 189–210.

Glick, Reuven (1998), 'Thoughts on the Origins of the Asian Crisis: Impulses and Propagation', paper presented at the Conference Asia: An Analysis of Financial Crises, 8–10 October. Proceedings to be published by the Federal Reserve Bank of Chicago.

Gordon, Wendell (1980), *Institutional Economics*, Austin, TX: University of Texas.

Greenspan, Alan (1998a), 'The Globalisation of Finance', *The Cato Journal*, **17** (3), Winter, 1–7.

Greenspan, Alan (1998b), 'Statement before the Committee on Banking and Financial Services, US House of Representatives, 1 October 1998', *Federal Reserve Bulletin*, December, 1046–50.

Hakkio, Craig S. (1994), 'Should We Throw Sand in the Gears of Financial Markets?', Federal Reserve Bank of Kansas City, *Economic Review*, second quarter, 17–30.

Haq, Mahbubul, Inge Kaul and Isabelle Grundberg (eds) (1996), *The Tobin Tax: Coping with Financial Volatility*, Oxford: Oxford University Press.

Hicks, Sir John (1982), 'Limited Liability: the Pros and Cons', in Tony Orhnial, *Limited Liability and the Corporation*, London, UK: Croom Helm.

Hieronymus, Thomas A. (1971), *Economics of Futures Trading*, New York: Commodity Research Bureau.

IMF (1998a), *World Economic Outlook*, May.

IMF (1998b), *World Economic Outlook*, September.

IMF (1998c), *World Economic Outlook and International Capital Markets*, December.

IMF (1999), *World Economic Outlook*, May.

Karpoff, Jonathan M. (1994), 'Short Selling', in Peter Newman et al. (eds), *The New Palgrave Dictionary of Money and Finance*, New York: Macmillan.

Khan, Mohsin S. (1987), 'Islamic Interest-Free Banking: A Theoretical Analysis' in Mohsin Khan and Abbas Mirakhor, *Theoretical Studies in Islamic Economics*, Houston, TX: The Institute for Research and Islamic Studies, pp. 15–35 and 201–6.

Krugman, Paul (1998), 'What Happened to Asia?', mimeo, January. http://web.mit.edu/krugman/www/disinter.html.

Lechner, Alan (1980), *Street Games: Inside Stories of the Wall Street Hustle*, New York: Harper and Row.
Madura, Jeff (1992), *Financial Markets and Institutions*, 2nd edn, New York: West Publishing Co.
Meltzer, Allan (1998), 'Asian Problems and the IMF', *The Cato Journal*, **17** (3). http://www.cato.org/pubs/journal/ci/17n3–10 html
Mills, Paul S. and John Presley (1999), *Islamic Finance: Theory and Practice*, London: Macmillan.
Mirakhor, Abbas and Iqbal Zaidi (1987), *Stabilisation and Growth in an Open Economy*, IMF Working Paper, Washington, DC: IMF.
Muhammad, Mahathir (1997), 'Highwaymen of the Global Economy', *The Wall Street Journal*, 23 September, p. C1.
Plender, John (1998), 'Western Crony Capitalism', *Financial Times*, 3–4 October.
Radelet, Steven and Jefferey Sachs (1998), 'The East Asian Financial Crises: Diagnosis, Remedies, Prospects', *Brookings Papers on Economic Activity*, New York: Brookings Institution.
Rix, M.S. (1965), *Stock Market Economics*, London: Sir Isaac Pitman and Sons Ltd.
Rogoff, Kenneth (1999), 'International Institutions for Reducing Global Financial Instability', *The Journal of Economic Perspectives*, **4** (13), fall, 21–42.
Roll, Richard (1989), 'Price Volatility, International Market Links and their Implications for Regulatory Policies', *Journal of Financial Services Research*, **3**, 211–46.
Sage, Marchand (1980), *Street Fighting at Wall and Broad: An Insider's Tale of Stock Manipulation*, New York: Macmillan. Marchand Sage is a *nom de plume* for the writer who is a sophisticated and successful veteran on Wall Street and hence does not wish to reveal his identity.
Schmidt-Hebbel, Klaus, Luis Serven and Andres Solimano (1996), 'Saving and Investment: Paradigms, Puzzles, and Policies', *The World Bank Research Observer*, 1/11, February, 87–117.
Schultz, George, Simon William and Walter Wriston (1998), 'Who Needs the IMF?', *Wall Street Journal*, 3 February.
Schwartz, Anna (1998), 'Time to Terminate the ESF and the IMF', Foreign Policy Briefing (48), The Cato Institute, 26 August.
Searth, Wan (1979), 'Bond Financed Fiscal Policy and the Problem of Instrument Instability', *Journal of Macroeconomics*, 107–17.
Shiller, Robert J. (1981), 'Do Stock Prices Move too much to be Justified by Subsequent Changes in Dividends?', *American Economic Review*, June, 421–36.
Siddiqui, Shamim A. and Mohsen Fardmanesh (1994), 'Financial Stability and a Share Economy', *Eastern Economic Journal*, spring.
Stiglitz, Joseph (1998), 'Boats, Planes and Capital Flows', *Financial Times*, 25 March.
Stiglitz, Joseph (1999), 'Bleak Growth Prospects for the Developing World', *International Herald Tribune*, 10–11 April.
Tirole, Jean (1994), 'Speculation', in Peter Newman et al. (eds), *The New Palgrave Dictionary of Money and Finance*, New York: Macmillan, pp. 513–15.
Tobin, James (1984), 'On the Efficiency of the Financial System', *Lloyds Bank Review*, July, 1–5.
Volcker, Paul (1979), cited in *Fortune*, 17 December.
World Bank (1998), *Policy and Research Bulletin*, April–June 1998.
Yeager, Leland B. (1998), 'How to Avoid International Financial Crises', *The Cato Journal*, **17** (3), winter.

COMMENTS

John G. Sessions

This is an important chapter which will help to disseminate the important lessons that the West can learn from the Islamic approach to economics and finance.

The chapter investigates the causes of the various financial crises that have hit the international financial system over the past two decades. Three key questions are asked. First, what is it that has enabled the continuation of macroeconomic imbalances, unsustainable exchange rates and unhealthy financial systems over such a prolonged period? Second, why have some of the countries that have followed sound monetary and fiscal policies also faced crises? Third, why have some of the apparently well-regulated financial systems also faced crises, and will greater regulation, supervision and transparency by themselves help minimize the volatility of the international financial system?

The author considers a number of causes for the crises, namely, financial liberalization; the bursting of the speculative bubble in asset prices driven initially by the excesses of financial intermediaries; and maturity mismatch whereby short-term international liabilities exceeded short-term assets. He comes down, however, in favour of inadequate market discipline as the ultimate root cause, focusing in particular on the rise in (especially short-term) debt. He cites three examples of the link between easy availability of credit, macroeconomic imbalances and financial instability – the East Asian crisis, the collapse of the US hedge fund Long Term Capital Management, and foreign exchange market instability.

The author concurs that the greater regulation that has been advocated by various commentators will help to alleviate some of the stresses. Regulation, however, cannot be relied upon totally: it is often difficult to reach a consensus on what and how to regulate. Even if there is agreement, regulation may be difficult to enforce because of the off-balance-sheet accounts, bank secrecy standards, and the difficulties faced by bank examiners in accurately evaluating the quality of bank assets; and bringing banks under tighter regulations may mislead depositors into thinking that their deposits enjoy a regulatory stamp of security.

A more fundamental remedy is argued to be a paradigm shift in favour of making both depositors and banks share in the risks of the business through the introduction of profit/loss-sharing.

I think the chapter makes a very valuable contribution to the literature. In particular I like the focus on macroeconomic finance aspects of profit/loss-sharing. This is an area that has been relatively neglected in previous research. I do, however, have reservations about some of the arguments put forward in the chapter:

1. It would be helpful if more statistical evidence were given in support of some of the arguments. For example, the author alludes to 'a reasonable amount of debt' but offers no guidance as to what this figure might actually be. Moreover, he argues that 'an excess [of short-term debt] tends to get diverted into speculation in the foreign exchange, stock, and property markets' but offers no evidence for this.
2. The fundamental premise that lenders will be more cautious under profit/loss-sharing ignores bankruptcy/collateral constraints under conventional Western loan arrangements. Banks are unlikely to lend to purely speculative projects if they are unable to guarantee a return.
3. The chapter focuses too much on the supply-side implications of profit/loss-sharing. It has been shown that profit/loss-sharing will affect the microeconomic demand for finance by acting as an efficient revelation device. The basic idea is that if the project outcome is stochastic, and if managers have an informational advantage regarding this stochasticity over investors, then a profit/loss-sharing contract between managers and investors will lead to a more efficient revelation of that information.[1] This could imply an increase in the demand for finance and a fall in the level of entrepreneurial effort and we could have a situation where borrowers are demanding more finance for, but supplying less effort to, risky projects. This could lead to similar problems of excessive, ill-disciplined finance as are claimed to occur under conventional lending contacts.
4. What are the implications for economic growth? If, as the author claims, banks will be more cautious under profit/loss-sharing, then how will this affect high-risk, high-return projects?

If these issues were also addressed, the chapter would make a very substantial contribution to both the Islamic and non-Islamic literature on loan *vis-à-vis* profit-sharing financing.

NOTE

1. See J.R. Presley and J.G. Sessions, 'Islamic Economics: The Emergence of a New Paradigm', *Economic Journal*, **104**, 584–96, 1994.

Index